Books of Merit

Water into Wine

TOM HARPUR

WATER INTO WINE

An Empowering Vision
of the Gospels

Thomas Allen Publishers

Toronto

Library and Archives Canada Cataloguing in Publication

Harpur, Tom
Water into wine : an empowering vision of the Gospels / Tom Harpur.

Includes bibliographical references and index.

ISBN-13: 978-0-88762-277-9

ISBN-10: 0-88762-277-1

1. Bible. N.T. Gospels—Criticism, interpretation, etc.
I. Title.

BS2555.52.H28 2007   226'.06   C2006-906995-6

Editor: Patrick Crean
Cover image: istockphoto/Olympus

The excerpts from *Egyptian Light and Hebrew Fire* in Appendix C
are by permission of the author, Karl W. Luckert, Ph. D.

Published by Thomas Allen Publishers,
a division of Thomas Allen & Son Limited,
145 Front Street East, Suite 209,
Toronto, Ontario M5A 1E3 Canada

www.thomas-allen.com

The publisher gratefully acknowledges the support of
the Ontario Arts Council for its publishing program.

We acknowledge the support of the Canada Council for the Arts, which
last year invested $20.0 million in writing and publishing throughout Canada.

We acknowledge the Government of Ontario through the
Ontario Media Development Corporation's Ontario Book Initiative.

We acknowledge the financial support of the Government of Canada through the Book
Publishing Industry Development Program (BPIDP) for our publishing activities.

11 10 09 08 07   1 2 3 4 5

Printed and bound in Canada

Dedicated to Joan and Bud
whose loving union blessed me with the
priceless gift of Susan.

If they say to you, "Where have you come from?"
Say to them, "We have come from the light, From the
place where the light came into being by itself . . ."

— THE GOSPEL OF THOMAS, Saying #50

Contents

Acknowledgment

I owe a debt of gratitude to my publisher and editor, Patrick Crean. His constant enthusiasm and commitment to the message of this book and his sensitive awareness of its potential to make a vital difference were a tremendous asset. Working with you, Patrick, was entirely a pleasure from start to finish.

Tom Harpur
Spring, 2007

Water into Wine

1

OUR JOURNEY BEGINS

The problem for and the function of religion
in this age is to awaken the heart.

— JOSEPH CAMPBELL, *Thou Art That*

ONE SUNDAY in the early 1970s, I was guest preaching to an Anglican congregation at a historic downtown Toronto church. The sermon was somewhat controversial in its thrust, and as I came down from the pulpit the rector was already on his way to the chancel steps. Turning to me, he said, "You can't leave it there, Tom." He then proceeded to disagree with every major point I had tried to make. The people gasped. Naturally, I responded with some gusto and we began an impromptu debate that lasted nearly an hour. Nobody left. Nobody even stirred. At one point I invited any who wanted to do so to join in, and several vigorously did. I still meet people today who were there and who say they have never attended a church service quite that exciting since.

In a way, this story parallels what has happened in the wake of my 2004 book *The Pagan Christ*. The response has been tremendous; most letter writers have expressed gratitude, but nearly all have said in one way or another, "You can't leave it there." Most of them wanted to continue the journey.

Those who read that book know that it sets out considerable, detailed evidence that the entire story upon which Christianity has rested for nearly two thousand years is based upon much earlier narratives, including one of humanity's earliest myths, that of Incarnation. In its simplest form, the doctrine of Incarnation is the understanding that deep in the centre of every person's being is a spark of the eternal fire of the Divine. It was that belief, I maintained, that formed the foundation upon which Christianity later was constructed. Specifically, to quote the words of the great psychoanalyst Carl Jung, it was demonstrated that "the Christian era owes its name and significance to the antique mystery of the god-man, which has its roots in the archetypal Osiris–Horus myth of ancient Egypt."[1] Since some conservative critics have attempted on various grounds to deny this Egyptian connection, I have included an appendix at the conclusion of this book with further striking, contemporary scholarship on the subject.

In the course of showing Christianity's deep dependence upon the ancient Egyptian wisdom, I concluded that there is no reliable, unambiguous historical evidence for an actual Jesus of Nazareth. This is not an easy conclusion to grasp for a Western culture deeply influenced by a literal, historicized version of the ancient myth—and for many it comes as a genuine shock. Many, on the other hand, have written to me to say that the question of historicity or non-historicity doesn't really affect their deeper spiritual understanding. Perhaps, at one level, it doesn't really matter that much. But it does matter—profoundly—when you look at the Church's past and realize the horrific consequences of literalism and the focusing of Incarnation in one putatively historical person. Millions have died because of it. Wars and torture have followed in its wake. The lives of countless millions have been controlled from cradle to grave by ecclesiastical powers as a result of such a dogma.

Essentially, what the historical approach has done has been to cut the individual off from realizing fully his or her own divinity within. This is of profound importance, because ultimately what matters is the subjective or inner meaning of the Jesus Story for each of us and for humanity at large.

The stance taken in what follows is that Jesus is a mythical figure. The Jesus Story certainly has of itself a long, tempestuous and incredibly complex history. But that is quite different from proving that the narratives themselves have anything historical about them. Arduous study shows that the "evidence" offered by professional apologists and many others for a Jesus of history simply doesn't stand up under critical examination. This particular emperor has no clothes, despite the fact that many scholars who should know better continue to argue that he does. The problem is that they become simply and hopelessly vague when asked to produce their evidence. The best they can do is to offer hearsay material, and that only of the flimsiest kind.

On the question of the current so-called "Third Quest for the Historical Jesus," Harold Bloom, the well-known American literary critic and bestselling author, comments: "Quests for the historical Jesus invariably fail, even those by the most responsible searchers. Questers, however careful, find *themselves* and not the elusive and evasive Yeshua, enigma of enigmas."[2] To my mind, they are like those looking for treasure down a deep well and finding only their own reflections in the water.

In his 2005 book *Jesus and Yahweh—The Names Divine*, Bloom says he is completely baffled, as a scholar, by the "human comedy" of this never-ending search. He describes reading the work of such prominent New Testament experts as Raymond Brown and Father J.P. Meier and wondering "why they will not admit how hopelessly little we actually know about Jesus. The New Testament has been ransacked by centuries of minute scholarship but all that labour does not result in telling us the minimal information we demand on any parallel matter." As for Flavius Josephus, upon whose shoulders the entire shaky case for Jesus' historicity is made to rest, Bloom bluntly, and rightly, states that he was "a wonderful writer and non-stop liar."[3]

While Bloom, without giving any reasons, somewhat paradoxically is prepared to admit that Jesus was "a more or less historical person," he believes nothing can be known for certain about him. He explains that what he means by this is that "everything truly important about him reaches me from texts I cannot trust." Part of the reason for this is that "there is not a sentence in the entire New Testament composed by anyone who had ever met the unwilling King of the Jews."[4] Before leaving this subject, I will say that in any criticisms received in the wake of *The Pagan Christ*, nobody has yet produced what any truly objective scholar would call convincing or verifiable evidence for a flesh-and-blood Jesus of Nazareth.[5]

Accordingly, there will be some commentary from time to time throughout this study on the historicity question as it becomes relevant to our main theme. However, that is certainly not the central issue here. Rather, it is this: what, when all is said and done, does the 2,000-year-old story of Jesus called Christ mean to you and me and to the wider world? This is the burning issue that the endless scholarly wrangling utterly obscures and for the most part fails even adequately to address. To get at that kernel of wisdom, we will treat the story here as it was originally, I believe, intended to be interpreted—as a myth of the highest order. Not just any myth, indeed, but the story of the evolution on this earth plane of each individual living soul. The fundamental thesis of this book is that the Jesus Story is your story and mine told in the light of eternity and of eternal values.

In the groundbreaking, still highly relevant television series by PBS called *The Power of Myth*, in which, during six fascinating one-hour shows, the famous mythologist Joseph Campbell was interviewed by journalist Bill Moyers, Campbell spoke about one of his favourite themes—the Hero with a Thousand Faces. He explained how all the greatest truths about who we are and what we are meant to be begin with a story. The story, or (to use the Greek word) *mythos*, is almost always, he said, a fictional account of the adventure(s) of a hero, someone who does daring and dangerous things for a cause, someone who goes out to speak and act courageously and then returns bearing his reward, whether material or spiritual. In the nearly universal god-man myth, the hero meets death or is swallowed by a monster only to experience rebirth and triumph at the end.

Each of us, Campbell argued, can learn from the hero's adventure because we are all likewise called to the going out and the coming back of the unique adventure that is our own life, from the moment of birth through maturity to death itself. The myriad myths of humanity can differ enormously from one another, and yet there are certain universal themes running through them all. The various trials and revelations experienced by the hero invariably call for a denial or "losing" of his or her own lower self, or ego, as the hero's consciousness is expanded and transformed. In Campbell's words, the important dimension of the story is the "interface between what is known" and the true source of all life and being. The myths, he declared, are meant to bring us eventually to a level of consciousness that is spiritual. Like dreams, they use the language of symbols and other imagery because they flow up from the depths of the unconscious and draw us ever upwards towards an ever-greater light. Greater light means fuller awareness of who we really are, and with that comes deeper appreciation of the presence of the divine light in other people around us. We become more sensitive to their hopes and longings, more compassionate to their struggles and their grief.

Given an approach like that, it is easy to see why Campbell, who died in 1987, called himself a "maverick" and why he had such difficulty with organized religions. Religion, ideally, should lift us into that greater light; it should connect us ever more solidly with the source of our very being and with one another. This is what people everywhere hunger and thirst for today. Yet history makes plain that religion has not always functioned that way. Carl Jung said that in a real sense religion has been humanity's creation as a defence against a genuine encounter with Transcendence or the Divine. To be quite specific, excessive literalism and the historicizing of that which was meant as metaphor and myth has too often led to religion as the great inhibitor of human growth, as the great oppressor of human freedom, a prison rather than a source of healing. Thus religion, Campbell said in a now-famous aphorism, can be defined as "mythology misunderstood."

The Pagan Christ taught that the Christian story is based upon an eternal myth of the gift of Christ consciousness, or of the divine flame, to every one of us. However, tragically, it is a myth that well over a billion people on Earth today still see as the literal story of a single individual who lived long ago in Palestine, who alone can be called the "Only Begotten Son of God," and who alone, by his death and Resurrection, can save us from the penalties of sin and death.

While the eternal mythos of the Christ within unites and binds all humanity together, this latter, exclusivistic, literal reading, and the insistence on an extremely questionable history, continues to rupture and divide Christians from other religions, from those of no religion and very often from one another. It's one reason why there are at least four hundred different competing Christian denominations and sects today. The return to the deeper, much more universal, mythological understanding is imperative as a condition for world harmony and peace. It is also, I deeply believe, the key to the survival of Christianity as a viable faith in the future.

I have found that the mythic approach to the Gospels, and indeed to the whole of the Bible, has enriched my faith and deepened it in ways I had scarcely imagined when I was a parish priest or a professor at the seminary. Nature is more alive to me—or I sense that I am a deeper part of it. Prayer, while much more informal and conversational—or more often deeply silent—seems more connected, more real. Trust in the mystery we call God is keener, more alive. The mythic way is the genuine path towards the goal of a renewal of faith in our time.

The question we will attempt to answer here, then, is: what do the Gospels themselves look like or "feel" like from that mythic and symbolic point of view? What happens when we drop the pretence that Matthew, Mark, Luke and John are varying complementary biographies of one man called Jesus of Nazareth and see these ancient texts for the allegories, parables, word pictures and myths I believe they were originally intended and understood to be? If sheer literalism leads to "blind faith," what kind of understanding and raising of consciousness flows once a mythical, metaphorical principle of interpretation is applied? The time has come to test this hypothesis and see.

Before I attempt to do so, however, let me be absolutely clear. This book is aimed at helping modern men and women to see the Gospels in a new light. In no way is it an attack upon Scripture or on other interpretations. In the Hellenistic world, sacred writings were widely interpreted as having an allegorical meaning. The literal sense was important in its limited way, but only as a "minor mystery" compared with the greater riches beyond. Another way of putting this is to say that sacred texts were understood to have both an *exoteric* and an *esoteric* meaning. The exoteric sense, the literal, was for beginners, those not yet ready to comprehend the real message. The true, or esoteric, meaning lay within or beyond the text itself.

There is abundant proof of this fundamental distinction in the pages of the New Testament, and in particular in Mark, the earliest of the four Gospels. In chapter 4 of Mark, after telling the very first of the parables—the parable of the sower, which is found in every Gospel—Jesus is asked about the meaning of the parables in general. The Gospel says: "When he was alone, those who were around him along with the twelve asked him about the parables." Jesus is then made to reply: "To you has been given the secret [in Greek, *mysterion*] of the kingdom of God, but for those outside, everything comes in parables . . ." In case we miss the point, the author/editor of Mark repeats it a few verses later. Verse 33 reads as follows: "With many such parables he spoke the word to them, as they were able to hear it; he did not speak to them except in parables, but he explained everything in private to his disciples." Matthew uses the same word as Mark for the secret but makes it plural—*ta mysteria*, the secrets or mysteries of "the kingdom of heaven." In other words, like all the other Mystery Religions of that period, early Christianity was based upon an inner or esoteric mystery teaching(s), which held the key to all the rest. The parables, then, are meant to communicate that essential mystery, while at the same time protecting it from being too readily seized upon and profaned by those of ill will.

When I was growing up in Toronto's east end, I attended a Bible class for youngsters of about ten to twelve years of age. There was one game we played at each session that gave me a gift that was to benefit and last me all my life; it was called Sword Drill. Each class member had a "sword," which was in fact a bible. You held it tightly in its "sheath" (under your arm) until the teacher called out a Bible reference. Instantly there would be a furious searching and turning of pages until the first to find the passage leapt up and read it aloud. Points were awarded and the competition was very keen indeed. It now seems simple or perhaps even naive. But it taught me how to find my way around in what can be a very difficult book, or rather, collection of books. It gave me a thorough knowledge of the literal text I can never forget. However, although it's a great place to start, one very soon longs and looks for something more. The vision that now follows has helped me as nothing else has done to find that something more.

There is one last thing I'd like to clarify before we go further: when I speak in this book of matter and spirit, or of the "spiritual" in contrast to the "material," I am not expressing or espousing some kind of ultimate dualism. Dualism holds that there are two essential (ontological) realities of good and evil, darkness and light, physical and spiritual. Zoroastrianism, for example, seems to be an expression of this. So was Manichaeism. That would mean that the body is evil (and some Gnostics went that far, affecting Christianity in the process) and only the soul is good. Ultimately, there is but one final reality, from which all else emanates. This Monad, another name for God, permits a cleaving into two realms so that, in the tension of opposites, Creation in all its manifold wonder takes place. Spirit and matter give birth to each other, and at the end of the eon or "age" all will be one once more. Neither is superior to the other. That is why matter "matters" and is a vehicle for the Divine.

2

THE MYTH AND YOU

*Finding the deeper meaning [of the Bible texts] is thus
the process by which God gradually, by means of parable
and metaphor, leads those to whom God would reveal
himself from the sensible to the intelligible world.*

— CLEMENT OF ALEXANDRIA[1]

Origin of the Gospels

SINCE THE PUBLICATION of *The Pagan Christ*, one question
that has intrigued and puzzled readers is just what the source
of the Gospels and the Gospels' Jesus actually was. Reading
as widely as possible has made me aware that there is nobody
today—no scholar or expert—who can give a definitive answer
to this question. The fact that we now know there were "many
Christianities" or Yeshua (Jesus) movements in, and in some cases
before, the first century has added greatly to the confusion and
uncertainty.[2] One theory, though, currently being discussed in
some popular writings, merits a great deal more research by Biblical scholars.

Philo Judaeus, who lived from about 20 BCE to 40 CE, was a
brilliant Jew by religion and a Greek philosopher by education
who lived in Alexandria, Egypt. He understood the books of the
Pentateuch (the first five books of the Bible) and other Hebrew

scriptures allegorically, and laboured diligently to harmonize them all with Platonic and Aristotelian philosophy. (It should be added that he and all the thousands of Egyptian Jews in Alexandria read the "Old Testament" in a Greek translation called the Septuagint, created roughly two hundred years earlier, in Alexandria.) His writing about the divine Logos, or Word of God, and about the "son" of God, for example, is thought by many scholars to have strongly influenced the author of the prologue to John's Gospel.

Be that as it may, it is the case that he writes also about a large group of devout Egyptian Jewish ascetics called Therapeutae, or healers, who lived near Lake Mareotis close to Alexandria. They were already well established long before Philo's time and had similar communities scattered around the Mediterranean basin in key centres. In his *De Vita Contemplativa*, Philo says they were also enthusiastic allegorizers of the Hebrew scriptures and, in addition, had arcane or esoteric writings of their own. Eusebius, Bishop of Caesarea in the fourth century, knew little or nothing of their origins but was struck by the similarities of their way of life to that of Christian monks.[3] He even speculates that the "writings of the ancient men who were the founders of the sect," referred to by Philo, "may well have been our Gospels and Epistles." This is an intriguing possibility. Epiphanius (*c.* 315–403) was a bishop and church historian who also linked the Therapeutae with the early Christians. He notes that the name Jesus (Yeshua, or "God saves") is similar to the Greek word *therapeutae*, a "healer" or "saviour." Godfrey Higgins in *Anacalypsis* says that the Therapeutae were physicians of the soul and had churches, bishops, priests and deacons all but identical with the Christians. He says they had missionary stations or colonies of their community in Rome, Corinth, Ephesus, Philippi, Colossae and Thessalonica, just as in the Pauline churches.[4]

In *The Pagan Christ*, I have documented the parallels between Osiris/Horus of Egypt and Yeshua-Joshua-Jesus in the New Testament. It is easy to see how allegorizing Jews, living in Egypt, could have made the shift. The Therapeutae could conceivably have been the original Christ communities and have first been called Christians at Antioch. What is certain is that there was widespread expectation in Jewish communities in the very early first century that Joshua or Yeshua the Deliverer might suddenly return to usher in a Messianic Age. Yeshua the Anointed One becomes Iesous Christos, or Jesus Christ, in Greek. His elevation to a central, mythical figure in Hellenized Jewish mysteries would have been a seamless transition.

But, it must be stressed again, nobody knows for sure how it all began.[5] However it happened, it is the "old, old story," this time in Jewish dress. To those who perhaps find it difficult to abandon a long-held opinion that every major religion must of necessity have its foundation upon a historical person, I commend the chapter "Can a Vibrant Religion Exist Without an Actual Founder?" in *Living Waters*.[6]

Before going any further, I would like to give here a very simple introduction to the Gospels, because I'm well aware that terms and ideas familiar to some readers are not necessarily shared by all. If you find it too simple or familiar, you can turn a few pages and get right into the book.

The Synoptic Gospels: Mark, Matthew and Luke

None of the Gospels have come down to us carrying the names of their "authors" or editors, and nobody really knows for certain who their final editors or "redactors" were, but I will use the traditional titles for the sake of simplicity.

It is important to know that Mark, Matthew, Luke and John and the rest of the New Testament documents were all written in

Hellenistic Greek. Greek was the lingua franca, the universal language of the educated class, in the ancient Mediterranean world,
ever since the conquests of Alexander the Great, who died in 323
BCE. Two things stand out when this fact is recognized:

1) It is agreed among scholars that the language in which any
   historical Jesus would have thought, spoken and taught was
   Aramaic. None of his teachings, however, have come down
   to us in Aramaic. Together with others, most notably the
   American critic Harold Bloom, I am amazed that more New
   Testament scholars are not wholly perplexed by this fact.
   Nothing, other than possibly five or six words, has been pre-
   served in the language actually spoken by a personage of such
   extraordinary standing in human history!

2) The Gospel of Mark makes no secret of the fact that the first
   disciples were uneducated fishermen. He even paints a picture of them as slow-witted at times. The idea that any one of
   them helped create and write a new literary form, a Gospel,
   needs to be put aside. None of the Gospels was written by an
   eyewitness. Paul, the earliest New Testament writer, never
   met a historical Jesus, only the mythic Christ.

So, nobody knows for certain when or by whom the Gospels
were created. It must be remembered that they were never "written" in the way a modern author writes a book. They are highly
edited works showing the evidence of having been compiled from
earlier collections of sayings and, I believe, ancient myths and
"miracle" plays depicted in the Mystery Religions.[7] Mark's Gospel
was by general scholarly agreement the first, written most probably sometime between 70 and 90 CE. Matthew was probably
written around 90 CE, Luke shortly thereafter. Because Matthew
and Luke contain nearly all of Mark and they can thus all be

viewed together, they are called the Synoptic (from two Greek words meaning "to see together") Gospels.

Since the finding of the Gnostic gospels at Nag Hammadi in Upper Egypt in 1945, it is recognized that there were at least twenty gospels circulating in the early centuries. Most were named after prominent Gospel figures to guarantee a feeling of authority and authenticity—that is, to ensure a readership. The Gospel of Thomas is the best known of these.[8] The four canonical (officially approved) Gospels were declared to be so by the Church during a lengthy process, and all others were hunted down and destroyed. The likely reason the books found at Nag Hammadi had been buried there was to escape the vigorous attempts after the Council of Nicaea, in 325 CE, to silence all but the official line.

Scholarly study long ago led to the conclusion that whoever "wrote" or were the final redactors/editors of Matthew and Luke had Mark in front of them when they wrote their Gospels because, between them, they reproduced the bulk of it verbatim. It should be noted, however, that they certainly don't treat Mark as the untouchable and inerrant Word of God, because at times they make specific corrections or depart from his account altogether. Mark includes no birth narrative ("his" Jesus is an adult from the very beginning), only a very few parables, and little other specific teaching of Jesus. There is no Sermon on the Mount. (Incidentally, the Sermon on the Mount becomes the Sermon on the Plain in Luke.) Also, Mark records certain (perhaps embarrassing) details—such as the cry of dereliction and forsakenness from the Cross—that Matthew or Luke either soften or, as I have said, leave out entirely. Mark frequently underlines as well the disciples' well-nigh total inability to understand what was happening.

In addition to Mark, Matthew and Luke seem to have another common source of material not found in Mark. The traditional hypothesis here is that this source, called Q (from the German word *Quelle*, "source"), was a "sayings" gospel with no story of the

Cross and Resurrection, much like the Gnostic Gospel of Thomas. Over the years, this hypothesis (no document has ever been found) has spawned many books and a plethora of Ph.D. theses, and it is still widely believed in by critical scholars. However, a formidable challenge to the theory has recently been issued by the scholar Michael Goulder of Birmingham, England, in an article in a prestigious scholarly journal titled "Is Q a Juggernaut?" In this article Goulder says that there is scarcely a Biblical scholar in Oxford today who would vouch for the authenticity of a Q document. He believes that the simpler explanation for the common non-Markan material is that Luke had Matthew as well as Mark in front of him when he wrote. [9]

The final element in both Matthew and Luke is material peculiar to each alone. This is generally referred to as L for Luke's and M for Matthew's. We must remember that the Gospel authors often were acting as redactors or editors, collating material from a range of sources, not all of them known to us today and many of them much more ancient than scholars from traditional backgrounds would care to admit. For example, there was a vast store of oral, as well as written, "wisdom" sayings that circulated widely in the ancient Near East, particularly in the Mystery Religions. The Mystery Religions were movements that restricted full admission to those who had gone through certain secret initiation rites, or mysteries. The most famous were those of Demeter in Eleusis in Greece, as well as those of Dionysus, Mithras, Serapis and Isis. The "parts" acted out and spoken by the sun god or central speaker in the many Mystery Religion dramas formed a part of this collection of "sayings," or Logia.

Why were four Gospels selected, and not three or six or eight? Irenaeus, the Bishop of Lyons around 190 CE, said there had to be four because there were four winds and four directions. This usually draws an indulgent smile from scholars, but there was a solid, though esoteric, reason behind the choice. For the ancients the number four was fundamental to the entire structure of life and the universe. The square, with its four sides, was the basis for any further elaboration in all forms of building, even the Pyramids. There were four major stages in evolution: the mineral, the vegetative, the animal and the human. Also, there were the four basic elements of water, earth, air and fire. This is the esoteric reason why the Egyptian sun god Horus had four sons. It is also behind the account of Jesus' choice of four fishermen as his chief disciples: Peter, Andrew, James and John. It was perfectly natural, even necessary, then, that this fourfold order of nature be followed in structuring the Scriptures for the new movement, Christianity.

John's Gospel

The last of the four Gospels, John, was probably composed around 95–100 CE, and is in a classification by itself. The vast differences between the Gospel According to St. John and the first three Synoptics have been commented upon by Christian scholars all the way back to the latter half of the second century. John may have followed some of Mark's outline, especially the Passion narrative, but his Gospel is so different that we are in an almost completely other world. From the very outset, John's Jesus is the Son of God in all his glory.

The differences between John and the Synoptics simply cannot be reconciled, much as some conservative scholars have tried. There are no parables in John. The account of the institution of Holy Communion, or the Mass, is missing completely, replaced by the washing of the disciples' feet on Maundy Thursday, as it has come to be called. Like Mark, there is no nativity story and no virgin birth. Instead of a birth narrative, we are told Jesus was the divine Logos with God, and part of God's being from eternity. The cleansing of the temple comes right at the beginning of Jesus' ministry in John, and not at the end, where the others all have it.

The amazing story of Lazarus is unique to John. In general, John's
Gospel has been called "the spiritual Gospel" because of the vari-
ous extensive and unique dialogues where the deep things of the
Spirit are discussed.

At the same time, the Gospel of John is undoubtedly the most
quoted of the four Gospels. It contains the famous text, John 3:16,
which is so often held up on a card by that person who always
manages to get a seat in the ball park right behind the catcher or
in the part of the arena where the TV cameras zoom in most frequently. The same text is found on signs of every size all along the
roads and highways of North America. It begins with the familiar
words "For God so loved the world . . ." It's the same chapter
that tells the story so loved and quoted by the more conservative
wing of contemporary Christianity, about the need to be "born
again." They misunderstand it completely in my view, but they
certainly use it a lot.

In discussing what is meant by being born again (or better, in
view of the Greek, "born from above"), in chapter 3 John makes it
abundantly clear that what is being talked about is the fact that all
humans are to have two births—the natural birth from "water," as
a human baby, and a second birth, which is spiritual. The "born
again" experience is that of recognizing one's true nature as a spark
of the Divine—the light that gives light to everyone coming into
the world. It has nothing whatever to do with what evangelicals
describe as recognizing one's status as a sinner and "accepting
Christ as Saviour." There is nowhere in the Gospels where this
condition for "becoming a Christian" is ever laid out in the manner,
for example, in which the famous Evangelist Billy Graham presents
it. The traditional church teaching that we all, by our very nature
as part of the human family, are contaminated by "original sin,"
that is, by the sin of our mythical forefather Adam—Paul says that
"in Adam all died" (because of his sin)—and that we add to this

by our own sinful acts, has been the basis for clerical control all down the ages.

It's important to remember that the idea of having a second birth is by no means unique to the New Testament. It was widespread in the cults and competing philosophies flourishing in the Greco-Roman world of that day. It even had its own term, *palingenesia*. In the Hermetic Literature (*Corpus Hermeticum*—recorded in the second and third centuries, but based upon Egyptian wisdom going back many centuries before that) the subtitle of chapter 13 is "On Being Born Again" and includes the "Hymn of Rebirth."[10]

Significantly, John's portrayal of Jesus and the whole story is, in fact, so different from the others that there were parts of the emerging ecclesiastical organization in Rome and elsewhere that wanted it rejected from the official canon of sacred scripture. One vivid way of describing this situation is to say that John's Jesus "walks about four feet above the ground." In other words, while this Jesus never categorically claims to be God (incidentally, this claim is not explicitly made anywhere in the New Testament), his status is one of great personal exaltation from the very outset. There is no Markan "Messianic Secret" here: there is no command not to tell anyone who he is. The Christology—the view of who Jesus is—is far "higher" in John than it is in Matthew, Luke and Mark. John's Jesus moves and speaks with the total authority of the central figure of the ancient mythos or mystery play, with no attempt to cloak or veil the fully allegorical nature of the drama. (For more on the differences between John and the Synoptics, see Appendix A.)

What are we to say to all of the above? The implications, it seems to me, are quite clear. While each of the Gospels is a mythical rendition of the Jesus Story, the Fourth Gospel is to my mind the most conspicuously so. Read literally, it is, with some brilliant exceptions, a laborious and quite unbelievable task. Taken fully in its deeper, spiritual sense as the drama of the soul in matter, it is a virtuoso piece of illumination and inspiration full of joy and glory and hope for all. I suggest that with all of this in mind, readers might want to get a good, modern translation—I prefer the New Revised Standard Version myself—and set aside the time to read John through. Don't do it in bits and pieces as if you were in Sunday school or church, but as a whole. Read it as you would any other book, remembering that the chapters and verses are artificial divisions introduced many centuries after the book first appeared. Read it allegorically as a parable about your own life's journey, and feel it come alive as never before. The message of this book is that Christ's journey is a metaphor for our own spiritual journey through life. Read as myth and allegory, the Gospels speak powerfully to that theme.

St. Paul

This book is concerned with the mythic meaning of the Gospels, but it must be kept in mind that the earliest writings of the New Testament are those of St. Paul, who was the major force in the establishment of Christianity as a universal faith. He wrote his epistles around 50–65 CE, about twenty years before the earliest Gospel. He knew only a mystical Jesus, and his approach is wholly mythical—that of the Christ within. Paul's knowledge of Jesus comes from visions and revelations; from the Old Testament (Paul viewed the whole of it as prophetic and as elucidating facts about Jesus); and from what was being said about the Christos in the Christian communities already in existence.[11]

The silence of Paul over the putative historical Jesus is virtually ear-shattering. But, because he does speak of Jesus Christ some two hundred times, the true nature of the problem escapes the average reader. He calls Jesus Lord and Son of God, but such titles already existed within both Judaism and the surrounding Pagan religions, and of themselves prove nothing. Paul presupposes that Jesus existed as a supernatural being before "God sent him into the world to redeem it." Such pre-existence on the part of the Logos and Sophia, or Wisdom, was part of Judaic thought at the time. It was also part of Gnostic thinking, and there is considerable evidence to support the view that Paul was a Gnostic. According to Paul, Jesus assumed flesh (mythically) sometime after the reign of David, from whom Paul says, following what the Old Testament prophesied, that Jesus, as a man, was supposed to have been descended.[12] In the myth, he was "made of the seed of David according to the flesh." This, of course, was part of the traditional view of what or who the Messiah had to be. In Romans too he terms him a Jew "according to the flesh" and, later, the scion of Jesse to govern the Gentiles.[13] As Professor G.A. Wells points out in *Did Jesus Exist?*, however, there were many centuries intervening between David and Paul, and the latter gives absolutely no indication in which of them Jesus' earthly life supposedly fell. It is all supremely vague and mystical. We remember that Osiris too in the myth had an earthly life but was wholly mythical himself. As the scholar G. Bornkamm has observed, it is "an astonishing fact" that Paul nowhere mentions Jesus of or from Nazareth, who was a prophet and miracle worker who ate with tax collectors and sinners. He never once calls him "Jesus of Nazareth."

Among other things, Paul is silent about:

- The Sermon on the Mount, and all the rest of Jesus' ethical teachings. He discusses ethical issues, even some doctrines familiar to us, such as "bless those who persecute you," but he gives them on his own authority, with no sign that Jesus taught the very same truths.[14] He appeals instead to passages from the Old Testament to support his teachings. The Gospel itself was already written in the pages of the Old Testament, according to Romans 1:2. He says there that the Gospel was "promised beforehand through his prophets in the holy scriptures."

- The virgin birth. Paul simply says Jesus was "born of a woman," but so too were the Pagan deities, for example Horus and his mother Isis. He never mentions the virgin birth.

- The Lord's Prayer. This omission is all the more remarkable in that Paul discusses prayer at length in chapter 8 of Romans and says plainly that Christians don't know exactly what to pray for and have to depend on the Spirit's praying within us with "groanings that cannot be uttered."[15]

- The temple cleansing—which is cited by all four Gospels.

- All the miracles that abound in the Gospels. In fact, he seems to deny that Jesus worked miracles, since he puts down that whole approach: "Jews demand signs [miracles] and Greeks desire wisdom, but we proclaim Christ crucified . . ."[16]

- He knows nothing of Jesus' command to go and baptize everyone, since he explicitly says: "Christ did not send me to baptize."[17]

- He fails to support his lengthy plea for celibacy by any reference to Jesus' reported praise for those who renounce marriage for the sake of the kingdom.[18]

- Even when writing about Jesus' death, he never mentions any of the trials, Pontius Pilate, Herod or Jerusalem. In 1 Corinthians, 2:6–8, Paul writes about the crucifixion of Christ by "the rulers of this age," but this is not a reference to any earthly powers. Rather, he is referring to the widespread view in the Judaism of his day that the world was in the grip of evil angels and other malignant forces.[19] Kittel, in his *Theological Wordbook of the New Testament*, says that by "rulers" Paul is not here referring to any earthly governors but to heavenly or spiritual ones.

Critical scholars agree that Paul gives Jesus' Crucifixion "no historical context" whatever, so that nothing is known from him as to where Jesus had lived, where he was killed, where he was buried or the story of his Resurrection. E. Kasemann, the distinguished New Testament scholar, has found that "the scantiness of Paul's Jesus tradition overall is surprising," to say the least, but adds that his silence over the circumstances of the Crucifixion, which is so central to his theology, is "positively shocking." G.A. Wells in *Did Jesus Exist?* notes that scholar W. Schmithals is on record as saying that Paul's silence about the entire substance of the Gospels is a "problem to which no satisfactory solution has been given during two hundred years of historical and critical research, and to the solution of which great theologians have sometimes not even attempted to contribute." They simply refuse to tackle the issue at all.

In addition to the above, the following facts need to be known more widely:

Paul's mention of James, the Lord's brother, does not necessarily mean a blood brother of Jesus.[20] The Jerusalem group of believers were called by Paul "the brethren of the Lord." Paul frequently uses the term "brother" for a fellow believer. Jesus, in this tradition, spoke of his close followers as his brothers, just as certain religious groups still do today, for example the Brethren churches. I even get letters from people wholly unknown to me that begin: "Brother Tom."

It is argued that 1 Thessalonians 1:6 says Christians received the Word in much "affliction" and so are imitators of Christ. This might seem to imply that Christ was known to have suffered, that is, on earth. But other gods had similarly been regarded as suffering—Osiris, Orpheus, Adonis, etc.

Paul speaks of the faithful as having "received Christ Jesus," in whom are hidden all the treasures of wisdom and knowledge. Wells notes this is "the purest mysticism" and that the knowledge of Christ comes from communion "with hidden powers or spir-its."[21] In 1 Corinthians 4:1, Paul designates himself and his fel-lows as the "stewards of God's mysteries," which was exactly the technical name for the stewards at the temples of the popular Egypto-Greek deity Serapis.[22]

Finally, Paul uses the language of mysticism and of Mystery Religions over and over again. He speaks of being in Christ, through Christ, with Christ, unto Christ, as suggesting some indescrib-able relationship between himself (or the believer) and Christ. It's a relationship, according to Wells, for example, that the context wholly fails to explain. The real explanation is that Paul knew only the mystical Christ, the "Christ in you, the hope of glory."[23]

Finding Personal Meaning in the Myth

Know what is in front of your face and what
is hidden from you will be disclosed.

— THE GOSPEL OF THOMAS, Saying #5

When I was in my teens I led a youth Bible class at St. Peter's Anglican Church in the heart of downtown Toronto. One of the favourite old-time hymns the young people used to ask for began with the words: "Who is on the Lord's side? Who for him will go?" The answer came ringing back in a later verse: "We are on the Lord's side; Saviour we are thine." It was a fine evangelical call to service for Jesus.

Later, however, in my first year at University College, at the University of Toronto, I happened upon the chapter in the book of Exodus from which the key words of the hymn were taken. It was chapter 32, where the mythical story is told of Moses' descent from the mountain bearing the two tablets of stone upon which God's "finger" had written the Ten Commandments. Moses dis-covers that in his long absence on the mountain the people have strayed and made for themselves the image of a golden calf. Moses throws a major temper tantrum, smashes the two tablets on the ground, seizes the calf and, after reducing it to powder in a fire, scatters the ashes upon water and forces the Israelites to drink it.

The true significance of all of this no doubt revolves around the author's awareness of the ending of the zodiacal Age of Taurus the bull and the beginning of the Age of Aries the ram. (Notice that in Genesis, when Abraham was about to slay his son Isaac, he was told to offer up a ram caught in a nearby thicket instead.) But it's what happened next that arrested my full attention. Here is the text itself:

> When Moses saw that the people were running wild (for Aaron had let them run wild, to the derision of their enemies), then Moses stood in the gate of the camp, and said, "Who is on the Lord's side? Come to me!" And all the sons of Levi gathered around him. He said to them, "Thus says the Lord, the God of Israel, 'Put your sword on your side, each of you! Go back and forth from gate to gate throughout the camp, and each of you kill your brother, your friend, and your neighbour.'" The sons of Levi did as Moses commanded, and about three thousand of the people fell on that day. Moses said, "Today you have ordained yourselves for the service of the Lord, each one at the cost of a son or a brother, and so have brought a blessing on yourselves this day." (Exodus 32:25–29)

I have never heard this part of the story read in church. The hymn, of course, like the Church in general, wholly slides over this horror—the total antithesis of common humanistic morality, never mind of the complete ethical teachings of the New Testament. Notice also another major but usually overlooked phenomenon: The "Lord" in the story is Yahweh, later to become God the

Father. The hymn, however, as almost always happens in unthinking, popular Christian theology, transfers the title "Lord" to the "Saviour," that is, to Jesus. In other words, the entire passage is twisted to suit the cause of "the Gospel."

Anyone familiar with the rest of Exodus and indeed the whole of the Old Testament will be fully aware that this passage about killing sons, brothers and neighbours, and being blessed in the process, is far from atypical. There are many scenes of greater gore and outright cruelty—even genocide—in these "holy" texts than the verses quoted here. It would be "flogging a dead horse" to begin to list the most heinous.

What is important to stress, however, is that none of this was actual history. The recording of real events was not, as cannot be underlined too heavily, the purpose or intent of the authors in every case. Archaeology supports what knowledge of ancient theological and philosophical practices has made abundantly clear: the many battles and the carnage depicted in the Bible, especially in the supposed conquest of the Promised Land—Canaan—never happened as actual fact. They were all part of the mythical surroundings given to the Israelites to glorify their past and to underscore the zealous, exclusivist nature of the tribal god they served. If even a fraction of the battles and slaughters described in the early books of the Bible had actually taken place, the "Holy Land" would today be ankle deep in ancient weapons and other signs of furious wars. It is not. Indeed, very far from it. Mythmaking, you see, didn't just suddenly start and stop with the stories of Adam and Eve in the Garden of Eden. It runs throughout the entire Bible, all sixty-six books, including all of the New Testament and thus throughout the Jesus Story as well.

But how, one asks, can ancient myth, even though understood as defined by Joseph Campbell as "what never was, but always is," speak to you or me in the technological era of the twenty-first century? In the coming chapters we will examine the familiar New

Testament Jesus stories and try to see where they came from and what they mean for our lives. As we do so, we will see the full nature of the spiritual encouragement and the solid grounds for conquering our fears that ring through them.

This encouragement, oddly enough, has most relevance where religion itself is concerned. Anyone who has thought about it knows there is a tremendous amount of fear involved wherever religion or spirituality are even mooted for discussion. I know many hundreds of people through letters as well as direct contact over the years whose entire experience of what is sometimes euphemistically called their "spiritual life" (but more accurately too often is their catalogue of neuroses) is ringed about with fear. There is fear of God's disapproval, fear of offending parents, relatives, friends, clergy and others. There is also deep-rooted fear of change of any kind.

This latter aspect deserves much more attention than it gets. There are millions walking about out there today whose inner spiritual growth has far surpassed anything they once knew, but who move in mortal terror of anyone else finding out. One woman reader of my newspaper columns wrote to say that she lives in dread some Sundays until the clock moves past 11 a.m. Only then can she relax, since it's now too late to make it to her local church. Most Sundays, however, old fears win out and she ends up seated in a pew well before the sacred hour. Such was her background that church attendance became so loaded with negative power that she is almost paralyzed by the idea of being free to choose to go or not go as an autonomous agent. She wrote that she resents the way the preacher "talks as though we all are five-year-olds" and then she feels guilty about being critical in the church and of the Church.

Not that failure to attend church necessarily means spiritual growth; it could mean the opposite. We all need to examine our religious beliefs and practices from time to time to see to what degree they are governed not by insight and spiritual freedom but by childhood habits and adolescent, ingrained taboos. For far too many even today, religion equals guilt—lots of guilt. Perhaps if more people like my friend could summon the courage to voice their feelings to the clergy, the quality of the preaching might improve. Certainly, not speaking up or just staying away does nothing to challenge the current infantilization of the laity.

It's painful to say, but the amount of superstition and fear of moving on that pervades much of the public mind when it comes to matters of faith and of spirit is profound. Yet, at the same time, there is an enormous fascination with spirituality. The towering success of *The Da Vinci Code* is a current testimony to this. The lesson learned by Peter is one for us all just now: "Fear not." Dare to leave the "boat," as we shall see he was once challenged in the myth to do, and move ahead! My hope is that this book will become the catalyst for just such a personal breakthrough for you.

3

THE VIRGIN BIRTH AND JESUS' CHILDHOOD

Deep at the heart of all that is, there shines
the beauty of a transcendent glory.

— ANONYMOUS

VIRGINS do not give birth to babies. Few people outside the Church need convincing of that today. Nevertheless, lest it be said that the mythical understanding being put forth here has already closed its mind against the possibility that God—however one expresses this ultimate mystery—can do anything, even to the breaking of the very natural laws which he/she created in the first place, some preliminary observations need to be made.

We know that stories of virgin births and/or other forms of supernatural births, of god-men and of illustrious heroes, were very much a part of the total milieu in the Mediterranean world of the centuries preceding and surrounding the emergence of the Christian movement. It was really a coded or esoteric way of saying that somebody was very special indeed. It was a metaphor in the ancient Greco-Roman world used to announce an entity of striking numinosity and power.

Early Christian apologists, in their disputations with Pagan critics, freely admitted there had been other virgin births. Horus, the ancient Egyptian saviour, was miraculously conceived, and Origen, in his famous debate with the Pagan philosopher Celsus, cites the story that when Plato was born of Amphictione, her husband, Ariston, was prevented from having intercourse with her until she had brought forth the child, which she had by the god Apollo.[1]

Similar stories circulated about Alexander, Apollonius of Tyana and dozens of others. There was an early tradition in the second and third centuries that the manger at Bethlehem was actually in a cave, and the symbol of supernatural births in this womb-of-the-earth-like setting also belongs to other ancient traditions. For example, the Greek god-man Adonis, whose death and resurrection after three days also came after the spring equinox on March 25, was born in a cave. So too was Mithras, whose cult is closely paralleled in early Christianity as well. Some second- and third-century Christian sarcophagi have carvings on them of the Nativity scene with the ox, the ass and the three Magi. The latter wear the hat of the god Mithras. The ass was traditionally associated with Seth, the brother and murderer of Osiris. It was also associated with the planet Saturn, a symbol for Israel. The ox or bull was for long ages the symbol for Osiris himself.

One of the clearest pieces of evidence that in the story of Jesus we are dealing with a mythical tradition lies in the two divergent accounts of the virgin birth found in Matthew and Luke. Incidentally, there are scores of scholarly treatments of the non-historicity of the "born of the Virgin Mary" phrase in the Creed, and only the most ultra-conservative of New Testament authorities would risk arguing today for taking it literally. Whether or not they believe in a historical Jesus of Nazareth, there is general consensus among

Biblical scholars that the birth narratives are Midrashic (interpretive) expansions of universal mythical themes. Nevertheless, it is important for our study to set out the major reasons for this overall agreement.

In the first place, the birth stories in Matthew and Luke are very obviously later additions to the original traditions about Jesus. The average uninstructed person who picks up a New Testament could well be forgiven for thinking that Matthew—who tells one version of the miraculous birth—is not only the first Gospel to have been written but also holds the earliest testimony in the book. Matthew's centuries-old position as the first of the four Gospels in any printed bible has lent immense authority to such a view. Of course, as anyone who has read even a little about the Christian scriptures knows, the Gospels together form a second, later stratum to the whole New Testament. The authentic letters of St. Paul are earlier than the Gospels by at least twenty to thirty years. What's more, the earliest of the four Gospels is that of Mark, written in Rome and usually dated sometime after 70 CE. I personally agree with those scholars who argue for a later date of about 90 CE, but conservatives, of course, try to push for not later than 70 CE, the date of the destruction of the temple by the Romans under Titus.

What is important about this matter of dating is that neither Paul nor Mark mentions a word about any virgin birth. Paul, who was the closest of all to the presumed origins, says in one passage that Jesus Christ was "born of a woman," but that is all. This is no evidence for historicity. The same, of course, was said by the Egyptians in their ritual myths about the god Horus. It was said of other mythic deities as well. Mark's Gospel significantly begins abruptly not with a newborn but with an adult Jesus being baptized in Jordan by John the Baptizer. Significantly, none of the other epistle writers in the rest of the New Testament cites a miraculous birth.

Perhaps most important of all, the Fourth Gospel, that of John, which even from the earliest times, as we have seen, has been regarded as the "spiritual" or "mystical" Gospel, also fails to mention the virgin birth. Instead, this author chooses to place Jesus' origins back before time was, that is to say, in the bosom of the Cosmic Source, or God. Hence the famous passage with which the Gospel opens—echoing the first verse of Genesis—"In the beginning was the Word [Logos], and the Word was with God, and the Word was God." More about that later.

Genealogies

The fact that a fictional tradition was gradually being established is attested to by the genealogies given to Jesus by the two sources that do speak of a virgin birth, namely, Matthew and Luke. Likely because the Gospel of Matthew was addressing the concerns of a mainly Jewish community, he traces Jesus' ancestry back to a beginning with Abraham.[2] He does so, significantly, in three groups of fourteen. Both numbers were of traditional, symbolical import. Together, they spoke of perfection. Luke reverses the order, beginning with Jesus himself and working backwards until he comes at last to Adam, whom he describes as the "son of God."[3] He was writing for a chiefly Gentile (Greek) community, and so, instead of emphasizing the Jewishness of Jesus, he stresses his universality. Jesus in this version comes directly from the first father of the race. Since Adam (most certainly) and Abraham (most likely) were also mythical figures, it's fairly obvious what's afoot.

But two other points must be made. There is absolutely no way the two genealogies can be made compatible, despite the contortions of some fundamentalist expositors. You just have to ask who Jesus' grandfather was alleged to be and check the texts for yourself. Secondly, and this seems to me to be the clincher against which logic can offer no acceptable solution, both of these lengthy and involved attempts end in a genuine debacle. Both are attempting to show that Jesus was of the Davidic lineage and thus a fulfiller of Messianic prophecy. The ancient traditions demanded that. But, since both are also at pains to show that Mary bore Jesus without intercourse with Joseph, the whole structure collapses with the admission that the Davidic bloodline came through Joseph, not her. Thus Matthew lamely concludes his list with: ". . . and Jacob the father of Joseph the husband of Mary, of whom Jesus was born, who is called the Messiah." Both genealogies thus become totally irrelevant as history. There is good reason why the unknown author of the first letter to Timothy, in chapter 1, verse 4, tells the young preacher to avoid giving heed to "myths and endless genealogies."

Son of a Carpenter?

Speaking of Joseph, the "father" of Jesus, it is highly revealing to consider how he has been depicted down the ages as a carpenter— making Jesus, on the surface at any rate, "the carpenter's son."[4] Mark, however, actually says that Jesus himself was a carpenter or stonemason: "Is not this the carpenter, the son of Mary?"[5] This is the reading of the bulk of the earliest Greek manuscripts. But there are also some manuscripts that say *the son of a carpenter*. This was the preferred text used by Origen in the second century and argued for in his famous dialogue with Celsus, the Pagan philosopher. Matthew's account quite plainly follows this textual tradition as well—he says "the carpenter's son." What is truly interesting, however, to those who see this all as eternal myth, is a truth elucidated by Carl Jung in his book *Symbols of Transformation*. Jung notes that not just Joseph but many, if not all, of the fathers of ancient heroes and/or god-men were artisans, carpenters or creative builders of one kind or another.[6]

According to an Arabian legend, Terah, Abraham's father, was a master craftsman who worked with wood. Tyashtri, father of the Vedic god Agni, was a cosmic architect, a smith and a carpenter. Cinyras, the father of Adonis, was also a carpenter. Hephaestus, the father of the many-faced Hermes, was the Greek fire god who made, among other things, Achilles' shield. Homer's hero Odysseus was a wily craftsman who planned and created the famous Trojan horse. This mythic theme, Jung points out, is also followed in folk tales everywhere, with the more modest woodcutter as hero or father of the same. In other words, the entire tradition of Jesus as a carpenter or the son of one is a clear sign, not of historical detail, but of mythical enhancement disguised as earthly fact.

Pagan Parallels

The third compelling argument against any possibility of history being behind the virgin birth is the obvious fact that, as already indicated, virgin births were a common feature of mythological solar and other deities or semi-deities in the ancient world. The reader is referred back to *The Pagan Christ* and the many other books cited there for further evidence that even the early Fathers of the Church felt some genuine embarrassment over the issue. Those deeply interested in the entire process whereby mythical characters become over the years the focus of seemingly historical trappings and an assumed historicity that is wholly unfounded upon actual facts of any kind should read Lord Raglan's classic 1956 study *The Hero: A Study in Tradition, Myth and Drama*.

The virgin birth part of the Jesus Story fails to ring true as history not least, then, because it is really part of a formulaic element in the tales of most major heroes from great antiquity. (So too is the element of the threat to the newborn's life. Herod's slaughter of the innocents—for which there isn't a shred of historical evidence—had many parallels. For example, at the birth of India's

Lord Krishna, King Kansa, a brutal tyrant, ordered the killing of all boy babies under two years of age.) But, in the case of Jesus, it has a remarkable, even central, esoteric message that for too long has been obscured by the furore over whether the virgin birth belongs to an authentically Christian faith or not. We need to move far beyond that theological debate now and explore what the inner meaning of the myth is saying to us about who and what we are.

The Meaning

By openly declaring that Joseph was not the actual begetter of Jesus, the Evangelists are saying that what mattered was not so much the natural side of Jesus' humanity, but the divine side or spark of the Divine within him. If we probe further, however, and see this notion as part of the myth of the human Self, or of every man and woman born into this world, what it says at the most profound level is that each human being's birth is a miraculous happening. We have a physical-psychical nature from our mother's womb, but we are also begotten of God. This is why John in his opening chapter underlines that those who receive the awareness of the Christ principle or light within themselves are "born not of blood, nor of the will of the flesh, nor of the will of man, but of God." We have a divine origin or a latent divinity within ourselves as a result of direct divine descent. As it says in the Book of Acts, "We are all God's offspring." This higher or more spiritual meaning is directly expressed in the prologue of John's Gospel, where he says: "That was the true Light, which lighteth every man that cometh into the world" (King James Version).

Thus, for example, Joseph Campbell sees the mythic meaning of the virgin birth as the coming to full awareness by each individual person that he or she is more than a human animal concerned merely with reproduction and material things. It is "the birth of the spiritual as opposed to the merely natural life," he says; the recognition that there are higher aims and values in living than self-preservation, reproduction, pleasure, the acquisition of money and things, and the struggle for power or status.[7] It's a birth in the heart, or the idea of being spiritually "born again" that Jesus spoke of and which has been so misunderstood by fundamentalists today.

So, the question posed to us by the virgin birth is not, Do you believe this literally? but, Have you truly experienced your own divinity within? Are you claiming your inheritance as more than a human animal—as a fully human being? To put this another way: Has the Christ principle been born in the manger of your consciousness? You don't have to be a Christian or a member of any church for this to take place. As the medieval mystic Meister Eckhart once said in a sermon: "It is more worth to God his being brought forth ghostly [spiritually] in the individual virgin or good soul than that he was born of Mary bodily."[8] As Campbell points out, this kind of virgin birth within is well expressed in St. Paul's statement in Galatians, "I live, now not I, but Christ liveth in me."[9]

The whole allegory of the humble but royal birth in a cave or stable was based upon the archetypal idea of the kingly nature of the crowning of our evolutionary development by the advent of self-reflective consciousness. The concept of a Messianic or Christly "coming" therefore is the result of the ancient sages meditating upon this new and higher degree of intelligence and self-awareness. The former, purely animalistic mode of life gave way to the potential inherent in a seed of divine mind implanted in the order of nature from "above," that is, by the mysterious omnipresence we call God. In reality, then, Christmas itself is, as the carol triumphantly announces, "the birthday of a king." But this "king" is not a single individual who is believed to have lived in Palestine some two thousand years ago, but the glorious birth within each one of us of divine Incarnation. As St. Paul puts it: "Christ in you; the hope of glory."

Thus, all the rites and practices of the churches at Christmastime are truly efficacious and meaningful only if the birth of the "Saviour Jesus" is understood as a symbol of the glorious "virgin" birth within ourselves. The joyful message is that Transcendence has broken into history and become part of every one of us. What we need is to have the eyes to see this glory within and all around. It is when we truly recognize who and what we really are that we are born again. As Hermes Trismegistus ("thrice great") says to his son Tat in the passage of the Hermetica already referred to: "I am not now the man I was. I have been born again in spirit."

At the Age of Twelve

One of the most obvious clues that in the Gospel narratives we are not dealing with anything resembling a biography of a historical person called Jesus or Yeshua of Nazareth is the fact that in all the Gospels except Luke there is a total silence about the entire period from Jesus' infancy until the beginning of his public ministry at about age thirty. This is wholly unlike any other biography ever written, and is a bedrock fact that the historicizers and other literalizers of all schools must face at some point. We are asked by them to believe that the Gospel authors and editors knew in minute detail what Jesus is alleged to have said and to have done over a space of from one year to about three years, but that at the same time they could not remember one single incident, occasion or saying from all the years between! It defies reason.

In his two-volume work *Ancient Egypt, The Light of the World*, the scholar Gerald Massey makes the telling point that this same vacuum occurs in the various accounts of many other mythical Messiahs. For example, there is no recorded deed or history of the Egyptian "Christ," Horus, between the ages of twelve and thirty years. Luke's exception, the story of Jesus being taken to the temple in Jerusalem when he was twelve, the approximate

age of incipient adulthood and personal responsibility to the
Torah, deserves a closer look. It is a highly instructive stage in
the unfolding drama:

> Now every year his parents went to Jerusalem for the festival
> of the Passover. And when he was twelve years old, they
> went up as usual for the festival. When the festival was ended
> and they started to return, the boy Jesus stayed behind in
> Jerusalem, but his parents did not know it. Assuming that he
> was in the group of travellers, they went a day's journey.
> Then they started to look for him among their relatives
> and friends. When they did not find him, they returned to
> Jerusalem to search for him. After three days they found him
> in the temple, sitting among the teachers, listening to them
> and asking them questions. And all who heard him were
> amazed at his understanding and his answers. When his par-
> ents saw him they were astonished; and his mother said to
> him, "Child, why have you treated us like this? Look, your
> father and I have been searching for you in great anxiety." He
> said to them, "Why were you searching for me? Did you not
> know that I must be in my Father's house?" But they did not
> understand what he said to them. Then he went down with
> them and came to Nazareth, and was obedient to them. His
> mother treasured all these things in her heart. And Jesus
> increased in wisdom and in years, and in divine and human
> favour. (Luke 2:41–52)

This passage reads clearly enough on the surface, but few stories in the overall drama are more frequently misunderstood and
distorted in the retelling, whether in sermons, popular writing or
Bible study, than this. It would be impossible to count the number
of times I have heard it skewed by clergy and others. In mistaken
zeal they cite the passage as evidence of Jesus' presumed unique

sonship and omniscience. We are told by them that he was found in the temple *instructing* the teachers and the authorities there. But such was not the case at all. Luke says simply that he was both listening to these experts and "asking them questions." True, we are told they were very surprised at his intelligence and at his answers to questions in the discussion.[10] But he wasn't *teaching* the teachers, as is so often supposed.

Luke himself gives his readers a hint that the story is symbolical/allegorical by using the formulaic, symbolical number three. Jesus' parents only notice he is missing and discover him in the temple *after three days*. In the Ritual of Egypt, Isis, the mother of the sun god Horus, searches for three days to find her son. As was noted in my earlier work, the number three gained its esoteric, symbolic meaning from the observed fact that for three days and two nights each month the moon is not visible from Earth. The moon was thought of symbolically as having congress with the sun at that time and as conceiving the new moon. Consequently, three became a symbol of any potent period of change or renewal. Hence the three days of Christ's entombment prior to the Resurrection.

But there are some other features deserving comment. What kind of parents, one might ask, would allow their twelve-year-old son, in what purportedly was his very first grown-up visit to an unfamiliar city and territory, such freedom of movement and lack of supervision as to not even notice he was absent for a whole day? The situation is all the more puzzling in that the text says they were actually on the move, returning through the dangerous country around Jerusalem (mainly wilderness or "badlands"), well before they began to search for Jesus in earnest.

Then there is the larger issue of historical credibility raised by the fact that, while Luke tells us Mary mused on her son's behaviour and treasured all these things in her heart, the subsequent narrative shows that she and his family in general had no idea of who he was really supposed to be. You would think that, having experienced a virgin birth herself and then observed her son's conduct and learned about his answers in the temple, Mary at least would have been well aware that something very remarkable was going on. Yet—especially in Mark, where on one occasion we are told his family came to get Jesus and take him home, "for, they said, he is beside himself" (is not well and may come to harm)— in the Gospels the immediate family are not shown as truly believing in him until after the Resurrection. This, of course, fits in completely with Mark's overall intention of showing that certain prophecies are being fulfilled. It was foretold that the Messiah would be rejected by even his closest friends and kin. Notice that some conservatives like to reason that, if this account were not really historical, the author would have left these negative details out through embarrassment. Why would anyone making up a story put in such a "clanger"? they query. However, they miss the point. As noted, the family's seemingly obtuse objections actually help make Mark's case. Only the true Messiah would be treated like that.

Fundamentally, however, the story relates to a deeper truth. What it reveals is that, as the age of responsibility is reached, one's deeper commitment, to the voice and stirrings of God both within and over all, comes to the fore of consciousness. The individual soul here radically begins its real "business," that of seeking to know and do the will of "the Father." "Jesus says to Joseph and Mary: 'Don't you realize I must be focused on my Father's concerns?'" (My translation.) In the ancient wisdom, the "father" was often a symbol of spirit and mind, while the "mother" symbolized the womb out of which spirit was born. But there was no hint of valuing maleness over the feminine. Far from it. Indeed, wisdom, personified—or hypostatized, to use the technical term— as Sophia, was invariably viewed as female. Sophia, or "wisdom" in Greek, is a feminine name. Mother, Latin *mater*, is the bearer of spirit. This story, then, is about the first solid step on the journey for all of us that ultimately, through much joy and struggling, leads to "home." There is a point where, however expressed, one decides to do the will of the "Father." Ego needs to begin to be controlled and made to serve a higher purpose than oneself. The road to spiritual maturity has begun.

Lest anyone expect that this road will be smooth or easy, let me hasten to say that it will require great courage and what the New Testament calls *hypomone*—tough endurance. The King James Version usually translates this Greek term as "patience," but this is only accurate in a very antique sense of that word. What it really means is the ability to stay with or under a heavy task or demanding situation. Life, as Scott Peck says in the very first lines of his giant bestseller *The Road Less Traveled*, "is difficult." The Buddha said so, the Gospels say so too. But, as I point out in *Living Waters*, the evolution of the soul is furthered much more by problems, doubts, anxieties—all forms of resistance to the Spirit within— than by purely halcyon days.[11]

There is a good reason why spiritually motivated people frequently experience "the dark night of the soul." I have certainly known such episodes of "dryness" in my own life, and can say without hesitation that they have, in retrospect, been times of genuine advance in self-knowledge and eventual victory over some mistaken ambition, pride or other weakness. Looking back at my life, I can see that the roughest terrain encountered has often been the most fruitful land I ploughed. The medieval alchemists tried to find ways of turning lead into gold. Understood esoterically, this was a metaphor for the inner spiritual soul-work involved for every one of us as we struggle by the grace of the God within to transform the leaden dross of all our foibles, all our neuroses and all our empty vanities into the pure gold of Christliness. St. Paul describes this process thus: "And all of us . . . seeing the glory of the Lord as though reflected in a mirror, are being transformed into the same image [that of the inner Christ] from one degree of glory to another; for this comes from the Lord, the Spirit."[12] That is what I mean by the concept of spiritual evolution.

As the well-loved hymn by Edwin Hatch puts it so aptly:

Breathe on me breath of God,
Till I am wholly Thine,
Until this earthly part of me
Glows with Thy fire divine.

4

TRANSFORMATIVE STAGES IN THE JESUS STORY

The letter kills, but the Spirit gives life.

— ST. PAUL, 2 CORINTHIANS 3:6

WE BEGIN HERE with the profound summation of spiritual truth once made by Valentinus, who was the author of *The Gospel of Truth*, one of the many Gnostic writings found at Nag Hammadi in 1945. He was a Gnostic Christian, later labelled a heretic, who was Egyptian but lived in Rome from approximately 135 to 165 CE (he founded a school there about 140) and had a very large following. He wrote the powerful, life-changing formula: "What liberates us is the knowledge of who we were, what we became; where we were, whereinto we have been thrown; whereto we speed, wherefrom we are redeemed; what birth is, and what rebirth."[1] However far from this central theme the discussion may at times lead us, this insight underlies the whole of our exploration from beginning to conclusion.

First, then, there comes an obvious question: If you take the literal/historical route, how long did Jesus' ministry last? In the schema according to Mark, followed by Matthew and Luke, the ministry lasts approximately one year. This is because deeply underlying the entire message is the ancient myth of the solar god in his yearly round. John's Gospel, however, which is, as we have seen, so unlike the other three in so many ways, seems to follow a three-year cycle. Scholars point out that in it there are at least three different Passover visits to Jerusalem. Since John's Gospel is the most "spiritual" and the least concerned to give even the appearance of verbatim reportage of a fully human being (in spite of the final chapter, which is an obvious appendix by a later hand), this Gospel can opt for the potent number three and at the same time focus almost the entire story on Jerusalem itself. In any case, the ministry lasted at most three short years.

As the great New Testament scholar Rudolph Bultmann once put it, John's Gospel is "all theology served up in the language of myth." Mark, the earliest Gospel, has been described as a collection of loosely knit anecdotes intended not as history but for edification and general evangelizing. Its mystery or the "secret" it reveals on the surface, literal reading is that Jesus is the long-expected Messiah and that the Kingdom of God will soon be a reality in the here and now. At a deeper, esoteric level, however, its message, as we have said earlier, is an allegory of the evolution of the soul in matter, the soul of every one of us. The Gospel begins with Jesus' baptism, which symbolizes the fact that to incarnate in the watery condition of the body is to be wholly immersed in the realm of matter. Just as Jesus descends into the waters of Jordan, so the soul of every one of us has descended into life in the body. The human body, as we know, is two-thirds water.

The Baptism

Few things, however, have been more distorted and misunderstood in the Christian religion because of a literal approach to the

Bible than the ritual known as the Sacrament of Holy Baptism. In the past, indeed, many have died because of bitter differences over how, when and how often it should be administered, to whom and by whom. Today, even the fast-growing crowds of the un-churched—those whom the retired Episcopal Bishop of Newark, John Spong, usually refers to as "church alumni"—still want their infant children "done," that is, christened or baptized. It is tradition-ally the key mark doctrinally of full membership in the Church; but, at the popular level, it is now commonly, for a growing number, little more than a social rite of passage and an occasion for a party.

Long ago, when I was a parish minister myself in the late fifties and early sixties, I baptized hundreds of babies and older children at my quickly growing suburban church, the majority of whom in all likelihood now belong to those swelling numbers who tell the census taker "no religion" when asked. I still vividly remember how weird it seemed at the time to be gazing down into the inno-cent faces of the tiny infant baptizands while reading from the prayer book service about their sinfulness and need for total regen-eration. It seemed a poor way to welcome these young "souls" into Holy Mother Church, or into the world in general for that matter.

I am reminded here of Joseph Campbell's anecdote in pro-gram 2 of *The Power of Myth*. There, in his commentary upon the way in which the Eden myth in Genesis shows nature as an enemy and God as opposed to nature, while man is seen as a disobedient sinner cast out of the Garden, Campbell told the story of the Zen Buddhist he once encountered in Japan. Remarking on this Gene-sis story, the monk said: "God against man—man against God; God against nature—nature against God. Funny religion!" Camp-bell noted that in the Japanese approach to religion there was no talk of depravity, a Fall from innocence, or original sin. They had a "mythology that includes all of life." He found it all a strangely liberating environment in which to reflect upon religion and its impact on our daily lives.

In the Gospels, the very first mention of baptism comes at the beginning of the Gospel of Mark's account. Without any of the preliminaries of the other Gospels, the drama commences with a quote from the Septuagint version (Greek translation) of the Old Testament: "See, I am sending my messenger ahead of you . . . 'Prepare the way of the Lord, make his paths straight.'" Then John the Baptist appears in the wilderness "proclaiming a baptism of repentance for the forgiveness of sins." It is clear that Mark deliberately took the Greek version of the quote, which is from Isaiah, chapter 40, rather than cite the actual Hebrew text, because it suited his purpose much better. He actually twists the original—which is about the return of the children of Israel from exile—and makes it into what it is not, a Messianic prophecy.

As one reads on, however, it is readily apparent that the personage Jesus presents at the Jordan does not proclaim himself as Messiah, or the Son of God; he announces instead the nearness of the Kingdom of God as being "the Good News [Euangelion] of God."[2] It's worth observing that "the Gospel" about which one hears so much in evangelical and other circles has nothing at this point to do with the kind of message that conservative preachers constantly proclaim. It's not about "the blood of Jesus," the Cross or even being "born again." The Mark text explicitly says the Good News is the reality of the Kingdom, the reality of God's presence in power in the world and intimately in one's life.

Before going any further, we should notice that earlier, in Luke's Gospel, he tells the mythical story of how Mary, upon learning that she is with child, goes to visit her relative Elizabeth. Though of advanced years and well beyond child-bearing age, Elizabeth has also conceived a son and is already in her sixth month.[3] Thus, we learn that John and Jesus were six months apart in age. From the point of view of the astronomical allegory, this is of crucial importance:

1) Elizabeth is yet one more example of the many women throughout the whole of the Bible who conceive in a miraculous fashion in their senior years. Abraham's wife, Sarah, the mother of Ishmael and Isaac, is one. You may remember she laughed at the angel's message. "So Sarah laughed to herself, saying, 'After I have grown old, and my husband is old, shall I have pleasure?'" In Hebrew, the name Isaac means "he laughs."4 The mother of Samson is another, as is Hannah, the mother of Samuel. The meaning is clear to those who understand the esoteric sense of it. We must return here to the belief of the ancients in several accounts that there were three evolutionary stages before the emergence on the scene of the human animal soul and finally the Christly or spiritual soul. First came the mineral, then the vegetative, then the animal, and finally, after "ages of ages," the dawning of self-reflective consciousness and the flame of divine fire within. The aged women reflect or portray this fourth or "late in time behold him come" theme, as the familiar Christmas carol puts it so well. We will see later also how the story of Jesus coming across the water "in the fourth" watch of the night—just before the dawn—makes the same point.

2) The sixth-months-apart aspect is making the significant point that, in the earlier astronomical allegory, the natural man, who rises under the sign of Virgo on the eastern horizon, gives way six months later to the spiritual man or Christ, who is born on that same horizon in the sign of Pisces, the fish. Eventually, as the evolution of our soul continues, the natural man is surpassed by the spiritual. This is the meaning behind the Baptist's words in John's Gospel: "He must increase, but I must decrease."5

Baptism Means Claiming Our Divinity, Not Removal of Sin

In Mark we read:

> In those days Jesus came from Nazareth of Galilee and was
> baptized by John in the Jordan. And just as he was coming up
> out of the water, he saw the heavens torn apart and the Spirit
> descending like a dove on him. And a voice came from
> heaven, "You are my Son, the Beloved; with you I am well
> pleased." And the Spirit immediately drove him out into the
> wilderness. He was in the wilderness forty days, tempted by
> Satan; and he was with the wild beasts; and the angels waited
> on him. (Mark 1:9–12)

That such a baptism had nothing whatever to do with sin is
transparent from both the text itself and from the fact that the
sinlessness of the Jesus character in the drama is vigorously
maintained in all of the New Testament.[6] In John's Gospel, the
Evangelist is in fact obviously embarrassed by this whole event
from that point of view and tries to explain it all away or at least
to downplay it. Water, as we have seen, symbolizes a number of
things, but principally it is the symbol of matter. Since our bodies
are made up largely of water, the soul was thought of as held fast
in a watery dungeon. It was a kind of death. When Jesus goes
down into the water, representing the divinity in every one of us,
his immersion symbolizes this central fact of Incarnation. The
soul accepts the lot and the struggle of being human—a blend-
ing of spirit and matter—in order to expand through experience
on this plane. Those who believe in reincarnation hold that it
may take several or even many lifetimes to gain all the experience
necessary for winning full spiritual maturity. My own view inclines

towards the belief that we continue to unfold and grow on higher spiritual planes beyond the grave. What is certain is that nobody can say for sure what form our future development will take.

But while John, as the natural man, baptizes—symbolically buries or clothes the divine spark or soul in the "tomb" of matter—so in turn the Christ figure is proclaimed as the element or agent by which the natural man will now be baptized or endowed with the divine Holy Spirit. This is why John the Baptist is made to say: "I baptize you with water but he will baptize you with the Holy Spirit." Significantly, Luke says here: "He will baptize you with the Holy Spirit and fire." The fire symbols the divine flame of intelligence and of potential Christhood. That is why, incidentally, baptism in water is accompanied by anointing with oil in some major branches of the Christian church, for example in the Orthodox Church. Oil ("thou anointest my head with oil," the Psalmist says) symbolizes this same reality. It is highly flammable and gives off a shine even when not ignited. It floats on water, that is, it rises to the top or the head, where reason and self-reflective consciousness were believed primarily to be embedded—and oil will even burn in the midst of the waters. In the watery "grave" of our material bodies, the "fire" burns on and nothing can ever put it out. This may be what the Gospel of Thomas's Jesus (Yeshua) means when he reportedly says: "I have thrown fire upon the world, and look, I am watching 'till it blazes."[7] Or again: "Yeshua said, Whoever is near me is near the fire . . ."[8]

In any case, St. Paul, whose thoughts and arguments can be extremely complex and at times virtually incomprehensible to an average reader, goes on at considerable length in Romans using the imagery of death, burial and resurrection in relation to our oneness with the mystical Christ. For example, in chapter 6 of Romans, Paul says: "Do you not know that all of us who have been baptized into Christ Jesus were baptized into his death? Therefore we have been buried with him by baptism into death, so that, just as Christ was raised from the dead by the glory of the Father, so we too might walk in newness of life." None of this, by the way, implies that Paul took any of this literally. His Jesus Christ is supremely a spiritual ray from the Father, as was Horus before him. All the action he describes takes place on a spiritual rather than an earthly plane.

In adult baptism, where there is a total submersion of the person under the waters, this burial and resurrection symbolism is of course more vividly portrayed than in the sprinkling of infants, though the symbolism remains the same. Once, long ago when we were going through one of my family's phases of attending a Gospel Hall form of worship (where the "whole Bible" was said to be preached and believed in), I took my place, at age twelve or thirteen, in the baptismal lineup at a tank at the very front of the church one Sunday evening. There, I had to endure the embarrassment of being nearly suffocated in front of some of my wide-eyed friends who had come along to observe the proceedings. The overzealous pastor got carried away and held me under unduly long as he simultaneously harangued the congregation. I emerged sputtering and half drowned. But as the proponents of infant baptism have always stoutly maintained, it's not really the amount of water that counts. This is true, if only they truly understand what the fundamental symbolism actually represents.

Put as simply as possible, the Christian rite of baptism is not about forgiveness of sins, original or not; nor, obviously, is it about enrolment in a certain exclusive, ecclesiastical "club." It's at the same time much more universal, much grander and yet simpler than any of that. The sacrament is one of celebrating and ritually expressing the basic datum of all religion, that of Incarnation of spirit in flesh. As St. Paul triumphantly exults: our bodies are the temple of the Holy Spirit. When a baby, for example, is baptized in the presence of all the congregation, what is really happening is that a fresh, incarnated soul is being symbolically welcomed into the whole human family. It's an occasion for all present to share in the rejoicing at our common, God-given inheritance.

That is truly the theme of the account of Jesus' baptism in the Gospels. As he comes up out of the water in the drama, he experiences a vision. The heavens are "torn apart" and the Spirit, in form like a dove, descends on him. Then the voice "came from heaven" saying that he was "my son, the beloved." Instead of the negativity inherent in the mention of sin, the voice says, "with you I am well pleased." The allegorical sense is crystal clear. The whole event is a claiming of our own divine descent. We are each declared to be the child of God, beloved by the very ground and source of all life. Instead of the pejorative, soul-killing labels the Church was to devise and pin on all its followers for centuries to come—of our "total depravity," our unworthiness even "to pick up the crumbs" under God's table—the pronouncement comes loud and clear of God's infinite pleasure in us.

This contrasts radically with the view of our humanity once elucidated by Reverend John Wesley, the great Methodist reformer. In Sermon 45 in the 1872 edition of *The Sermons of John Wesley*, he thunders: "This then is the foundation of the new birth—the entire corruption of our nature . . . everyone born into the world now bears the image of the devil in pride and self-will." That is really a classic statement of the dogma of original sin, the notion that, because of Adam's alleged "fall," humanity is forever tainted by that act of disobedience. Humanity, according to St. Augustine, was a "massa damnata," and only the death of the sinless Son of God could ever set that right. This theology gave the Church enormous power and control over people's lives, and it still looms large in too much Christian preaching today.

Nearly two thousand years of controlling people by constantly harping on their ungodliness and sin has produced predictably poor results. One can only speculate about how differently millions

upon millions would have felt and behaved in countless genera-
tions had they been told from the very beginning: "You are my
much-loved offspring with whom I am pleased indeed." To create
loving people, you need to have children who are told of their true
nature and potential—and then are truly loved. The implications
of this more spiritual understanding of baptism for the churches
are potentially transformative on a grand scale. There really is
some very Good News to proclaim! But new baptismal liturgies
or services have to be created to replace the negative formulae of
the past.

Nazareth

When Mark says that Jesus came from Nazareth and was baptized
by John, it's the only time he explicitly mentions the place that
has come to be universally regarded as Jesus' hometown. A few
verses later, an unclean spirit is said to have addressed him as
"Jesus, the Nazarene" (and Jesus is referred to as a Nazarene three
more times in this Gospel), but there the meaning is quite different. It probably has nothing to do with a place name. As Professor
G.A. Wells, in a lengthy and detailed discussion, points out, the
term "Nazarene" is used in some extant documents as "the title of a
sect." It is thus the equivalent of saying "George the Methodist"
or "Tom the Anglican."[9] Notice that Mark does not tell us that
Jesus actually came from or grew up in Nazareth. According to
Luke, Mary and Joseph lived there—they went to Bethlehem for
the birth—but Matthew's birth narrative differs sharply at this
point. In Matthew's version, their "house" was in Bethlehem. To
keep the Nazareth connection, however, Matthew has the whole
family go there after the highly symbolic return from Egypt following the death of Herod. In his usual formula, Matthew says this
was to fulfill an Old Testament prophecy that "He will be called a
Nazorean" (the King James Version again translates the Greek

here as "Nazarene"). But there is no such prophecy in the entire Old Testament!

I will not weary the reader with the incredibly detailed and complex discussion and debate over the possible significance of the fact that Mark and Luke call Jesus "the Nazarene" while Matthew, John and Acts always call him "Jesus the Nazorean."[10] In any case, early Jewish followers of the Christian way were called by both terms. In none of the Gospels, however, does Jesus apply either term to himself. He is depicted rather as an itinerant prophet who called no town or village his home. He is Everyman.

Today in modern Nazareth, the Roman Catholics, with their huge Basilica of the Annunciation, allegedly built over the site of the grotto that was Mary's home, are still engaged in a long-running dispute with the Greek Orthodox Church. The latter claim to have the true site of the Annunciation at their Mary's Well Church, about half a kilometre away. But in such matters, of course, since it's all mythical, absolutely nothing is certain. There are rival places for most of the "holy" sites in Israel that are touted today as genuine places where "events" in Jesus' life are held to have occurred. Fighting over which religious group has control over what "sacred spot" is a major and ongoing scandal.

There is a good reason for discussing the alleged Nazareth connection, but as is becoming clear, the issues are far more complex than a surface examination suggests. Study of the records reveals that it is even quite possible there was no village or settlement at a place called Nazareth in the first century CE. For example, there is no mention of a village or town called Nazareth in the Hebrew Bible, nor in the works of Josephus (who wrote during the first century CE), nor in the Talmud. Yet both of the latter sources give lengthy lists of Galilean settlements. Josephus lived for some time in the region. According to *The Encyclopedia of the Dead Sea Scrolls*, Nazareth "is not mentioned in the Hebrew scriptures (nor in any Hebrew literature prior to the seventh or eight century CE)."[11]

Among recent books raising doubts over this whole issue is *The Fabrication of the Christ Myth* by the Jewish author Harold Leidner.[12]

My own examination and summary of the voluminous scholarly discussion over whether or not Nazareth was a hamlet at the putative time of Jesus' childhood suggests that the general archaeological picture would appear to indicate the existence of a very tiny village wholly devoted to agriculture that originally came into being in the course of the third century BCE.[13] So, I believe there most likely *was* a village called Nazareth in the first century CE. But its connection with any historical Jesus is at best obscure.

The reason St. Paul, who mentions the term "Jesus Christ" about two hundred times, never once writes of or calls him "Jesus of Nazareth" was undoubtedly because he himself had never heard of such a place. Its use by Mark and the other Evangelists appears ultimately to me to have its roots in theology, not geography or history.

The Temptation— Testing in the Wilderness

Mark's Gospel

Mark, as we have seen, has no real chronology. His work is not a biographical "life" of a historical person. Consequently, he covers this up and regularly connects scenes that were unconnected in his sources (or his creative imagination) with the Greek word *euthus*, which means simply "immediately." That's what happens right after his description of the experience attributed to Jesus at the River Jordan at the hands of John the Baptist. Aware now of his true, essential nature as God's child or "son"—"the Beloved" with whom God is well pleased—we are told, "And the Spirit *immediately* drove him out into the wilderness." Mark then continues:

"He was in the wilderness forty days, tempted by Satan; and he was with the wild beasts; and the angels waited on him."

When we look at the parallel descriptions of this episode in Matthew and Luke in a moment, we will see just how abbreviated and condensed this pericope (the technical, scholarly term) or passage really is here. But for now I suggest that you try to put aside all previous conceptions and misconceptions gained from whatever source—early Sunday school lessons, old sermons, or even recent readings of the text—and see the narrative through fresh eyes if you can.

Consider, first of all, that there were no witnesses to this "event." You know at once you are in the presence of the mythical when there is no precision whatever regarding time or place and no possibility of eyewitnesses. The Evangelist is simply recounting or creating the story or mythos. The wilderness here, as it is time and time again throughout the Scriptures, is also simply an allegorical manner of speaking. It is a metaphor for the soul's life in the body on this plane of existence. We are spiritual beings in the "wilderness" of bodily existence. Incidentally, the wilderness wanderings of the Israelites in the Old Testament uses the very same metaphor. The mention of his being with "the wild beasts" is a unique feature of Mark and again is a pointed reminder that we have an animal nature that cannot be hidden or ignored even though, notice carefully, the text clearly emphasizes our spiritual nature by saying that it was not chance but the Spirit that "drove" him out for the wilderness testing. This clash of Spirit and our animal nature is not just inevitable, however; it is absolutely essential for any possibility of growing and evolving into the complete beings of light we are destined one day to become. This can be costly and painful. But, it should be added, we are not, somehow, wholly on our own; there is the ideal model of the Christ figure in the Gospels to inspire us on our journey.

Everybody knows what is probably the most familiar passage in the entire Bible. Nearly every wedding one attends these days has it as a primary reading. It is Paul's famous Hymn to Love in 1 Corinthians:

If I speak in the tongues of mortals and of angels, but do not have love, I am a noisy gong or a clanging cymbal. And if I have prophetic powers, and understand all mysteries and all knowledge, and if I have all faith, so as to remove mountains, but do not have love, I am nothing. If I give away all my possessions, and if I hand over my body so that I may boast, but do not have love, I gain nothing.

Love is patient; love is kind; love is not envious or boastful or arrogant or rude. It does not insist on its own way; it is not irritable or resentful; it does not rejoice in wrongdoing, but rejoices in the truth. It bears all things, believes all things, hopes all things, endures all things.

Love never ends. But as for prophecies, they will come to an end; as for tongues, they will cease; as for knowledge, it will come to an end. For we know only in part, and we prophesy only in part; but when the complete comes, the partial will come to an end. When I was a child, I spoke like a child, I thought like a child, I reasoned like a child; when I became an adult, I put an end to childish ways. For now we see in a mirror, dimly, but then we will see face to face. Now I know only in part; then I will know fully, even as I have been fully known. And now faith, hope, and love abide, these three; and the greatest of these is love. (1 Corinthians 13)

What must be realized is that, while Paul never met a historical Jesus, he had in his heart and teaching a vivid portrait of the Christ within—the goal of all human striving. In other words, this is not just a hymn to love, it's an explicit, detailed picture of what God intends us to become. Anyone can talk about "beings of light," but this sculpts out the steps we need to take to get there.

How long does this "wilderness" testing go on for? Well, the text of Mark says Jesus was there in the wilderness for forty days. But, as was described more fully in *The Pagan Christ*, in the Bible this is a fully symbolic number. Here it refers to the whole of life. Our entire life is a "test in the wilderness." Forty always types, or represents, a period of incubation—as of seeds prior to blooming, or of a birthing process of some sort. A human fetus takes forty weeks to develop fully from conception. Jesus, acting out here the drama of the soul of every one of us, is then put to the test by Satan. It should be understood that Satan too is symbolic. He represents the necessary, opposing force in the yin and yang of life. Without the tension of opposites—Satan on one hand, "the fallen angel of light" or Lucifer, and the Spirit together with the "good angels" on the other—the soul would have nothing to push against, nothing to develop its spiritual muscle on.

It is worth pondering that much that we consider evil in our lives frequently has to be seen and understood in a far deeper and broader context. Without it, without the struggle with pain and suffering, we would be greatly weakened and impoverished.[14] That's why St. Paul could say that when he was "weak," he found he was being made stronger by the enabling or "grace" of God.

Throughout the entire spectrum of evolving forms of life on this planet, you can witness this fundamental principle at work. All advancement and gain comes through the "pain" of the clash of opposites. Without this, everything would turn literally and figuratively to a kind of mush. Carl Jung said about this basic inevitability of human living: "The sad truth is that man's real life consists of a complex of inexorable opposites—day and night, birth and death, happiness and misery, good and evil . . . Life is a battleground. It always has been, and always will be; and if it were not so, existence would come to an end."[15] That's why not only Jesus but Zoroaster, Horus, Hercules, the Buddha, and every hero ever known has had to pass through a series of tests or trials, from killing dragons to slaying giants. You can see the same process working in the saga of Frodo's trials in Tolkien's trilogy *The Lord of the Rings*, or in the story of Luke Skywalker's adventures in the well-known *Star Wars* series of films. The adventures of Harry Potter echo the same theme. It is worth noting that Horus had three "fights" with his uncle and enemy Seth, just as there are three temptations from Satan in the Jesus story. The Buddha also had a threefold temptation to meet and overcome. His tempter, in the tradition, was the *Kama Mara*, the Sanskrit words meaning "lust" and "death."

Two observations are important before we move on to the fuller and later accounts in the other two Synoptic Gospels. Firstly, there is an echo of a very familiar Old Testament narrative in the mention by Mark that angels ministered to Jesus. In chapter 19 of 1 Kings there is a story of the prophet Elijah going into the wilderness and, experiencing a deep depression in which he actually asked that he might die, we are told he was ministered to by an angel. Mark could well have expected those familiar with the Septuagint (Greek) version of the story to see the parallel.

Secondly, in reference to Satan or the Devil, Lord Raglan in *The Hero* makes a powerful argument that the general public is almost wholly unaware of the extent to which past figures of note, almost universally regarded as "real" or historical, are in actuality the product of ancient myth and drama. He writes: "The history of the Devil affords an interesting example of this process [whereby a dramatic figure in a ritual of some kind becomes historicized]. Originally, it would seem, he was a ritual character who wore the horns of a bull or goat . . . and so the Horned Man became the antagonist of the Hero. Eventually he stepped out of the ritual into real life, and became what to millions he still is, a figure far more real than any historical character has ever been to anyone."[16] Extreme literalists would do well to read Raglan's book. For example, speaking of the Jewish traditions embodied in the Old Testament, he writes: "It is a necessary part of the thesis I am putting forward in this book that whoever regards the Old Testament as a historical work, in the sense in which we understand history, entirely misunderstands its character."[17] These words precisely describe the situation reflected in the New Testament as well.

Matthew's and Luke's Accounts

Matthew, like Luke, expands upon the scant two-verse version of the Temptation in Mark by giving us the nature of the wilderness testing in a highly stylized, three-act drama. Again there is no hint of any specific time or place other than an immediate connection with Jesus' baptism by John and his new awareness of having an adult relationship as a beloved "Son" with the ultimate ground of all being we call God.

Both these authors mention that Jesus was led into the wilderness *by the Spirit* and that the actual testing came at the end of forty days of fasting. Both attempt to bring a little reality—not to say a ray of humour—by saying that after such a long time without food "he was famished." Both agree on the first "temptation" about turning stones into bread, but they reverse the other two. Matthew places the pinnacle-of-the-temple ordeal first, followed by the offer of "all the kingdoms of the world," while Luke does the opposite. Apart from this and the fact that Luke, whose theology lays a greater stress than the others' upon the work of the Holy Spirit, says that Jesus returned from the Jordan "full of the Holy Spirit," the two accounts are virtually identical.

Certainly anyone at all familiar with myth will recognize instantly that that's precisely what we are encountering in these familiar stories. Again there is no hint of any witnesses or of "he told us" or "we were later told." Besides, the vignettes themselves are wholly otherworldly, supernatural and visionary in feel and texture. There is no real suggestion of these being biographical details or historical facts. However, the mythical formation of the temptations as it has been developed in these two Gospels seems at a surface glance so obvious and, as it were, even heavy-handed that the inner meaning has been lost to millions of literalizers down the centuries. What, we can well ask, is the relevance of the temptations for the evolution of our own souls in today's world?

I'd like to preface the answer to that question with a personal observation from my own life and from my observations of the lives of others. It is almost always just after my most exalted moments of highest spiritual experience or insight that sudden testing or temptations to doubt, to fear, to entertain negativities, can strike. The same can happen after a moment of high accomplishment. Life, it seems, wants to level us out or block us in some way. It's a time to be watchful and mindful of past times when similar moments have come and have been overcome. Jesus is being tested precisely because he has just had a peak experience of ultimate reality at the baptism in Jordan. You will find this phenomenon on your spiritual journey too.

Temptation #1:
Misuse of Spiritual Power for Selfish Ends

Then Jesus was led up by the Spirit into the wilderness to be tempted by the devil. He fasted forty days and forty nights, and afterwards he was famished. The tempter came and said to him, "If you are the Son of God, command these stones to become loaves of bread." But he answered, "It is written, 'One does not live by bread alone, but by every word that comes from the mouth of God.'" (Matthew 4:1–4)

Of course, it hardly needs saying that none of us will ever be faced with the literal question of whether or not to turn stones into bread. The inner meaning clearly lies hidden from profane or easy rendition. Obviously, though, the clue is revealed by the nature of the response to the riddle. The allegory sets up a reason for quoting the Scripture, "One does not live by bread alone, but by every word that comes from the mouth of the Lord."[18] Here, in a total reverse from those times when it is given a spiritual sense, bread as a symbol connotes all that can be summed up under the term "materialism" in its widest usage.

Suddenly, then, the passage is timely, up to date, piercingly relevant to even the most modern of readers. What is being described is always the greatest of all temptations for the human being, this creature of spirit and matter destined to be forever one. We are constantly tempted to use our Christos endowment for selfish, crude ends. It is particularly the case for those of us privileged to be living in the so-called "developed" regions of the world. The temptation is pervasive, at times exceedingly blatant, at times deceptively subtle, but it is there, as the popular jargon has it, 24–7. Life in the body, being a spiritual entity in a material world—with all its glories and its shame—means to be incessantly bombarded by the siren call of money, celebrity, the paraphernalia of success, and an ever-increasing, soul-destroying consumerism that all but drowns out the "still small voice" that brings the creative, challenging word, the inner prompting, the life-sustaining essence flowing from "the mouth of God."

Only you or I can put that challenge into the specific personal terms our own unique life situation demands. But face it we must. Those who attempt to live "by bread alone" are in the end destined to faint and drop by the way. Any individual, culture or empire that tries for long to defy this spiritual law will ultimately implode and die.

Temptation #2: Testing God

> Then the devil took him to the holy city and placed him on
> the pinnacle of the temple, saying to him, "If you are the Son
> of God, throw yourself down; for it is written, 'He will com-
> mand his angels concerning you,' and 'On their hands they
> will bear you up, so that you will not dash your foot against a
> stone.'"[19] Jesus said to him, "Again it is written, 'Do not put
> the Lord your God to the test.'" (Matthew 4:5–7)

This time we find that the Devil (the Greek word used is *diabolus*,
"deceiver") quotes Scripture too and is answered by another
quote. This, like Jesus' first response, is from Deuteronomy.[20]

Again the dramatic imagery of the editor/author is purely imaginative, figurative and hypothetical. As in the first temptation, the
Christos persona is faced with an even greater test than that of a
spectacular use of spiritual powers. Notice that the tempter begins each of these two seductive invitations with the powerful
though tiny word "if." He says, "If you are the Son of God . . ."
The fundamental issue is really about doubting the truth of one's
confirmed experience of the inner Christ. And this is a temptation
that confronts one time and again throughout the whole course of
one's life. It comes in many forms—sometimes straightforwardly
as the temptation to "show off" spiritually, to vaunt one's allegedly
profound spirituality in some audience-pleasing mode or fashion,
only to realize one has fallen into a foolish trap; but more often it
comes in the shape of second-guessing, dark, self-betraying doubts
about the reality of the Divine within. At one level you know you
are God's beloved child, but at another, sometimes even simultaneously, there is the sudden, strong temptation to question it.

All of us have experienced this at one time or another. We get
waylaid by low feelings or other distractions and forget our true
inheritance. That's why a key part of any true religion—a part

too often ignored today—is to remind us of who we truly are: pilgrims who have come from the Light and are moving ever, however haltingly, towards it again.

There are millions today, unfortunately, whose understanding of God remains at the level once attained in Sunday school or confirmation classes in childhood or early adolescence. They regard the divine mystery, if they think of it at all, as a kind of supernatural adjunct to their technology-wrapped lives and so attempt to "put God to the test" constantly by bargaining processes masquerading as prayer. "If you'll help me ace this exam, I'll do this and that or I'll cease doing, or saying, the following . . ." Or, "If you'll heal me/my child/my partner"—and here the only limit is one's imagination—"I'll do/give/forgive/attend the following . . ." We ignore God for 99 percent of the time and then, when a crisis looms, quickly try to "put him to the test." This may seem to be perfectly natural. But, on deeper reflection, one realizes it is based on an infantile theology that would make God out to be much less than God. It's an attempt to render the Divine a mere instrument of our wishes, whims and caprices. It's a betrayal of a fundamental trust that we are beloved beyond all telling and that all that we have or are or ever hope to be is in his/her care.

Temptation #3: The Lust for Power

> Again, the devil took him to a very high mountain and showed him all the kingdoms of the world . . . and he said to him, "All these I will give you, if you will fall down and worship me." Jesus said to him, "Away with you, Satan! for it is written, 'Worship the Lord your God, and serve only him.'" (Matthew 4:8–10)

Matthew keeps this as the third temptation while Luke has it in second place. I believe Matthew's instinct was right. This is the greatest seduction of all to the soul in matter—as the entire history of our species bears eloquent witness. As such, it makes a fitting climax to the unfolding allegory. The lust for power, as the Viennese psychiatrist Alfred Adler argued and as competing philosophies down the ages have consistently maintained, is the aspect of the shadow side of *Homo sapiens* that has wrought the most havoc.

Its clamping grip twists the lives and deeds of not just the rich and the ruling elites; it bites to some degree on all our personalities in insidious and deceptive ways. We all have a lurking lust for power of one sort or another. Some of us succeed in hiding it or even mastering it more than others. For those who achieve high political status, its tentacles wrap more tightly than the bark on a tree. One has only to go down a list of the major players on the global political scene over the past thirty years to see the horrific consequences—and to see that religious-sounding regimes can succumb as quickly as the rest when the lure of greater power trails past. There are, for example, deeply sinister overtones to the current quest for "a new world order" by some religiously backed power brokers in the United States. But the struggle for power over others can be found in all too many marriages and families; it can be found at the office; it looms wherever and whenever people relate to others. It frequently and nastily occurs in church congregations. I have witnessed this as a parish priest at very close quarters indeed. The microcosm of these smaller struggles is mirrored alarmingly in the macrocosm of the whole story of our humanity.

The very sad truth is that, because the Church has for centuries read and preached about this temptation—and the two others—as if it were a literal event in the life of a divine, miracle-working Saviour who was the wholly unique, Only-begotten Son of God, very few, and least of all political leaders, have truly seen or felt the impact or relevance of the temptation of power for their own lives. Church leaders themselves have often missed the point.

In a lifetime of participation in the Anglican Church, first as a layman, then as a priest and a professor at a major seminary, I have never heard a sermon or an exposition on what are generally called "the Temptations of Christ" that really made sense or that in any concrete manner was made applicable to my own life. The story always seemed to me to be alien and remote from my own concerns and questions. Yet for years, whenever the relevant passages in one of the Gospels were read by the officiating priest and he concluded by saying, "The word of the Lord," I was as quick as anyone there to join in responding, "Thanks be to God." The entire process seemed, on reflecting, to be next to mockery. However, once the scales were removed from my eyes and I saw for the first time that it was my soul and that of the person next to me that were being thus allegorically addressed and challenged, I felt as though there was a wholly new, undreamed-of dimension being revealed to my innermost being. It became indeed a Word with life-changing, transformative impact instead of a series of dead, unreal letters on a page about a distant, unreachable paragon of long ago.

Having praised Matthew, we will conclude with Luke. He ends his account of the Temptation thus: "When the devil had finished every test, he departed from him *until an opportune time*." I have put the final four words in italics because they convey the important truth that the testing of our spiritual selves never ends on this plane of existence. As with Seth and Horus in the Egyptian mythos, the struggle between Christ and Satan, understood allegorically, never finishes while we are in the physical body; it is an essential part of the schooling or "making" of our souls. Mark says it was the Spirit that "drove" Jesus into the wilderness for testing. It is part of a divine plan. We notice also that Luke continues his narrative with the words "Then Jesus, filled with the power of the Spirit, returned to Galilee . . ." Each victory in the unending conflict brings an added blessing and furthers the growing of the Christ within.

Choosing the Twelve Disciples

The Four Fishermen

As Jesus passed along the Sea of Galilee, he saw Simon and his brother Andrew casting a net into the sea—for they were fishermen. And Jesus said to them, "Follow me and I will make you fish for people." And immediately they left their nets and followed him. As he went a little farther, he saw James son of Zebedee and his brother John, who were in their boat mending the nets. Immediately he called them; and they left their father Zebedee in the boat with the hired men, and followed him. (Mark 1:16–20)[21]

I have set out in full this, the earliest version of the calling of the four fishermen to be disciples, to let the reader see just how wholly unlikely it is as history. Mark's Greek is awkward here, as the expression "as Jesus passed along the Sea of Galilee" in the NRSV makes plain. He wants to give his readers a sense of knowing local detail, but does so clumsily and unconvincingly. The Sea of Galilee is a sizable body of water and one doesn't just "pass along" it, as anyone who has been there knows. Also, without much more background information, the idea that four men whom he had not even met would suddenly drop their life's work on the spot at first call from a stranger in order to "follow" him makes little sense. That puzzled me when I first read it as a teenager, and at a surface level it still could do so today.

This same improbable scenario is repeated almost verbatim by Matthew. Luke, however, most probably writing at a later date, is aware of the problem and attempts to make the mythos seem a little more logical by first having Jesus provide a miraculous catch of fish. He stages the scene by saying that once, when Jesus was standing by the "lake of Gennesaret," the crowd was pressing in on him. So, observing two boats on the shore, he got into one belonging to Simon and asked him to put out a little way from shore. Then he taught the crowd from the boat. When he finished, he told Simon Peter to launch out to deeper water and lower his nets for a catch.

We are told that James and John were partners of Peter and Andrew, and that the four of them were all "amazed" at their sudden success after having spent a night catching nothing. According to Luke, Peter was so overwhelmed by this seemingly supernatural occurrence that he fell at Jesus' knees and said: "Go away from me, Lord, for I am a sinful man!" Jesus ignores the reference to sin and tells him, and presumably the other three fishermen, that they are not to fear, "from now on you will be catching people." So they beached their boats and "they left everything and followed him."

Even thus expanded, the story lacks historical plausibility. It should be remembered here that Horus, the Egyptian saviour figure, also had four sons who were described as fishermen in that ancient myth. Significantly, in the story of the life of the Buddha in the Pali canon, about 80 BCE (set down in Ceylon five centuries after the events described and, according to Joseph Campbell, five hundred miles away from their location), Buddha also chooses his followers immediately after his time of threefold temptation.

The Twelve Stages of Growth

In *The Pagan Christ* the fully mythical nature of the twelve disciples was discussed at some length. It is my contention that they were no more historical human beings than was their leader. What is noteworthy is that, although there are four places in the Gospels

where a list of their names is given, a closer look reveals that no
two of these lists agree in all respects. What is more, the majority
of those named are cited only to pass into virtual oblivion later.
Only a handful of them appear more than once in the narrative.

Peter is the one disciple whose "persona" or role in the drama
adds most to any feeling of the story being about flesh-and-blood
people. In a sense, he is representative of most of us. We can identify with his projection of human weakness, for example his impet-
uosity—wanting to walk on water and then sinking through fear;
his desire to prevent Jesus from heading into inevitable trouble by
urging him not to go up to Jerusalem for the Passover; his being
the one to blurt out, "You are the Messiah," in answer to: "Who
do you say that I am?" Then too there is the opposite pole, the
shame of his threefold denial during the Passion, according to St.
Matthew, of even knowing Jesus at all. We feel his pain as he goes
out and "weeps bitterly" when the cock crows and Jesus' prediction about him comes forcibly home to him. Later, by the time
Acts was written, well into the second century, he had indeed
become in the story the "rock" his name plainly signifies, preaching fearlessly, and it was upon faith like his, we are told, that the
fledgling churches were founded.[22]

Apart from Peter, the characters of the rest of the disciples are
not rounded out, and they for the most part are not heard from
again. The truth is that twelve is a special esoteric number appear-
ing throughout the Bible and other ancient books: the twelve sons
of Jacob, the twelve stones that Joshua was ordered to set up in the
dried-up riverbed of the Jordan, the twelve pieces into which
the concubine's body was cut up in the Old Testament story, the
twelve Urim and Thummim on the breastplate of the High Priest,
the twelve baskets of fragments after the feeding of the five thousand, the twelve months of the solar year, and numerous other
examples.[23] In the kingdom of light, according to later Manichaean

theology, the father of greatness is surrounded by twelve eons and 144 eons of eons. [24]

In the central, ancient, divine-human drama, the twelve aspects or powers of the solar deity were personified by twelve characters. In the Christian myth these came to be represented by fishermen because in ancient theology the astronomical Avatar or Redeemer coming roughly about 250 BCE entered in under the equinoctial precession sign of Pisces. Hence he became titled as Ichthys, the Greek word for "the Fish." Jesus came as Yeshua or Joshua, meaning "God saves." But we find that Joshua of old was described in the Bible book that bears his name as "the son of Nun," and Nun is "fish" in Hebrew.

What is important in any mythical reading of the Gospels is that the twelve disciples of Jesus esoterically "type" or symbolize the twelve powers of spiritual light energy and intellect to be gradually unfolded in our own human evolution in twelve stages or levels of growth—all of which was represented or imaged by the twelve signs of the zodiac. No ancient religion can be understood without reference to the role of the zodiac in the evolution of the cosmos and of the human.

In the Ritual of ancient Egypt, the soul had to pass through twelve dungeons, each guarded by a god, in each of which it was kept captive until the god opened the gate. He would not open it until the soul could say his name. The dark jail cells allegorize the state of the soul embodied in matter. The meaning was that we remain prisoners of a particular power or faculty until we are able to open up our ability to make use of and take command of its powers. The jailer is ignorance, and knowledge (*gnosis*) is the sole key to release.

The thinking of the ancient sages was that, just as the sun has to pass through the twelve signs of the zodiac in the great precession of the equinoxes, so too each human soul must advance through twelve stages of being and of enhanced spiritual cognition one at a time as it evolves into the fullness intended by Divine Mind. In some accounts this occurred over many lifetimes in a cycle of rebirths; in others it was in this world and the next. Each level affords specific experience—a new stage of spiritual aware-ness—to be added to the final complete and twelvefold unity. Some adepts call this the acquisition of the twelve intelligences. Each of us is thus eventually destined to become a Christ who nurtures, instructs and trains his or her own "twelve disciples" within the parameters of his or her own individual personality.

In my earlier work I outlined in detail some obvious parallels between the followers of the solar deity Horus and the disciples of Jesus. It is sufficient here to point out, for example, that just as Jesus purportedly gave his disciples the authority and power to raise the dead, we can read in the Pyramid Texts: "Horus has given his children power to raise you up [from the funeral bier]." His twelve attending astronomical powers are termed "saviours of the treasures of light." Along with Horus, they also are described as accompanying him to earth as sowers of the seed and then later as reapers of the divine harvest of souls intended for heaven.

In the four Gospels, rather like the followers of Odysseus in Homer's famous *Odyssey*, the disciples are shown to be very reluc-tant and somewhat slow-witted learners. Jesus often is critical of their lack of insight and awareness. This is an allegorical reflection of our own recalcitrance and dullness of spirit in gradually getting mastery over the animal-based drives that mire us down in indo-lence and mediocrity when it comes to our spiritual development. We too need frequent reminding that the Spirit may be willing in and of itself but the "flesh"—because of our immersion in matter—is weak.

The Temple Cleansing

Then they came to Jerusalem. And he entered the temple and began to drive out those who were selling and those who were buying in the temple, and he overturned the tables of the money changers and the seats of those who sold doves; and he would not allow anyone to carry anything through the temple. He was teaching and saying, "Is it not written, 'My house shall be called a house of prayer for all the nations'? But you have made it a den of robbers." (Mark 11:15–18)

Matthew and Luke follow Mark's text very closely here.[25] However, John's Gospel adds a significant detail not found in any of their versions of the story. Before coming to that, though, it needs to be said that nothing illustrates better the dangers and the theological errors that open up when you take a historical and literal approach to Gospel texts than this scene in the narrative. Anyone who takes the time to consult Google, for example, putting in the words "temple cleansing" and "Jesus," will find hundreds of thousands of hits—everything from serious commentary to pious sermons to racist and anarchist rants. The fact that Jesus is said to have driven out the moneychangers is taken by some as justification for violence in the name of Christ.

For example, one site on Google named "Jesus at the Gym" tries to make a strong case for a physical or muscular kind of Christianity, and offers such vapid insights as "Jesus was no wimp." One site tries to make a case for Jesus as an anarchist, a "libertarian vigilante." Another site under the heading "Aryan Nations" uses the story as a justification for its extreme racist views with phrases such as "the people of Judea were an inferior and insane racial horde of polluted stock." It calls Christians who would be peacemakers "feeble and worthless pacifist retards." There is everything, from those who call themselves eco-justice activists to animal rights activists who emphasize the fact that (in their view) Jesus liberated the animals when he drove the sheep and cattle from the temple precincts.

The incident of the temple cleansing has always been a focus of controversy and debate between liberals and conservatives. The reason for this is that while the Synoptics—Mark, Matthew and Luke—put the story right at the end of Jesus' ministry, where it is said to have been the final cause of the plot against his life, John's Gospel places it starkly at the very beginning. Liberals make the case that you can't trust Gospel chronology in the light of this discrepancy, while conservatives strive mightily in their contention that there is no problem at all. In their view the solution is simple: there were two temple cleansings, one at the beginning of the ministry and one at the end. They have no idea, apparently, of how strained this kind of reasoning and seeking-harmony-at-any-price appears.[26] Chronology in and of itself is definitely not a primary concern of the authors at this or any other point in the story.

As hinted at the outset, John adds one other significant aspect to the controversy over this passage by including the colourful but, for many, highly problematic detail that Jesus "made a whip of cords" to use in driving "all of them out of the temple, both the sheep and the cattle." In other words, he made and used heartily a sort of weapon, hence the websites of those who would try to justify a more violent kind of faith. The whole picture is further complicated—for the literalists—by the fact that changing the hated Roman money, with its imprint of the emperor upon it, into temple coinage was in fact expressly required by Jewish law. The Talmud states clearly that beginning on the first of Adar, the month before Passover, a proclamation was made to the people that they should prepare the Shekalim. "On the 15th day of Adar, moneychangers were sent out to collect the Half-Shekel [of silver] for its donation . . . On the 25th day of Adar, moneychangers were installed in the Temple itself to help in the collecting of the Half-Shekel donation."[27]

Explicit instructions about the various animals and doves (for the poor) to be sacrificed in the temple to fulfill all the various ritual requirements for all pious Jews—burnt offerings, sin offerings, offerings at the birth of babies, and much more—were part of the Torah and explicitly described in the Book of Leviticus. For example, Leviticus 5:7, speaking of an offering to expiate specific "sins," says: "But if you cannot afford a sheep, you shall bring to the Lord, as your penalty . . . two turtledoves or two pigeons, one for a sin offering and the other for a burnt offering." In other words, Jewish law itself necessitated the presence both of the moneychangers and of the various merchants selling sacrificial cattle, sheep and doves. It was an entirely legitimate activity. It is true, however, that the people themselves were aware from time to time that there was chicanery and price-boosting going on. Evidence from both Josephus and the Talmud attests to this. The charge, then, that the house of God had become a "den of thieves and robbers" was not wholly without basis.

The Meaning for Us

It is worth observing that the Synoptic writers use this purported event to refer back to an Old Testament saying about "My house shall be called a house of prayer" while John gives it a prophetic nuance by quoting instead the saying "The zeal of thy house will consume me." However, putting all of the above discussion aside for a moment, let us come directly to what I am convinced is the allegorical intent behind this act of the spiritual drama.

St. Paul, writing much earlier than any of the Evangelists, speaks quite openly and plainly about the true temple of God, that is, the heart and mind, the inner person or soul of each one who has realized the true nature of the Good News, the "mystery"

of "Christ in you, the hope of glory." Unlike the Evangelists, whoever they were,[28] Paul lived at a time when the second temple was
still standing in Jerusalem and the ritual sacrifices were going on
there.[29] But, in 1 Corinthians 3:16, he virtually trumpets aloud to
the young believers there, "Do you not know that you are God's
temple and that God's Spirit dwells in you?" And, lest anyone
think this is a single reference, in 6:19 of this same epistle he says
again: "Or do you not know that your body is a temple of the Holy
Spirit within you, which you have from God, and that you are not
your own?" The true temple of God, then, that which has to be
cleansed and kept as a "house of prayer," is nothing more, or less,
than our own innermost selves. Each of us is more truly God's
"temple" than even the finest cathedral or mosque.

The exciting thing about this truth is that it resonates with the
solid witness of other ancient spiritualities as well. You cannot
read the Upanishads, for example, without realizing that the Vedic
or Hindu scriptures teach above all that the holiest shrine, the
greatest temple, the most sacred place on earth, lies wholly within
the innermost being of each of us. That is the place to be kept
cleansed and pure from all that would distract or mire us down or
rob us of our true divinity. Listen to the Nashiketa Upanishad:
"Smaller than the smallest, greater than the greatest this Self
[divine presence within] forever dwells within the hearts of all."
Again: "Both the individual self and the Universal Self have entered
the cave of the heart, the abode of the Most High . . ." And
finally: "This Brahman, this Self, deep-hidden in all beings, is not
revealed to all; but to the seers, pure in heart, concentrated in
mind—to them he is revealed."

The same truth could be illustrated from the mystical sages in
all religions. This is the real, inner message of the temple cleansing, but the scholars, the preachers and the amateur apologists—
all eager to argue over and justify their own literalistic readings of
the text—miss the truly universal message it seeks to convey. As

Joseph Campbell so often sought to persuade his readers and listeners, religious stories and religious symbols are continuously "chronically misread," and the result is that nothing but divisions and barrenness of spirit are the harvest. He taught that one of the biggest problems with Christianity today is that it still does not teach people how to relate to and forge a relationship with "the deity residing in you," within the temple of your very Self.[31] The misreading of the cleansing of the temple by the Church down the ages is a classic illustration of this problem.

Preaching the Theme of Judgment

When Charles Darwin wrote in his diary that he gave up his belief in orthodox Christianity because he had come to see its teachings about hell and eternal punishment for the unsaved as a "damnable" doctrine, he was reacting, to my mind, as any sane, rational person would do today. Nobody who really believes in a truly loving, ultimate God can accept with equanimity one who has prepared a place of torment for any of his or her children. What do we do, then, with the many passages in the Gospels and the rest of the New Testament that all too graphically depict scenes of judgment and horror where, it is said, there will be weeping, wailing and gnashing of teeth in flames of hellfire? Here, perhaps more than at any other point in our attempt to grasp the inner meaning for our lives of the sacred writings, we need to keep a tight hold on our basic premise that metaphor and allegory is the supreme key to understanding the Bible.

None of the passages, including the most explicitly lurid, that describe God's judgment on human wrongdoing or the end of this cycle (wrongly translated as "the end of the world") are to be taken literally. This is where even the great Albert Schweitzer erred in his watershed book *The Quest for the Historical Jesus* (1910). Schweitzer rightly said that the Jesus of orthodox Christianity was a chimera produced by rationalism and liberalism combined. He posited instead a wild kind of apocalyptic, eschatological (dealing with end times) preacher who believed in an imminent end of the age. His Jesus, accordingly, preached only an "interim ethic"— thus enabling Schweitzer to avoid the seeming contradictions and/or impracticalities of many aspects of such teachings as the Sermon on the Mount. According to this "take," Jesus was wrong and died in vain. (Incidentally, much later in his life, Schweitzer altered this extreme view and took the ethical teachings of the Sermon much more seriously, as expressing abiding principles.)

I know full well that many of the passages on judgment and end times are difficult to interpret, and some modern preachers have contorted themselves almost gleefully twisting and turning these passages into alleged blueprints for a coming Armageddon of one kind or another. Playing the politics of fear to the hilt, they have attracted a wide popular following. But, once the allegorical approach is taken, together with a more honest appraisal of the full text, a quite different, and in my view a much more spiritual and compassionate, understanding emerges.

The End Is Now

One thing the literalists have not been sufficiently candid about is the undeniable fact that, whatever the content of the apocalyptic "clips" in the Gospels may be, there is always the catch (for them) that the speaker, Jesus, insists that the time for it all to happen is not in some distant future, but now, that is to say, at the time of pronouncement.

For example, chapter 13 of Mark, called "the little Apocalypse," speaks of the destruction of the temple (there is scholarly agreement that this was obviously written after the event had already happened at the hands of the Romans in 70 CE) and sparks the question about end-time unfoldment. The description that follows is probably a stock piece of "floating" apocalyptic litera-ture, a popular genre of the day, but what is absolutely crucial is verse 30, when quite abruptly Jesus is made to say something that puts it all in context: "Truly I tell you, this generation will not pass away until all these things have taken place." To underline the seriousness of this highly significant rider to all that precedes it, he adds: "Heaven and earth will pass away, but my words will not pass away." Clearly the author(s) was tipping his hand that what was said was what was meant. This was no far-off event (say, two thousand years ahead), but something immediate.

There are several other similar pronouncements in similar contexts that could be produced, but the point needs no further elaboration. The wording in all the passages referring to Gehenna, to Hades, to lakes of fire and all the rest is clearly pictorial and allegorical, and the timing is always immediate or very close at hand. My own interpretation of it all is that judgment, the conse-quences of all our words and actions, takes place always in God's time, which is eternally now. Nothing has done more to weaken moral fibre and to dull the edge of the human struggle for control of the animal part of our nature and for soul evolution than (1) the belief that there is some kind of vicarious atonement always avail-able for forgiveness of every sin; and (2) the teaching that any consequences of present moral turpitude will come only in some far-off future.

It's my conviction that the message of the Gospels—through metaphor, allegory and myth—is that our daily struggle against selfishness, greed, lust, envy and all the other "sin which does so readily beset us" is the true Battle of Armageddon that we must all face. It follows that since "as a person sows, so shall he reap," the karmic law of action and effect means that we feel and register the results of any wrongdoing in ourselves, right now.[30]

I also see it as highly significant that in John, the latest, most mythical and sophisticated of the four Gospels, there is no mention whatever of a fiery "hell." The Gospel of Matthew is indeed darkly obsessed by the themes of judgment and "furnaces of fire," but he had his own existential reasons for piling on terrible imagery of coming punishment. Modern New Testament scholarship has shown that the particular life situation in the early Church that this Gospel was written to address made a strident polemic against the Pharisees and the synagogue inevitable. The author and editors, facing bitter rivalries, felt forced to heighten elements in the materials they were handling to the point of becoming extreme. Professor F. W. Beare in his commentary on Matthew questions whether any of the imagery about a hell of fire was ever used by a presumed historical Jesus at all. Notably, St. Paul never makes any mention of hell. And Origen, the great Alexandrian Bible scholar and theologian, roundly criticizes the foolishness of those who read scriptural passages about end time or ultimate judgment in any crudely literal way. He was, like myself, a universalist who believed God would in mercy ultimately reconcile, restore and bring all his Creation to himself.

Understood properly, then, not as a description of a literal fact but as a metaphor, language about the end of the world is intended to lead us into a new way of experiencing the dynamics of being alive and aware here and now. Theologian Dr. Eugene Kennedy has written: "The end of the world comes every day for those whose spiritual insight allows them to see the world as it is, transparent to transcendence, a sacrament of mystery, or, as the poet Blake wrote, 'infinite.' The end of the world is, therefore, metaphoric of our spiritual beginning rather than our harsh and fiery ending."[31] Once you catch the vision that the Divine is incarnate in you and in all Creation around you, the world as it once was no longer exists. You are "born again" or, to quote St. Paul, you have become "a new creation." You see it all with new eyes. The Gospel of Thomas expresses it best where it has Jesus say: "The Kingdom will not come by expectation. The Kingdom of the Father is spread upon the earth, and people do not see it." In other words, the "end" is now.

The Transfiguration

A man is a god in ruins.

— RALPH WALDO EMERSON, *Nature* (1836)

I have a confession to make. The Feast or Festival of the Transfiguration, which occurs in the calendar of the church year on August 6, never held much appeal for me. The reason for this probably goes back to my earliest years as an unwilling member of a youth Bible class. I didn't know what the word "transfiguration" meant then, and I think that helped create a somewhat negative response that was hard to shake off later when I understood the term quite well. The *Canadian Oxford Dictionary* defines it thus: "1—a change of form or appearance. 2 a—Christ's appearance in radiant glory to three of his disciples . . . b—the festival of Christ's transfiguration." It was not always observed as a special day. According to the *Oxford Dictionary of the Christian Church*, general observance of the Transfiguration goes back to 1457 when Pope Callistus III ordered its universal celebration to mark a victory over the Turks at Belgrade on August 6, 1456. The earliest written version of the incident in the New Testament occurs in chapter 9 of Mark.

As we read, we are again alerted instantly here, as Mark leads into his account of the Transfiguration, to the non-historicity of the text. For example, the text has Jesus once more make a prediction about the future that very obviously was not fulfilled. They—the disciples—did not in fact live to "see that the kingdom of God" had come with power. In the last authentic words of this Gospel, in chapter 16, verse 8 (the rest is a much later attempt to forge an ending), the story describes the disciples as left numbed by fear when the tomb was found empty. In 2005, Bart Ehrman in his *Misquoting Jesus* set out the evidence for believing that the so-called "longer ending" of Mark, with its appearances and the Ascension story, was never part of the original Gospel. But, be that as it may, here is Mark's Transfiguration account:

> And he said to them, "Truly I tell you, there are some standing here who will not taste death until they see that the kingdom of God has come with power." Six days later, Jesus took with him Peter and James and John, and led them up a high mountain apart, by themselves. And he was transfigured before them, and his clothes became dazzling white, such as no one on earth could bleach them. And there appeared to them Elijah with Moses, who were talking with Jesus. Then Peter said to Jesus, "Rabbi, it is good for us to be here; let us make three dwellings, one for you, one for Moses, and one for Elijah." He did not know what to say, for they were terrified. Then a cloud overshadowed them, and from the cloud there came a voice, "This is my Son, the Beloved; listen to him!" Suddenly when they looked around, they saw no one with them any more, but only Jesus. (Mark 9:1–8)

From the scholar's point of view, Mark is the initiator or creator of this remarkable Transfiguration story, and Matthew and Luke repeat their versions with but a few minor additions or changes. Luke's account, for example, echoing the experience of Moses on Mount Sinai in Exodus, says that "the appearance of his face changed" as well as his clothes. What is really important is that Moses and Elijah—representing the Law and the Prophets—are seen in the vision talking to Jesus. It is a form of mythical confirmation that the old and the new are truly one revelation.

But Was It History?

Tradition has it, of course, that this was a historical event, and today's visitors to Israel are duly taken to visit or view Mount Tabor, a hill that, while only about seven hundred metres in elevation, nevertheless towers over the surrounding Plain of Esdraelon in the Lower Galilee. (It was clearly visible on the eastern horizon for the first full day of my 1976 hike for the *Toronto Star* from Nazareth in the north down the Jordan Valley to Jericho and eventually Bethlehem.) Some authorities, however, have argued for Mount Hermon, a much higher mountain in Lebanon to the north, while yet others say it was the Mount of Olives just east of the old city of Jerusalem. That the latter could have been in the mind of the original author of this episode seems to this writer the most likely of all, since this part of the Gospel has all the "feel" of a resurrection-like piece of the overall fictional drama. The "east" or "eastern mount" was in the ancient mythos always the point of departure from this earth-plane for the glorified soul. The fact, however, that we are clearly being prepared for an allegorical treatment is shown by the way Mark's story begins. His use of the phrase "after six days" and the going up into a nameless "high mountain" in a wholly unspecified region are standard symbols in ancient theology, as we have already seen.

Further evidence of the allegorism involved is to be found in the way in which, in sacred traditions, other avatar or saviour figures are also said to have been transfigured or "set ablaze like the sun." The Buddha had his transfiguration after ascending a mountain in Ceylon where the heavens are said to have opened, flooding all around him with a great light. The glory of his person shone forth with "double powers." Indeed, he shone like the brightness of the sun and moon together. In the ancient Ritual of Egypt, Horus, the sun deity whose life so fully anticipated all of the Gospel story, is described in similar terms. For example, "Horus gives thee the gods; he makes them come to thee; they illumine thy face," the Ritual says. Matthew tells us that Jesus' face "shone like the sun," in other words like that of a sun god, and Luke implies the same when he says, "the appearance of his face changed and his clothes became dazzling white."

Philo, the first-century Jewish philosopher-sage who interpreted allegorically the whole of the Pentateuch (the first five books of the Old Testament), in his commentary on Moses's vision of God on Mount Horeb says that his soul and body were blended into a single new substance, an immortal mind essence having the appearance of the sun. In the account of Moses receiving the Ten Commandments in Exodus, we read that the "skin of his face shone"—so much so that on descending from the mountain after forty days and forty nights (that number forty again) he had to wear a veil on his face lest the people he spoke with be blinded by the brilliance. The theme of divine or semi-divine personages suddenly being revealed in dazzling, sunlike glory, I repeat, is common in many ancient myths and religions. In his well-known play *The Bacchae*, Euripides describes how the god Dionysus first appears as a disguised stranger in his old homeland of Thebes. Later, however, he reveals his true identity, and his people cry out: "But look! Who is this? It is Dionysus come himself, no more disguised as mortal, but in the glory of his divinity."[32]

Understanding the Transfiguration

Earlier, in chapter 13 of Matthew's Gospel, we read that "Then [at the end of all things] the righteous will shine like the sun in the kingdom of their Father." In other words, in the final deification of the soul—the soul of every one of us—there will be what can only be described as a glorious transfiguration. This brings me directly to the meaning of this whole "act" in the divine drama of the evolution of the soul. First, though, it should be pointed out that as early as the third century, in Egyptian Gnostic Christianity, there was a document called the *Pistis Sophia* ("Faith Wisdom") that purports to record instructions given by Jesus to his disciples at the end of a twelve-year sojourn on earth following the Resurrection. It clearly describes the Transfiguration as following rather than preceding the Resurrection. Personally, I agree with those scholars who are convinced that the Transfiguration story is really out of place where Mark, followed closely by the two other Synoptics—John in his Gospel omits it entirely—has put it. It really marks the final stage in soul evolution, the climactic transition from mortal to divine. Thus I'm convinced it is or was a resurrection story that got misplaced.

This is by no means an idiosyncratic view of my own. This suggestion has in the past been supported by some of the most widely acclaimed of New Testament scholars; for example, by Heinrich Meyer (1800–73), Julius Wellhausen (1844–1918), Adolf Harnack (1851–1930), Alfred Loisy (1857–1940), Maurice Goguel (1880–1955) and, the most renowned of them all, Rudolph Bultmann (1884–1976). One of the most contemporary of scholars to put the case that the Transfiguration story in Mark could well be out of place here, and is actually "pointing to the very earliest vision" that gave rise to the Easter faith, is the noted New Zealand professor emeritus of the Victoria University of Wellington, Lloyd Geering.[33]

Jesus' Transfiguration or glorious change of appearance, then, is deeply symbolical of our own eventual metamorphoses fully into beings of light. As St. Paul says, it will happen suddenly, "in the twinkling of an eye," and "we shall all be changed." This story in the end is really a glyph or metaphor of our ultimate glorious destiny as the perfected sons and daughters of God.

5

MIRACLES OF WHOLENESS

You lift up the soul, O God, and make the eyes sparkle.
You give health and life and blessing.

— ECCLESIASTICUS 34:20

I CANNOT DESCRIBE the great sense of intellectual and emotional relief that first flooded over me when I realized at last that all of the healings ascribed to Jesus in the four Gospels are, in fact, acted parables or allegorical dramas. I can still remember the sense of release I felt when I first read Origen's assertion that "the chief value of a miracle is not that it happened, but the truth allegorically symbolized therewith."[1] From driving out "unclean spirits" to raising the dead, Gospel miracles are powerful witnesses not to a superhuman, magician-like wonder worker or to God dressed up in the disguise of a Galilean peasant, but to the efficacy of the spiritual powers latent in every one of us. There was a time in my student days, long ago, when I took the miracles quite literally and missed their subjective meaning for my own life, and at the same time created huge intellectual problems for my faith.

I found when ministering to people in a parish that I was far from being alone in this. You see, if one takes them literally, one has to ask what kind of alleged human being are we reading about?

Raising the dead, walking on water, turning water into wine, multi-plying loaves and fishes, opening the eyes of those blind from birth, stilling storms and all the rest of the miracles are plainly not the acts of a flesh-and-blood human person. They are far removed from the realm of even remote possibility as actual occurrences. Yet the New Testament read literally appears to assert them as facts.

However, even if all rational thought about that aspect of the issue is suspended for a moment, how could one then justify the limitation of the benefits associated with such godlike power to remove all human suffering and need, such control over the forces of nature, to the comparatively small number of people said to have been affected by it at one brief period of time in the Gospels? Why not heal all the lepers, all the lame? Why not feed all the hungry and poor, and so on? Why wait so long to make a brief appearance on the earthly scene? It made no sense at all. But, once crude literalism is put aside and you realize that the entire Jesus Story is a mystical drama with a whole range of symbols meant to relate us to the evolution of our own innermost selves, these mira-cles can come alive with fresh power, immediacy and significance. Instead of being an inhuman God-in-disguise, one who really always had "four aces up his sleeve," we see in Jesus a portrayal or model type of our own inner Christ principle or Christ conscious-ness. If we apply the allegorical or symbolical sense of each mir-acle to our own lives, then they illustrate beautifully the many steps in the full realization of our own innate divinity. We have the divine healer within ourselves, the "Spirit of love, of power, and of a sound mind," to quote St. Paul.

Healing Lepers

Whenever the Bible speaks of leprosy and lepers, the term used—Hebrew *sara 'at*—is an imprecise one covering a range of skin dis-eases. According to *Religions of the Ancient World*, leprosy as cited in Scripture "probably encompassed a large variety of diseases that produced a discoloration of the skin."[2] Anyone who takes the trouble to consult the lengthy discussion of the disease as set out in great detail in chapters 13 and 14 of the Book of Leviticus will quickly realize the imprecision, and indeed stark superstition, surrounding the subject. For example, in chapter 14 it expressly says that a house could have leprosy and that it could taint even the walls and plaster, all of which would have to be scraped before the home could be pronounced "clean" again. But modern medicine defines true leprosy (Hansen's disease) as caused by the organism *Mycobacterium leprae* and characterized "by skin sores, peripheral nerve damage and progressive debilitation. Disfigurement and loss of toes or fingers are caused by the lack of feeling in the affected areas and hence (mostly inadvertent) damage by accidental injury or other trauma." While leprosy remains a serious problem worldwide today, it is "not very contagious," contrary to the thinking behind attitudes towards lepers in the Bible, and responds quickly to specific, inexpensive medications.[3] Today, it could and should be eradicated completely.

Whatever modern medical science may know about the specific bacterium based disease called leprosy, nevertheless it remains true that in the Biblical text it is the ultimate symbol of being ritually and socially unclean and thus wholly unfit for any of the norms of ordinary living. To be a leper was to be cast out, shunned and condemned to the status of a pariah. The Book of Numbers, chapter 5, verse 2, illustrates the point as we read how "the Lord spoke to Moses, saying: Command the Israelites to put out of the camp everyone who is leprous . . ." Consequently, leprosy becomes allegorically the symbol of man's need for the healing and cleansing touch of the Divine. It stands for all that would block our being at one both with others around us and with the god within. That's why one of the most moving stories of healing in all of the Hebrew Bible tells how a great but non-Israelite army captain called Naaman "suffered from leprosy" and was ultimately led to total healing through the intervention of the renowned prophet, the successor to Elijah, named Elisha.

The whole story of how a young captive Jewish girl became the chief actor in the narrative—it was she who told her mistress, the wife of Naaman, about Elisha's remarkable healing gifts—is one of my personal favourites from the Old Testament. It is found in chapter 5 of the Second Book of Kings. But its significance here relates to the way in which it sets the precedent and the tone for healings of lepers in the Gospels. As we have seen already, most of what the Gospels' Jesus does in terms of miracle has already been anticipated by various sun god–like characters in the Old Testament—and before that by other ideal "types" of the god within, such as Horus of Egypt. If the prophets healed lepers, Jesus must be shown to have healed them too.

All of this brings us to Luke, where ten lepers are "cleansed":

> On the way to Jerusalem Jesus was going through the region between Samaria and Galilee. As he entered a village, ten lepers approached him. Keeping their distance, they called out, saying, "Jesus, Master, have mercy on us!" When he saw them, he said to them, "Go and show yourselves to the priests." And as they went, they were made clean. Then one of them, when he saw that he was healed, turned back, praising God with a loud voice. He prostrated himself at Jesus' feet and thanked him. And he was a Samaritan. Then Jesus asked, "Were not ten made clean? But the other nine, where are they? Was none of them found to return and give praise to God except this foreigner?" Then he said to him, "Get up and go on your way; your faith has made you well." (Luke 17:11–19)

There are several points being made by this story or vignette of a quite remarkable healing. Firstly, the ten men are quite conscious of their need. It has a name and they know it. They have faced their condition—unlike the situation into which we so often drift, where we will do anything rather than face up to or name our need for transformation or renewal. The first step to recovery for alcoholics, we know, is naming or admitting to their addiction. The lepers verbalize or plainly express their longing to be whole. They are immediately told as a result to take a daring step. Lepers claiming to be cleansed, whole and fit for reabsorption into the life of the community and the nation had to pass a rigorous inspection by the priests. While still in the grip of the disease, the ten are told to behave as though they did not have it—as if they had already been made whole.

At this point comes the central thrust of the allegory. We read: "And as they went, they were made clean." That is how it is with each of us in our spiritual journey. It's not a case of sitting around waiting for our prayers to be answered, of keeping everything on hold while we wait for some special sign or epiphany to inspire us. It's a matter of immediate obedience to the Spirit's prompting from within. As a writer, for example, I know how very tempting it is to postpone research, or to put off actually sitting down alone in a room and making a beginning. There are always a hundred excuses: I'm not in the right frame of mind, the topic is too ill defined, I don't know where to begin. I once knew a reporter whose slogan was: "I'll research that." In fact, he used to say, "I love research. It can go on and on. It's writing that bothers me!" You will be able to supply comparable situations from your own life. From my experience, I find that when I make a beginning—when, like the lepers in our story, I assume that the Spirit is going to be there leading me and granting me grace—something significant starts up almost simultaneously. As has been well said by many contemporary self-help gurus, once you make a committed beginning to a creative project, the universe "comes onside" and works along with you. It was "as they went" that the lepers were made clean.

Finally, there is the surprising conclusion to the narrative when, of all the ten who were healed, only one—the least likely of them all because he is a double leper, a despised Samaritan—comes back to give thanks. He is told to get up off his knees and "go on your way; your faith has made you well." This does not mean that he alone was left cleansed and whole. All ten of them were the recipients of divine grace and bounty, as indeed is every one of us whether we give thanks or not. All of us have been blessed by the gift within of the "light that gives light to every person coming into the world"; we have each of us the presence of the Christ or Higher Self or "image of God" at the core of our being. But if there is no genuine recognition of this pearl of great price, this bit of yeast that leavens the entire loaf, this mustard seed that is to spring up into a mighty tree, then we miss out on entering fully "into the joy of the Lord." We may miss out on the blessing of being made "master over many things" because of our faithlessness over what was less.

The allegorical sense of this story of the lepers glows with meaning at many levels. Not least of these is the blessing that comes with daily, even hourly, recognition of all there is to be grateful for. I was impressed a few years ago, at a large luncheon gathering in one of Toronto's major downtown hotels, to hear the quiet testimony of Sir John Templeton, one of the most successful businessmen of our era. He told the audience that he had made it a practice for many years—he was in his early eighties at the time—to begin each day, even before getting out of bed, by thinking of five things for which he truly was thankful to God. This is not a guarantee of success in investments, but it does bring spiritual rewards of untold worth.

The Healing of a Paralytic

We come now to a story told by the three Synoptic Gospels about a paralytic man who was brought to Jesus for healing. Mark tells it earliest, in chapter 2. Interestingly, verse 1 says that Jesus "was at home," and yet it was not in Nazareth but in another town some distance away on the Sea of Galilee, called Capernaum. There was, Mark says, such a crowd around his house as he taught that the whole entrance was jammed full of people. Nobody could get in or out. Then some other people came, four of them carrying a paralyzed man on a litter. Frustrated by the throng, they lifted the man up onto the roof, removed some of the tiles and lowered him down on his mat. Jesus, seeing their faith, told him his sins were forgiven and said: "Stand up, take your mat and go to your home." The man stood up and, picking up his mat, "went out before all of them."

Some scribes who were there tried to start an argument over the alleged "blasphemy" of Jesus telling the sick man his sins were forgiven, but the real point to be made here is that the man's paralysis speaks to our own fears and inner blocks. How often in life do we find that we are locked in on ourselves, unable to move forward, unable to take some important step or decision, paralyzed in some way? What the text is saying is that the Christ within us can, if called upon, unbind the shackles that prevent our progress. The "sins" or mistakes that brought about our temporary paralysis can be forgiven—without the intervention of clergy or others—and we can be empowered to take up our bed or mat and move on and out. We need not look above us or around us or seek some far-off, distant deity. It is the Christ in us who, as Paul says, gives us the sufficiency within to do all things.

I remember so well a point in my own life where I seemed paralyzed by fear, loneliness and a growing sense of despair. It was during the second year of my four years of graduate and post-graduate studies many years ago. For a variety of reasons, partly a growing sense of just plain homesickness, partly a weariness with too much study, I was feeling depressed and wanted very much to throw the whole thing up and quit right there. (I was overseas at Oxford, and it was back in the days when trips home and even

phone calls were out of the question because of the expense.) Late
one night I was returning to my room across a darkened quad
with a dread foreboding that I would soon pack up and go home.
My prayers had seemed all in vain—I felt spiritually paralyzed.
But just then somebody began to play the organ in the otherwise
empty chapel in the far corner of the quadrangle. I listened, and
tears came to my eyes as I recognized an old hymn that was a
favourite of my father's. Somehow, though I can't even recall after
all these years what hymn it was, God spoke to me through it.
A realization shone in my mind and heart of just how proud my
father was that his son was studying at Oxford, and of how it
would disappoint him so if I were suddenly to drop out and give
it all up. Somehow the Spirit moved the logjam in my heart and I
felt a great surge of fresh courage and determination to stay the
course. I slept well for the first time in many days that night—and
never looked back. The paralysis within was gone.

Evil Spirits

Anyone who reads through the Gospel of Mark and takes it as a
literal history has, in addition to facing the intellectual difficulties
already referred to at the beginning of this chapter, to come to
the conclusion that Jesus did little else than go about performing
exorcisms. The very first miracle of healing in chapter 1 of Mark
illustrates the point:

> Just then there was in their synagogue a man with an unclean
> spirit, and he cried out, "What have you to do with us, Jesus
> of Nazareth? Have you come to destroy us? I know who you
> are, the Holy One of God." But Jesus rebuked him, saying,
> "Be silent, and come out of him!" And the unclean spirit,
> convulsing him and crying with a loud voice, came out of
> him. They were all amazed . . . (Mark 1:23–27)

Taking such passages, indeed the entire set of descriptions of healing miracles in the Gospels—from the many cleansings of leprosy to the raising of the dead—at their surface or apparent value as objective descriptions of factual events has unfortunately led down the ages to more gullibility, superstitions and cruel excesses than almost any other influence. (As an example, think of the killing of thousands of "witches" by the Church in the sixteenth and seventeenth centuries in Europe, or the scandalous hanging of a score of innocent men and women in the witch hunt at Salem, Massachusetts, by rigidly religious Puritans in the late 1600s.)

Indeed, looking always for the "miraculous" in physical and mental/emotional healing or in other realms has tended to glorify blind faith and ignorance at the expense of an intelligent following of the true miracle of natural law. By encouraging a constant seeking for the "supernatural" in life instead of the study and application of the wisdom embedded in the laws and workings of the world of nature, the true majesty and divinity of the fixed order all around us have too often been diminished or ignored. Thus religion has frequently found itself in foolish opposition to the gift of intelligence and true science when in fact the real miracles of healing are to be found there.

The truth is that any teaching or belief that harms or diminishes humanity's faith in and reliance upon the utter trustworthiness and unchangeability of the laws of nature as discerned by reason actually hinders our evolution as a species. It erodes our sense of stability and constancy in the universe. It introduces, in fact, a note of chaos if some arbitrary feat or intervention by an externalized deity can abruptly abrogate these very laws of life and action. The whole of religion is brought into disrepute when such magical thinking replaces our God-given, innate reason and respect for unchanging truth. But there is a lot of magical thinking in religious circles today.

During my life's work, first of all as a parish priest in a suburb of Toronto, then as a seminary teacher and finally as a journalist covering religion at every level, I have personally witnessed time and again the havoc wrought by the follies of an extravagant supernaturalism in the ranks of the blind believers in would-be "miracle" workers. What this means for the reader here is that it is only by seeing the Gospel miracles for what they are, symbolic dramatizations of spiritual myths, that they can be kept from destroying the very foundations of a rational understanding of life itself. Taken as history, they can end up as little better than embarrassing nonsense. To quote Alvin Boyd Kuhn, whose thinking was explored in *The Pagan Christ*, a lot of religious thinking is unfortunately grounded "on a contempt for natural law."

He goes on to make an observation I had come to much earlier myself, that it must "basically be assumed that if spiritual law in some measure transcends natural law, it does so by fulfilling and consummating it, not by negating it." True, spiritual law can mould natural forces to its aims and purposes—as we use a machine or, for that matter, our own bodies. But it never disregards or contradicts the laws of either machine or body. Further, I would add that when in the realm of medicine or anywhere else it appears that the laws of nature have been shunted aside or transcended in some way, the more rational explanation is that there are deeper natural laws at work in or through the phenomenon that as yet still lie beyond our present knowledge. A miracle such as a spontaneous remission of a "terminal illness," for example, in my thinking simply points to an unknown or a hidden law that science has yet to discover.

What the Bible miracles really are intended to illustrate, then, is the fully wonder-working power of the Christ in us to transform our ordinary mortal life and to bless our animal bodies as well as our souls with divine beauty and the glow of health. The true healing that we all seek as individuals and as a race can only be found as the spirit of the Christ in us (by whatever name we choose to call it) subdues our warring lower instincts and brings us into harmony with nature, others and ourselves. The real miracle comes, I am convinced, when you realize that the Transcendence that lies at the heart of the cosmos and that radiates through every molecule of being in the universe lies at your own heart's core. The rapture of the eternal is waiting to be grasped and known by each of us, here and now. As Eastern theology states it: "Thou art that!" In Sanskrit, the phrase is rendered as *Tat Tuam Asi*, "You and I and Ultimate Reality are one." This is what Joseph Campbell once described as "electrifying" Good News, but alas, you rarely hear it in our churches.

An examination of a few more of the Gospel "miracles" can now be made. They all have their parallels in other ancient sacred literature where other god-men do almost exactly the same. Horus in ancient Egyptian lore, for example, opened the eyes of the blind and the ears of the deaf, and made the lame to walk again. The Hebrew Old Testament has, as stated earlier, many healings and wonders that are consciously paralleled by the New Testament authors.

The Demon-Possessed

The text of Mark, which contains the most primitive stratum of Gospel teaching in the New Testament—following, of course, Paul's much earlier witness—presents Jesus primarily as an exorcist, driving out demons from people on every side. The first chapter of Mark, verse 39, sets this out most clearly: "And he went throughout Galilee, proclaiming the message in their synagogues and casting out demons."

Only the crudest of literalism down the ages has, with often terrifying results, interpreted this as an expulsion of actual satanic forces. What is pictured or symbolized by these demonic influences are precisely the same drives, influences, complexes, obsessions and compulsions that we have in mind when we speak metaphorically of a person's inner "demons" distracting, wasting or paralyzing his or her life. As spiritual beings enmeshed in matter, with all the weaknesses that flesh is heir to, we are often too easily caught up in currents and forces that threaten to take control or to turn us into courses of thought or action which disrupt our inner harmony and spill over into our behaviour towards others. Without healing, these forces can at times break out into antisocial or even criminal behaviour. History is full of examples of the horrors made possible when individuals or even whole nations succumb like a herd to the grip of the lower animal instincts within us all. Perhaps the most perceptive book I have ever read on the issues at stake for humanity in all of this is Carl G. Jung's slim volume *The Undiscovered Self*, in which he says that a mere change in the neuronal workings in the minds of a few key leaders could easily plunge the world into a nuclear night. Anybody who has never faced the reality of the shadow in their own life and psyche would do well to read this book. It's a real step in fulfilling the admonition of the ancient proverb "Know thyself," and consequently a significant rung in the ladder of personal, soul progress.

The Demoniac

The story of the demoniac who said his name was Legion, "for we are many," vividly told in chapter 5 of Mark, illustrates in a powerful way just how encountering the Christ can transform an individual—or an entire society. The exact place where it happened is not essential to the story. Study of the earliest manuscript evidence reveals confusion over whether the spot was called the country of the Gadarenes or the Gerasenes. This was no doubt due to the problem presented by the fact that Mark's account says there was a body of water close at hand but Gadara is several kilometres from such. Mark in his version has one demoniac; Matthew, who likes to double things where possible, says there were two.[4]

But the chief points are these: the man was utterly out of control; he lived among tombs, which is to say that, like many religionists today, he surrounded himself with the bones of the past; he was a danger even to himself—"he was always howling and bruising himself with stones." Significantly, Jesus confronts him with a blunt question: "What is your name?" We know that, in many cultures, naming something was often thought of in the ancient world as the first step in gaining mastery over either an object or, indeed, another person. The fairy tale of Rumpelstiltskin is an illustration of the same idea. The elaborate tale, which originated in Germany (where he is known as Rumpelstilzchen), comes to a happy conclusion when the queen discovers the dwarf's name and so wins release from a promise made under duress to give him her first-born child.[5] The sick man in our story is also compelled to face his illness, to put a name on it before he can be healed. What is revealing in the symbolism of what follows is that the dispossessed evil spirits are made to come out and depart from the man beside a body of water, and that they should ask to be freed to enter animals considered to be gross and unclean. "And the unclean spirits came out and entered the swine; and the herd . . . rushed down the steep bank into the sea, and were drowned in the sea."

It is worth observing in passing that Mark expressly says there were "about two thousand" pigs in the great herd that dashed themselves down into the sea. In the Eleusinian mysteries, according to Freke and Gandy's *The Jesus Mysteries*, a crowd of some two thousand initiates on one occasion were required to bathe in the sea with a herd of swine. The purpose of the ritual was to transfer any taint of animality and evil from the initiates over to the pigs. The pigs were then sacrificed by being driven over a cliff into the waters. The neophytes were at once declared pure and totally renewed.[6]

Water itself signifies the watery domain of the physical or material body, as do the pigs. The realm of the human is to be ruled by the Christ Spirit; the activities of primordial lusts and instincts were relegated to their true abode. It is significant to recall at this point that in the final Egyptian tableau of judgment in the Hall of Judgment, any person who failed to pass the high ethical standards required was immediately delivered over to the Typhonian beast—a composite of pig, crocodile and hippopotamus. This signified rejection for that moment or cycle as the soul was forced to descend back into the body of the animal to gain further experience before ultimate deliverance or "salvation."

There are at least two high points in Mark's account here. The first is when the swineherds run off and return with a crowd from the "city." They came to Jesus "and saw the demoniac sitting there, clothed and in his right mind." The healing was complete. The second is the ending where the former demoniac begs to be allowed to remain with Jesus but "Jesus refused, and said to him, 'Go home to your friends, and tell them how much the Lord has done for you, and what mercy he has shown you.' And he went away and began to proclaim . . . how much Jesus had done for him; and everyone was amazed." There is a great truth there. Nobody who has come to the realization of the Christ within, and who has experienced the power of that inner consciousness to drive out the "demons" and restore true healing, can refrain from making it known—certainly not by pious preaching to or cajoling of others, but by a quiet and radiant witness day by day. There is nothing at all wrong—and indeed much that is right— in being eager and able, when called upon, to give "a reason for the hope that is in you."

Nature Abhors a Vacuum

In both Matthew and Luke there is an important pericope, or brief story, ending in a pronouncement or warning that is of considerable importance for one's own spiritual life. It is a piece of wisdom that was "floating" in the sea of material available to the Evangelists, and has no specific connection to anything other than the fact that they place it in the general vicinity of a preceding discussion of whether or not Jesus is casting out demons through the power of the evil one himself. This provoked the well-known dictum that if Satan casts out Satan, how can his "kingdom" survive?[7]

Here is the story I have in mind as found in Luke's account:

> When the unclean spirit has gone out of a person, it wanders through waterless regions looking for a resting place, but not finding any, it says, 'I will return to my house from which I came.' When it comes, it finds it swept and put in order. Then it goes and brings seven other spirits more evil than itself, and they enter and live there; and the last state of that person is worse than the first. (Luke 11:24–26)

One doesn't have to believe at all in the reality either of a Satan or of "unclean spirits" to grasp the deep truth of what this imagery is bringing home to us. A particularly poignant example of what it is all about is revealed to me every time I hear about or from people who have come to the point where all the religious dogma of their past, with its guilt and other burdens, as well as whatever comfort it brought, has suddenly crashed or been totally rejected.

Many today find themselves precisely in that place. The religion they learned in their youth or the beliefs that seemed to work for at least a while are suddenly thrown into question or fail badly to meet the tests of life. Or people become overwhelmed by the sheer weight of the varying opinions on religion now flooding our media. Too often they then throw out everything. Their "house" is swept clean and empty. But a terrible vacuum remains; there is often a haunting sense of loss. They discover all too quickly that we are all spiritual beings and that there is an inner "space" in us that will be filled—one way or another. What is being said in this brief story is that we must find our true spiritual core and allow it to overflow within. Otherwise its place will eventually be taken over by other "spirits"—the spirit of raw ambition, of lust for material possessions, the spirit of false and misleading doctrines, of cynicism or even despair. If, as I believe, it is true that we do, so to speak, have "a God gene" or are "hard-wired" for God, then we must beware of the kind of gods we worship once we have rid ourselves of past idols. Right now in the Western world exactly this kind of crisis is upon us. The old gods are being driven out. And they need to go. The burning issue is what will rush in to fill their place. It's a personal issue, but it is also societal, and ultimately global as well. It has particular relevance for the churches.

The Man Born Blind

As he was walking along the street in Jerusalem, Jesus saw a beggar, a man who was "blind from birth." His disciples, like too many pious people still today, at once jumped to the harsh assumption that such a disability was obviously somebody's fault. "Who sinned?" they ask. "This man or his parents?" This question has been taken by some over the years to imply a general belief in reincarnation since, if the man sinned—and he was born blind—it must have been in a previous life. However, in Judaism at that time, it was considered possible for a person to "sin" in utero, in the womb of the mother. In any case, Jesus is portrayed as going beyond the entire notion of illness as punishment, and the author of the Gospel shows the real purpose of his allegorical tale: the blindness will be the occasion for "God's works" to be revealed. Making a mud plaster with saliva and earth, Jesus is said to have spread it over the man's eyes and to have told him to go and wash it off in the pool of Siloam. John says in an aside, "Siloam, which means Sent." So there is allegorical symbolism throughout. He's sent; he washes himself; he returns able to see.

There is more to this story of the man born blind, however, and it's worth reading again in full. You can find it in chapter 9 of John.[8] Nevertheless, for our purposes here, this abbreviated account is sufficient. The point is that this blind beggar is every human who has ever lived. We are each of us born blind to the fundamental reality of who we really are. Plato recognized this centuries before the Christian era. It is partly what he was talking about in his theory of Reminiscence, where he taught that all learning is really a kind of remembering of what we once knew. We do not see or understand that we are in our true inner selves sparks of primordial fire from far beyond time itself. We are thus blind both to our true identity and to our true potential. It is only when we encounter the empowering presence of the Christ principle or Christ consciousness in our innermost being that our intellectual and spiritual "eyes" are fully opened. Or, as the Gnostics put it, we have been roused to total wakefulness. We can then echo perhaps the most telling line in this man's story. Pressed and harassed by the rigidly religious about how, when and why—and by whom—he was healed, he says simply: "One thing I do know, that though I was blind, now I see." By this "sign," the Evangelist expresses his hope that we may each of us be able spiritually to say the same.

We are all of us blind in some ways, deaf in others, and plagued as well in the course of our lives by drives or moods or "spirits" that sometimes lead us astray. We grow lame and walk at times with a limp. We all need the inner ministrations of the Spirit of God as we struggle onwards to become ever more fully who we really are.

The early Fathers of the Church, including Origen in the second century, said that whatever healings and other miracles Jesus performed in the Gospels were but typical and symbolical of what he would do in the Spirit; and that the bodily diseases he healed were not to be understood other than as infirmities of the soul that are to be cured by him as an immanent Spirit. Once that profound truth is firmly grasped, it opens up a new and sane vista as one reads of people being cleansed of the outward scourge of leprosy, freed from the tyranny of a variety of "demonic" possessions or, as in the case of Jairus's daughter in Mark, raised from death to life.[9] In the case of the raising up from the dead of Lazarus in John's Gospel—a story based upon the coming back to life of the Egyptian god Osiris—this was indeed the most potent, final symbolic act of all. As we have already seen, death was the metaphor of the soul's life in the body on the material plane. The body was the tomb of the soul. To be raised to life meant to be brought to a full awareness of one's true spiritual condition. As St. Paul thunders: "Awake, thou that sleepest, and arise from the dead, and the Christ shall give you light." That is the true "Easter of the heart" we all need, not once or twice at some special moment of conversion, but all through our lives on this earthly plane.

Raising the Dead

Horus of ancient Egyptian mythology had the power to raise the dead, as we have seen, and in *The Pagan Christ* there is a detailed account of the close parallels between the raising of Lazarus by Jesus in John's Gospel and the much earlier story of Osiris. For John it is the seventh or crowning "sign" of the sevenfold powers of the Christ. But in the Hebrew Bible, in a well-known passage in chapter 17 of the First Book of Kings, the great prophet Elijah also demonstrated the same authority in restoring to life the son of the widow of Zarephath, near Sidon. The text says: "Then he stretched himself upon the child three times, and cried out to the Lord, 'O Lord my God, let this child's life come into him again.' The Lord listened to the voice of Elijah; the life of the child came into him again, and he revived." Consequently, there is no surprise when we come to the Gospels and read in chapter 7 of Luke about the widow of a place called Nain having her son brought back to life again right in the midst of the actual funeral procession. When Jesus bid him to rise, we are told "the dead man sat up and began to speak."

In chapter 9 of Matthew an even more striking passage describes the bringing back to life of the young daughter of "a leader of the synagogue"; there is again here no mention of any specific place. This episode is notable because the story of the one miracle contains within it an even more revealing story of recovery from disease. First, though, Jesus is told about the little girl's death, and he responds to the man's request—"come and lay your hand on her, and she will live"—by taking his disciples and following the father to his home. When he gets there and sees the commotion of the mourners and a general crowd, he tells them all to leave, "for the girl is not dead but sleeping." We are told they laughed at that, but "he went in and took her by the hand, and the girl got up." Then the Evangelist adds the traditional refrain "and the report of this spread throughout that district."

The literal reading of this kind of miracle obviously makes Jesus out not to be a human being at all, but a God-in-disguise walking the earth. The liberal view, on the other hand, holds that he was a remarkable person about whom, over time, wonderful tales and legends grew and blossomed. These, it is argued, must be stripped away to get at the "historical Jesus" behind it all. The buzzword here is "demythologize." This approach may seem to appeal to reason, but it does so at the expense of wholly eviscerating the text of its fundamentally empowering meaning.

My contention throughout, as in *The Pagan Christ*, is that, contrary to popular belief, the mythos, a deep archetype in universal human consciousness, came first, and seemingly objective additions to it were made to illustrate or to convey its full significance. We need to "remythologize," restore the mythical dimension and examine its meaning. The story is symbolic of deeper, hidden realities that reveal timeless truths. The ancient theologians, we know, saw death and sleep and kindred conditions always as metaphors of the soul in its unawakened or unenlightened state. It is the coming to consciousness of the Christ spirit or Christ principle that brings light into the darkness, that rouses one from sleep or raises the "dead" to life. The Christ draws near and the girl is brought back to life. The dawning of awareness of the presence of the inner Christ "kick-starts" our dead minds and hearts into newness of life. That's what this miracle is all about.

The Miracle within a Miracle

But what of the miracle within this story of the little girl? It must be set out in its brief three lines of narrative. It follows immediately after Jesus got up to go to the little girl's home:

> Then suddenly a woman who had been suffering from hemorrhages for twelve years came up behind him and touched the fringe of his cloak, for she said to herself, "If I only touch his cloak, I will be made well." Jesus turned, and seeing her he said, "Take heart, daughter; your faith has made you well." And instantly the woman was made well. (Matthew 9:20–21)

While the story of the synagogue ruler's daughter illustrates the power of Christ consciousness or spirit at the level of the individual, this concise anecdote is the mythic unfoldment of a much wider and deeper perspective on the evolution of the human soul. In its cryptic elegance it sets forth a picture of one of the most fundamental moments in our history.

In the text, the woman—who frequently represents matter (Latin *mater*, "mother")—is described as "suffering from hemorrhages for twelve years." We have already seen how the number twelve plays a prominent role everywhere in ancient sacred literature. The bleeding is continuous, but for a specific, preordained or appointed duration. It symbolizes the earth or nature or matter's inability to conceive a certain specific "child" or fruitage. As long as a woman continues to menstruate, no conception has taken place, nor can it. However, once the symbolic woman of this story touches the hem of Jesus' garment, that is, once contact with the Christly principle or divine force has been made, the blood flow ceases. She is made well. What this portrays is the moment long ago when the time had come in evolution for the bringing to birth in humanity of self-reflective consciousness and the inner Christ. This story, then, is in reality a variation upon the same theme expressed in the mythic story in chapter 3 of Genesis, when the eyes of Adam and Eve were opened and true consciousness was born.

The glorious truth is that this whole experience of coming back to life or of birthing the Christ child can happen to us today—I repeat, not just once in some blinding flash of supposed supernatural intervention, but daily. This inner divinity, the Atman or the inner Christ, is the Holy Spirit, the inner flame or ray—the Psalmist's "lamp unto our feet." As St. Paul says in his second letter to Corinth, "For it is the God who said, 'Let light shine out of darkness,' who has shone in our hearts to give the light of the knowledge of the glory of God in the face of Jesus Christ."[10]

We should remember, though, that this by no means grants us assurance that life will always be an exultant, mountaintop experience. We are spiritual beings living on the cross of material existence. That's why to the words just quoted Paul adds immediately this reminder: "But we have this treasure in clay jars [earthly bodies], so that it may be made clear that this extraordinary power belongs to God and does not come from us. We are afflicted in every way, but not crushed; perplexed, but not driven to despair; persecuted, but not forsaken . . ." The mystical death of Jesus on the Cross is for Paul always a potent symbol for our own taking up of the "cross" of life on the material plane to follow his path.

By the way, it is commonly assumed that because Paul spoke of Jesus' death on the Cross, he was referring to a historical event. Recent studies, however, have examined the evidence more closely in the light of the Apostle's obvious Gnostic characteristics. He was in reality a Gnostic-type Christian, and the Gnostics held the view that the supernatural and other "events" in the Gospels were but earthly descriptions of what transpired in higher, spiritual realms. The actual, physical death of God was totally unthinkable for them—and for me. True reality was found in the "pleroma," or fullness of the heavens. In the Hermetic literature of Egyptian origin in the second century CE, this was termed "the tabernacle of the zodiacal circle."[11] That's why, as we saw earlier, although Paul teaches that Christ was crucified, he never mentions when, where or by whom. In other words, he gives no historical context whatever because for him it was a supremely heavenly or spiritual "event."

6

NATURE MIRACLES

*The biography of a spiritual teacher is not an account of
historical facts . . . . It is a symbol of the spiritual biography
of that man, and all the elements of the biography are symbolic.
Just through reading them properly you learn the message.*

— JOSEPH CAMPBELL[1]

Jesus Walks on Water

FOR TWELVE YEARS, between 1971 and 1983, I covered
religion stories at home and around the world as religion
editor for Canada's largest newspaper, the *Toronto Star*.
One of the more unusual incidents on this beat occurred in 1982.
When it was announced that Reverend Billy Graham and his team
were planning to come to Toronto for a major week-long crusade, my editors decided to send me out to Graham's headquar-
ters in Minneapolis. The plan was for me to meet Graham there
and travel back with him to Toronto on the jet. I was to inter-
view him at length for a front-page story for the following day,
the eve of the crusade. It all went extremely well. Graham, whom
I had come to know personally over the years from previous meetings and interviews, graciously invited me to sit with him for the
entire flight and answered questions over a wide range of issues,

from legalizing marijuana to John Lennon's remarks over a decade earlier about the Beatles being "more popular than Jesus."

It all made for a great story, which ran as scheduled as the leading headline at the top of the front page the next day. What particularly pleased my editors was Graham's willingness also to meet with me the following morning on the boardwalk on Toronto's waterfront. Remembering a memorable photo of the Evangelist that ran in the British tabloids about twenty-five years earlier, on the eve of his first London crusade at Harringay Arena—he was in an athletic outfit and jogging in Hyde Park—I took a photographer along to try for something similar. I wanted to catch a shot of him running on the boardwalk by the lake with the CN Tower and the rest of the city's skyline behind.

Graham showed up with his press officer and gamely agreed to jog a little for us. A small crowd of onlookers gathered as Graham ran two or three short laps while the camera clicked. The press officer and I were talking when suddenly a look of horror came over his face and he ran down to the water's edge, shouting, "No! Stop!" I turned around and saw Billy Graham, socks and shoes off, walking out on a stone retaining buttress that was just exactly flush with the surface of the lake. The photographer had apparently observed that a couple of seagulls standing out on it looked for all the world as though they were standing on the surface of the water itself. He knew at once what he wanted to do.

The press officer and I were alarmed. Apart from the fact that neither of us wanted a photo simulating Graham walking on water, there was the serious risk of the Evangelist slipping and falling on the algae-covered, smooth and slippery stone surface. We were hugely relieved when we saw him getting off and wading ashore. Those photos turned out remarkably well. They could have caused a sensation, but the *Star* never ran them. As far as I know, they're still in some obscure file and safe from prying eyes.

It might have made a great illustration, but newspapers and their editors often have better judgment than they are given credit for.

What we're leading up to, of course, is one of the best-known stories in the Gospels, the one where the disciples, rowing hard at the oars, in the darkness of night and in the midst of a storm, suddenly see Jesus walking on the sea. They are terrified, thinking, with some justification, that they are seeing an apparition of some kind. Jesus speaks to them with a characteristic "Don't be afraid," and thus assures them who it is. Peter, with typical rashness—he is the one who always in the drama portrays some of our most human frailties—yet still holding doubt, says, "Lord, *if* it is you, command me to come to you on the water." Jesus says, "Come," so Peter gets out of the boat and "started walking on the water, and came toward Jesus." But then he notices the roaring wind and the waves. We are told "he became frightened," and he begins to sink.

This passage from Matthew again is not a literal account of any event.[2] It is pure myth. But it's absolutely brimful of meaning for the evolution of your spiritual life and mine. In the first place, in ancient scriptures the sea has multiple significance as a powerful metaphor. It is the mother—Latin *mare*, French *la mer*—of all life. It is no accident that most of the saviour figures of antiquity have a mother whose name is Mary, Meri, Maya or some other variation of this. Water, as we have seen, itself esoterically signifies matter.

But in addition, the sea, with its vast, unruly powers, strange creatures and hidden depths, often in the Bible metaphorically signifies the deep, roiling, unruly passions of the unconscious within us or the savage powers of various antagonistic forces without. This is true, for example, in the Psalms, where the Psalmist at one point cries out, "All thy waves have gone over me," or again, "deep calleth unto deep." In Habakkuk 3:15, God is said to have walked "through the sea." Jesus, the Buddha and Horus of ancient Egypt all are said to have walked on the waters of the sea. In fact Buddha walked on water on several different occasions, according to the tradition.

Jesus on Ice Skates?

An incredible testimony to the tendency of our secular culture to literalize and/or demythologize the Jesus Story at every turn appeared in the press by a kind of synchronicity just as I was completing this passage. In the Ideas section of the *Toronto Star* of Sunday, April 9, 2006, there was this extraordinary headline: JESUS CHRIST ON HOCKEY SKATES! It sounded like a weird Canadian-style blasphemy until you read the story below. It told how a professor of oceanography at Florida State University had conducted an inquiry and had come up with an allegedly scientific explanation of how the "miracle" of walking on water might have occurred. Writing in the *Journal of Paleolimnology*, a Canadian science journal, a Dr. Doron Nof and his colleagues said that unusual freezing processes probably had iced over parts of the freshwater Sea of Galilee. They elaborated with details that are irrelevant here, but the end claim was that Jesus probably had walked not on water but on surface ice. At a distance it would have been easy for the disciples to have been misled.

This same kind of crude mistaking of myth for history seduces some scientists with predictable regularity every Christmas when they try mightily to come up with an explanation for the Star of Bethlehem. In such cases it is the scientists who end up sounding and looking every bit as foolish as the most extreme of the Bible literalists. The mystical star is a regular part of the esoteric message in much of ancient mythology. Nobody in antiquity with even a small amount of education took the star as a fact of life. A garbled reading of the myth always leads to distortion and missing the inner meaning altogether.

To "walk on the sea," then, is to symbolize control over all the varied psychological and other forces that seek to overthrow our spirit and hinder us in the upward evolutionary path to far fuller maturity and joy. The text says the Christ—the spark/flame of spiritual consciousness in us—came walking over the sea in the "fourth watch," just before sunrise. The ancient sages knew, as we have seen, that there were four stages of our development and of evolution in general. First came the mineral stage; then the vegetative; next the organic or animal; and then, in the middle of the fourth stage or "watch"—the human—comes the dawning of self-reflective awareness. This brings the power to choose between right and wrong and the capacity to intuit the Divine.

This power, then, this gleam of the divine fire in everyone, has, when nurtured and fanned to full flame, the dynamic to calm our most dreaded fears and to rescue us from drowning utterly beneath the stresses and, at times, catastrophes of our daily lives. We can inwardly converse with or pray to this Higher Self (what Socrates called his Daemon) within and be reassured. The message is clear: to "walk over the waters" of life, one must learn to keep one's inner eye upon the Divine within and without. The motto of the Gospels' Jesus figure is always "Be not afraid," and it still speaks powerfully to us today. I am often asked, do I still pray? Yes, daily—I have no choice. But not the old "give me, give me" of my youth addressed to some external "big guy in the sky." Most often it's the prayer of affirmations or, even oftener still, the prayer of silent waiting upon the voice within.

The Miracle of Loaves and Fishes

The setting in chapter 6 of Mark is idyllic—a hillside by a quiet lake. Harried by the crowds, Jesus tells the Apostles to come away to a desert place and rest awhile. So they go by boat to "a deserted place."

According to Mark, however, the crowds not only saw what was happening but also "hurried there on foot from all the towns," and did so in such an expeditious manner that they somehow managed to arrive "ahead of them." The exaggeration here is quite clear, as is the complete vagueness as to time and place. Mark very obviously is simply arranging an "event" for dramatic and theological reasons. So, Jesus went ashore and, having compassion for them "because they were like sheep without a shepherd," he began to "teach them many things." Notice that, as so often in this Gospel, Mark teases us by saying Jesus taught, yet wholly neglects to tell us what these teachings were. Apart from the Parable of the Sower, his Gospel is virtually lacking in detailed teaching content of any kind. As some scholars have put it, Mark is simply a Passion narrative with a kind of lengthy introduction.

Then the text says that, because it had grown late and they were all in a deserted place, the disciples asked Jesus to send the crowd away so that they could walk to the nearest village or town and buy something to eat. Jesus responds by bidding them give the people something to eat. Naturally they are somewhat surprised and even shocked, and ask whether he expects them "to go and buy two hundred denarii worth of bread" and feed them all. This sets up his question, "How many loaves have you?" We're not told how by Mark, but the disciples quickly "found out" and said, "Five, and two fish." The total number, seven, is—as always—symbolical. It generally symbols perfection. Consequently, Jesus tells them to seat the people "in groups on the green grass." They sat down in groups of hundreds and of fifties, we are told.

Here is the verbatim text of the "miracle" that followed, from Mark:

Taking the five loaves and the two fish, he looked up to heaven, and blessed and broke the loaves, and gave them to his disciples to set before the people; and he divided the

two fish among them all. And all ate and were filled; and
they took up twelve baskets full of broken pieces and of the
fish. Those who had eaten the loaves numbered five thousand men. (Mark 6:41–44)

We should notice that, in following Mark, at this point Matthew
heightens the scale of the miracle by ending it with the words
"And those who ate were about five thousand men, *besides women
and children.*" That would mean, taken literally, that possibly as
many as fifteen thousand mouths were filled.

Mark, not content with this remarkable feat (according to the
literalists), presents the reader swiftly with a second or repeat miraculous feeding of a crowd only two chapters later, in chapter 8.
This time it involves 4,000-plus people in another deserted spot.
You would think that the disciples, remembering the feeding of
the 5,000-plus, would have known the drill by now. Instead, they
again ask naively: "How can one feed these people with bread
here in the desert?" We need to read the full passage:

In those days when there was again a great crowd without
anything to eat, he called his disciples and said to them, "I
have compassion for the crowd, because they have been with
me now for three days and have nothing to eat. If I send them
away hungry to their homes, they will faint on the way—
and some of them have come from a great distance." His disciples replied, "How can one feed these people with bread
here in the desert?" He asked them, "How many loaves do
you have?" They said, "Seven." Then he ordered the crowd
to sit down on the ground; and he took the seven loaves, and
after giving thanks he broke them and gave them to his disciples to distribute; and they distributed them to the crowd.
They had also a few small fish; and after blessing them, he
ordered that these too should be distributed. They ate and

were filled; and they took up the broken pieces left over, seven baskets full. Now there were about four thousand people. And he sent them away. And immediately he got into the boat with the disciples and went to the district of Dalmanutha. (Mark 8:1–10)

Clearly, though ultra-conservatives argue otherwise, these two stories are a doubling up by Mark of a single original tradition. He may simply have been following the tradition laid down in the Old Testament that two witnesses are needed to establish the truth of any incident or case at law. We simply don't know. Significantly, both Luke and John omit the second feeding altogether. In John's account, however, the cameo detail is added of the small boy with his lunch of five barley cakes and two fish (again the number seven). He offers them to be shared. These latter are then multiplied for all, with twelve baskets left over.

How Is This Possible?

That the meaning of this story, common to all four Gospels, is clearly not historical but theological is plain to anyone who reads it in the context of the lengthy discussion of Jesus as the bread of life that follows it in chapter 6 of the Fourth Gospel. History or actual event has nothing whatever to do with what the miracle is saying. On the surface, of course, the five different versions of miraculous feeding in the Gospels appear to describe an astounding magical trick worthy of characters in a Harry Potter book or the fabled Merlin of old. Those who insist that these are literal narratives to be taken at face value—since every word is the inspired Word of God—are thus compelled to believe in an impossible, magician-like Jesus who is a kind of superman and as such totally unlike the ordinary flesh-and-blood humans whom he ostensibly came to "save." This is not what the overall message of the New

Testament is about, since it insists at the same time throughout that, like Osiris in the Egyptian myth, he was one of us in every way—except for sin. If one can simply close one's eyes and swallow, then this kind of supposed supernatural intervention in the normal workings of nature makes a crude, superficial kind of sense. But most thinking persons will either shrug it all off or scoff at the credulity required.

Thomas Jefferson long ago found a way to deal with the dilemma such stories present to those who value reason as one of the highest gifts of God: he simply took his scissors and eliminated all such miracles and other traces of the supernatural from his New Testament. Scholars with a great deal more Biblical sophistication—such as Rudolph Bultmann—and most liberal Christians in his wake have taken the path of demythologizing. They recognize that the passages in question are certainly not history; they are mythical in nature. Their solution therefore is to remove the entire myth mentally rather than with a cutting tool. The true myth as a bearer of timeless truth is thus not understood in its proper role and function but dismissed as an accretion to what little remains as a putative "core account."

Some of the other attempts to deal with these miracles would be risible if they were not so sadly far-fetched. For example, C.S. Lewis, in his book *Miracles* and elsewhere in his apologetic writings, tries to save the day by pointing out that in the multiplication of loaves and fishes God (whom he seems to equate with Jesus, even though neither St. Paul nor the Gospels ever go that far) was merely speeding up into a brief moment of time what he does in the fertile fields and in the oceans every day by natural means. I have great respect for Lewis as a professor of English and as a former courageous and articulate defender of Christianity against non-believers, but it must be said that he was neither a Biblical scholar nor a theologian. His eager explanations of miracles explain nothing; they simply add to the mystification.

Even worse than the former Oxford don's tangled explications
are the feeble attempts of liberal preachers to tiptoe around the
problems raised by resorting to such rosy explanations as—for
example—that John's account gives us the real clue. The boy who
brought forth his lunch set such a moving, altruistic example for
everybody else who was there that they all dug deep into their
pockets and packs to bring out their own lunches and fixings and
put them together for a kind of open-air potluck supper on the
greensward. It's what in England one would call "a nice try," but
there's absolutely nothing in the text to suggest this. Though it
suits those who would reduce the Gospel themes to polite middle-
class moralizing, the point of the story is not that good things
happen when everybody shares their resources.

Bread in the Wilderness

What is really going on here, then, and is it possible for a modern
reader to discover a way to read these accounts in any deeply
meaningful way? There is, and it depends again wholly upon taking
what is mythological as purely mythic in nature and content. If you
like, to use a term I have employed earlier and which I strongly
recommend, we have to *remythologize* the Gospels, not demythologize them, and then try to see what the myths are intended to convey. It is precisely the mythic element in the healing and nature
miracle stories that bears the timeless truth so necessary and relevant to the plight of each of us today. That's where the true glory
breaks through. To be robbed of this consistently, as many churchgoers are, is to be denied the very water of life that religion is supposed to offer.

The truth is that none of these feedings actually happened.
There has never been found—and never will be—even so much
as a single letter home from anyone at that period saying they
were present at such "events" and were witnesses of such marvels

and portents. But the truths these stories contain are timeless and essential for our spiritual understanding and growth today. (Keep in mind as we proceed that symbols and myths in ancient sacred writings often are multivalent, that is, they have many levels of meaning, some of them at times even apparently contradictory. Take, for example, Lucifer. His name means "light-bearer" and he was the bright and morning star; yet he also symbols that mythical character Satan or the accuser, the Diabolos.)

First of all, we should remember that one of the concerns of the authors of the New Testament was to present the Jesus character in the drama as a second Moses. There had been a prophecy of one being raised up who would be "like unto Moses," only greater. That's why, as we will see shortly, Matthew has Jesus give the fictional Sermon on the Mount: Jesus, the second Moses, must give a new law from a mountaintop just as Moses had brought down the law from Mount Sinai. That's why Jesus went as a baby to Egypt (in the story) and was then called "out of Egypt" just as Moses had been. That's also why there was a threat against the baby Jesus as there had been a threat against the baby Moses before. Just as there was a Joseph, who was a dreamer, in the original account of how Moses eventually came to be in Egypt, so there is a Joseph and his dreams in the birth narratives in the Gospels. Similarly, in order to be seen as truly equal to and greater than Moses, Jesus must be shown working miracles, for example feeding the multitudes just as Moses had persuaded God miraculously to feed the Children of Israel during their sojourn in the desert. Moses saw to it that manna, a miraculous food, was provided from heaven. So too, then, Jesus is depicted as providing bread in the wilderness.

Our Deep Hunger

But that is only a tiny beginning on what the feedings of the thousands was about. To go further in this, we need to look more

closely at what is involved in all the esoteric imagery about bread.
It plays a prominent role in the mythologies of ancient Egypt and
elsewhere in the ancient world.

Before we do that, though, notice that, in Mark's description
of the feeding of the four thousand, Jesus says the crowd has been
fasting or hungry for three days. The number three, as we saw
earlier in this study as well as in *The Pagan Christ*, occurs with an
amazing frequency throughout the Bible. It is often significant
as marking a period of conception, of new beginnings, new life.
Jonah was three days in the fish's belly, Jesus was raised on the
third day—as were Osiris and Adonis—Moses asked Pharaoh
to allow the Jews to go a three days' journey into the wilderness to
worship their God. The astronomical feature behind all this, as
we have seen, was the monthly three-day period when the moon
is not visible from Earth and was thought to be conceiving the
fresh new moon from a mythic congress with the sun. But from an
evolutionary standpoint, three stood for the periods of development before the fourth stage—the coming of the Christ principle,
Divine Mind, in every human being.

So, the three days that the crowd went hungry allegorically
denote the three previous steps. They speak to us of the stage in
our evolution when humans were symbolically hungering in the
wilderness for the Christ mind that the bread of the miracle represents. Notice that the number of the loaves and the fish comes
to seven. Seven, again, is the number of perfection, but it is also
the symbol for the seven stages of unfoldment through which life
must pass in completing every cycle, and so on and on. Made up
of three plus four, seven contains the basic numbers for the entire
universe. Four is the number for the square—the basic building
block and foundation for all the more intricate structures; three
is for the triangle in addition to what has already been said above.
Most importantly, three times four makes the crucial number

twelve, which, among so many other things, denotes the various figures of the all-important zodiac above.

Bread is deeply connected in the ancient symbolism with two "houses" or signs of the zodiac, Virgo and Pisces. Most are aware that Pisces is the house of the fishes by name, but it is much less well known that Virgo in the esoteric symbolism of old, based upon astronomy/astrology, was called the house of bread. This is because, when the constellation of Virgo rose on the eastern horizon at midnight on December 24, it was believed that she bore on her left arm the Christ child or the symbol of the Christhood principle coming as a gift to all humanity, and in her right hand Spica, which is the brightest star of all in this constellation and which in Latin translates as "a spike" or "an ear of corn/wheat." So, symbolically, the coming of the Christ is the coming of heavenly bread. This is why in the Fourth Gospel, in the context of the miracle of feeding the five thousand, the author speaks allegorically of Jesus as the bread of life: "For the bread of God is that which comes down from heaven and gives life to the world."[3]

Like Horus before him, Jesus says, "I am the bread of life." In other words, the divine principle incarnated in each of us is, if recognized and fully appropriated as our very own, the secret of life itself—not just physical life, but life immortal, life for evermore. This is what all the New Testament language about eating the body of the Christ truly signifies. There isn't the slightest intention of conveying—what would have been truly abhorrent to any Orthodox Jew then or now—a literal sense of actually eating anyone's flesh or body. This was a fully Pagan (Egyptian and Greek) metaphor and totally foreign to the traditions of Judaism. The same could be said of the whole idea of a dying and rising godman; it too had Pagan and not Jewish roots. In fact, few things can be said to be less in accord with the traditions of Judaism than this.

Holy Communion

The sacrament of Holy Communion, or the Eucharist, is therefore a ritualized, symbolical, spiritual "feeding" upon the divine energies flowing into us in the living reality of Incarnation through the indwelling Spirit of God. The careful recording of the fact that there were many fragments of bread and fish—twelve basketfuls—gathered after the "miracle" denotes the truth that it was by fragmentation into individual units that the Christ principle was initially imparted to each of us, and that none of it will ever finally be lost. As the ancients said, "The gods distribute divinity." Moreover, there is a profound reason why the Gospels of Matthew and Luke say that Jesus was born in Bethlehem, apart from the fact that Bethlehem is the prophesied place where the Messiah is to be born. *Beth Lechem* in Hebrew means "the House of Bread." Similarly, long before him, Horus's birthplace in Egypt was Anu, the place of "multiplying bread."

The Sign of the Fish

In the ancient wisdom of the sages, every one of us had two mothers, one to give us natural birth and one to give us spiritual birth. At this level of the symbolism, Virgo, the "house" of bread, is the first of these and Pisces, the "house" of fish, is the second. In esoteric thought, man's body houses the two mothers; the body is a double house of bread and fish. As St. Paul says, "There is a physical [natural] body and there is a spiritual body." Because, in terms of evolution, a fish, the first organism recognized as able to breathe while submersed in water (matter), was a symbol of incarnation—a spiritual essence "swimming and breathing" in a material, or watery, body—it was an obvious choice as a Christian term.

The Gospels' Jesus is marked by Piscean symbols. In the catacombs, the sign of the fish was a secret token of Christian presence, and in the artwork one sees crossed fish on a plate on the altar or two fish crossed on the Christ's forehead or at his feet. For a considerable time in the early centuries Christians were known by the Romans as *Pisciculi*, "Little Fishes." They were thus members of the fish cult. The Greek word for fish, *ichthys*, forms an acrostic for "Jesus Christ the son of God our Saviour." There is a strange story in Matthew.[4] Jesus tells Peter to go to the sea and "cast a hook." Then he is to open the fish's mouth and find a coin in it. This simple illustration once again makes the point that the fish—organic life breathing in water and so symbolizing the human living in a watery/material environment—nevertheless carries something of great value within. It is an esoteric glyph or image of Incarnation—something golden in what seems made only of matter.

Whenever I reread these mythological accounts of the "miraculous" feedings and am made aware again of the exalted meaning carried beneath the surface words, I feel much as I do when at a Eucharist or Mass my mind is able to pierce through the literal exterior to the truth underlying all the pomp, symbolism and ritual. There is a profound gratitude to the mystery we call God for his lavish grace and generosity in giving of the divine flame to dwell in my heart and life. Knowledge and experience of this, through thinking about it often and through meditation, is the true "bread" on which my soul nourishes itself and is daily sustained. At Communion, I find I can usually shut out all the extraneous accretions and literalisms of the ritual—not to mention the piling on of verbiage as if God needed reminding of all "his wondrous acts" in the past—while concentrating or meditating on this. I recommend that readers of these pages do the same. We need rituals that are meaningful. In spite of much in the service that may put you off or at times be even intellectually offensive, you can lose yourself in the wonder of the divine gift so freely invested in us all. We come together to "re-member"—to restore the unity of the divine "body" of the original gift.

Changing Water into Wine

As we have seen, John, or the Fourth Gospel as it is called to differentiate it from the three Synoptics, calls the miracles attributed to Jesus "signs." In other words, then, the author wants to make it perfectly clear that the meaning of the signs, of which significantly there are seven in his Gospel, is symbolical or allegorical. This includes the healing of the blind man and other healings already discussed. Still, down the ages into the literalisms of today, the vast majority of ordinary Christians have simply assumed they are meant to bear a pedestrian literal sense—and the clergy, for the most part, though knowing better themselves, have done little to avoid the misunderstanding.

This issue can be clearly seen in the very first sign or, in Greek, *semeion* that John describes as beginning Jesus' public ministry, in chapter 2 of his Gospel. He tells us that "on the third day"—a formula with which the reader is by now well acquainted—there was a wedding in a place called Cana of Galilee. This story is very familiar to Bible readers. Mary, the mother of Jesus, is said to be attending the celebration, and Jesus, along with his disciples, has been invited as well. (The writer assumes we know that Jesus had a group of disciples already, although in John's version he has only so far named the four we meet in chapter 1: Peter, Andrew, Philip and Nathaniel.) In any case, the wine supply gives out suddenly and Jesus' mother reports this embarrassing detail to her son.

She is met with what many scholars agree is a rather sharp response: "Woman what business is that either of yours or mine?" The NRSV translates it: "Woman what concern is that to you and to me?" This is followed (rather lamely, it appears to me) with the words "My hour has not yet come." Most people would not have been reassured by such a response in "real life," but Mary is depicted as taking what seems like a rebuke for a full consent to act, because she then immediately says to the servants: "Do whatever he tells you."

At this point we are told there are six stone water jars "for the Jewish rites of purification" standing nearby. Each one, according to John, holds "twenty to thirty gallons." Jesus commands the servants to see that they are filled "up to the brim." Then he instructs them to draw some out and take it to the chief steward or head waiter for tasting. As soon as he has done so, the steward in turn calls the bridegroom and says the well-known words "Everyone serves the good wine first, and then the inferior wine after the guests have become drunk. But, you have kept the good wine until now."

All who are familiar with not only the Judeo-Christian Bible but also the other "Bibles" or sacred writings of the ancient Near East will know that wine symbolism is an almost constant theme. All the gods of antiquity were gods of wine, from Horus of Egypt to Dionysus or Bacchus of ancient Greece and Rome. As noted in my book, *The Spirituality of Wine*, wine, grapes and the vine are mentioned hundreds of times in the Old and New Testaments together. Wine, being a composite of spirit (fermentation) and matter (water), was the perfect symbol of the miracle of Incarnation, a complete type, glyph or analogue of the Christ in each of us.

Earth Forces Become Divine

We have already seen a fourfold progression in our evolution from the mineral, the vegetative, the animal and finally the human. This latter, human phase was in turn thought of as progressing through seven stages, the final or seventh (meaning perfection) being that of the coming of the indwelling Christ. The six water pots thus represent the hidden, earthy or elemental stages in the incarnational development of the Christ principle in matter prior to the

seventh stage, the full blossoming on the human plane that the
Jesus persona models or fulfills. This "coming" or final stage,
which is the spiritual heritage belonging to every member of the
human family, is, when claimed or fully recognized within, like
the vast difference between ordinary existence and truly being
fully alive; it's like the difference between a really good wine compared with plain water. In passing, it's interesting to notice that
when Mark describes the transfiguration of Jesus, in chapter 9, he
tells us that it also happened "after six days."[5] Again the meaning is
symbolical and has nothing to do with actual chronology.

Since in many ways John is widely recognized by scholars as
the most anti-Judaism of the Gospels (it's misleading to say "anti-
Semitic," since presumably the author is Jewish), it's not surprising that the editor can't refrain from making the point that the jars
were for use in various Jewish rites of cleansing, such as of the
hands before meals. This illustrates in his view (since they now
contain wine) the superiority of the Christian version of truth to
that of the parent faith. But that's not (thankfully) his main objective in the story. It's plainly to make certain from the outset of all
that he has to say that the message of Jesus is like the "divine mania"
of which Plato wrote, the intoxication of mind and senses with a
living experience of the presence of God in our midst and in our
hearts. It's as different as water and wine. That's what the inner
meaning of this passage now brings home to me as I read it. No
longer is it the semi-magical act of a distant "hero," but an illustration of the impact on one's life made possible by awakening to or
laying hold on the reality of the Christ mind and spirit too often
left dormant or unrecognized at the centre of one's own being.

Notice that there were "six stone [or earthen] jars." Jesus, symbolizing the seventh or transforming power, comes to transform
the nature that had been put together by the first six outpourings
of primal life into a higher spiritual status. The Christ always
is given the task of converting or transfiguring the six lower ele-

mental or "stone"—earthy—forces into divinity. Just as a single ray of light passing through a prism breaks into seven colours, so too in both the natural and the spiritual realm basic processes were thought of as ultimately forming a sevenfold stream of development from the source of all being.

We know that Horus of Egypt turned water into wine and was a god of wine, but to get something of the full texture of the cultural and religious background of what John is expressing in the story of the wedding at Cana, here is an excerpt from the famous play by Euripides called *The Bacchae*. It's about another god of wine, Bacchus or Dionysus:

Next came the son of the virgin, Dionysus,
bringing the counterpart to bread, wine
and the blessings of life's flowing juices.
His blood, the blood of the grape,
Lightens the burden of mortal misery.
When, after their daily toils, men drink their fill,
sleep comes to them, bringing release from all their troubles.
There is no other cure for sorrow. Though himself a god,
it is his blood we pour out
to offer thanks to the gods. And through him,
we are blessed.[6]

The vivid metaphor, then, of changing water into wine is really a powerful way of stating what the Jesus Story is about: the transformation that happens when the secret of being wholly alive and awake as children and bearers of the Light within breaks in upon us. This alone, according to John, is the key to a life lived "more abundantly."

7

THE SERMON
ON THE MOUNT

*History is not the primary referrant of our
[religious] symbols, but our own inner selves.*

— JOSEPH CAMPBELL, *The Power of Myth*

The Greatest Sermon Never Preached

EVERY DECEMBER during the twelve years, from 1971 to
1983, when I was the religion editor for the *Toronto Star*,
I had one of the most precious opportunities and privileges
any journalist could dream of. As long as there was a story there,
I could travel anywhere in the world I wished, usually accompanied by a photographer, to gather material for a front-page series
as a Christmas special. This took me to Calcutta, to Bethlehem,
and to the High Arctic, to mention a few trips. But one of the most
remarkable and memorable was that leading to the 1980 series
headlined as A TALE OF TWO MOUNTAINS.

The mountains were Mount Sinai, where Moses is said to have
received the Ten Commandments, and the Mount of the Beatitudes, where Jesus is widely believed to have given the Sermon on
the Mount. We camped out in both places, and I had the experience of reading the Beatitudes in my worn Greek New Testament

while looking out over the Sea of Galilee. The "mountain" is in fact a rather low hill, but even with tourists coming and going, attracted to the lovely Roman Catholic church on the brow of it, the peace and tranquility of the spot are not to be denied. As I read in silence, a service was in progress led by some Franciscan clergy and I distinctly heard, in French, the immortalized opening lines: "Blessed are the poor in spirit, for theirs is the kingdom of heaven."

We are thus on very familiar—and holy—territory in what follows. More has been written and preached about what has come to be universally known as the Sermon on the Mount (even though a shorter version in Luke is said explicitly to have been on a "plain") than any other part of the Bible. Here again a quick look at Google on the Internet will instantly bring up close to two million hits or references of some kind. To cover even a small percentage of the varying opinions and interpretations of scholars, preachers and a host of others on the Sermon's nature and content would take not just a whole book but indeed a good-sized library of many volumes. While it contains much that is sublime, the "Sermon" also has its share of problems, some contradictions, and intellectual as well as moral challenges of various kinds. [1]

To put the matter as simply as possible at the outset, the "Sermon" is believed by most Biblical scholars to be actually a compendium of widely varying wisdom and other sayings, ranging all the way from the Beatitudes themselves to the Lord's Prayer, the golden rule, and the parable about the wise man who built his house upon the rock while the foolish man erected his on sand. There are three full chapters in all (chapters 5 to 7 of Matthew) and some 110 verses.

All that can be done here with any thoroughness is to acquaint the reader with some of the most outstanding features and to interpret the most crucial teachings, the Beatitudes. In the first place, the Sermon is praised to the skies by almost everyone and taken as the pure essence of Christian orthodoxy. However, I have found over the years that very few of those who laud it most highly have ever bothered to read it in its entirety, let alone attempted to ponder its total message. Its high moral tone is simply assumed. A closer look reveals some high ideals and some excellent guideposts for our spiritual unfolding, but it also raises some problems.

Some Background

The earliest writer in the New Testament never once mentions the Sermon on the Mount (or its variant, that on the plain in Luke). Paul, as is well known, never explicitly mentions any of the teachings of a putative historical Jesus except for one, and that saying is nowhere to be found in the Gospels at all! It occurs in the Book of Acts: "It is more blessed to give than to receive." His recital of Jesus' words over the Last Supper was "received from the Lord"— in a vision, in other words—and is a formula widely believed by scholars to have been based upon the Mystery Religions. What is more, Mark, the earliest Gospel, written sometime after 70 CE, makes no mention of any such sermon either. Nor indeed does John, the latest and most highly developed (in terms of Christology, or elevation of doctrine about Jesus) of them all.

Without drawing the issue out unduly, it can safely be said that the Sermon is a completely artificial construct by the redactors or editors of Matthew and that its setting is also likewise wholly fictional. In other words, it was produced by several "hands." My former New Testament professor, Frank W. Beare, who wrote a classic commentary on this Gospel, believed it was the product of what he called "the School of Matthew." The earliest commentator to address the question of where the Sermon is supposed to have taken place is Jerome (342–420 CE) in his commentary on

Matthew, where he says merely that it was on some mountain or other in the Galilee.

I consulted *The Catholic Encyclopedia* on the issue, and after considerable toing and froing its conclusion is that nobody knows for certain what place or mountain was supposedly involved. Matthew says simply, "When Jesus saw the crowds, he went up the mountain." The reason for the lack of detail, of course, is that here, just as wherever "the mount" or a "high mountain" is cited in Scripture, the meaning is in truth purely symbolical. It carries the same meaning as when the Egyptian creation account or myth speaks of the mount that rises up out of the soup of nothingness, the Nun, and becomes terra firma, which is to say, the earth itself. Nobody knows where the Sermon took place, then, because it never literally took place anywhere.

This may seem a slightly shocking statement at first, but that it is factual can be confirmed by a few additional observations. Those who regard Christianity as a wholly original, "made in heaven" kind of faith may dispute this all they wish, but the truth remains that chapters 5, 6 and 7 of Matthew—the longest continuous monologue in all of the New Testament—do not contain wholly original concepts or teachings. Scholars over the years have dissected it all verse by verse, and there is nothing in this purportedly unique "constitution of Christianity" that cannot be found pre-existing in either the Hebrew scriptures (the Old Testament), the Talmud, Midrash or the Mishnah, or, much earlier yet, in the teachings of ancient Egypt. For example, loving one's neighbour as oneself is the key teaching of the Gospels' Jesus. But if you read Leviticus 19:18, for example, you will find it had been part of Jewish teaching for centuries: "You shall not take vengeance or bear a grudge against any of your people, but you shall love your neighbour as yourself." In the aphorisms in the Book of Proverbs, which often bear a close affinity to their Egyptian predecessors, it is also made plain that you are to do good, that is, act lovingly towards all, including your enemies.

Proverbs and Ecclesiastes are two Old Testament books based upon the "wisdom" traditions from the ancient world. It's interesting to find that in his *Discourse Against the Christians*, the Pagan philosopher Celsus (*c.* 180 CE) cites the Gospels' Jesus saying, "It is easier for a camel to go through the eye of a needle than for a rich man to enter the Kingdom of God." Celsus comments on Plato (who lived four centuries before Christ): "Yet we know that Plato expressed this very idea in a purer form when he said, 'It is impossible for an exceptionally good man to be exceptionally rich.' Is one utterance more inspired than the other?"[2]

There are whole scholarly texts totally devoted to showing the real roots of Sermon on the Mount teachings. Some New Testament scholars have spent a lot of time trying to demonstrate that the variations between some of Luke's parallels in his Sermon on the Plain and the sayings found in Matthew are due to common sourcing in various levels of the hypothetical—and now hotly disputed—"sayings document" called Q, mentioned in chapter 1.[3] But this is largely a waste of effort. Clearly, wherever he found them, Matthew adopted a huge collection of wisdom sayings—and there were at the time, as already indicated, many circulating in the ancient Mediterranean world of ideas—and, as Papias informs us, he put them together "as best he could." Luke, whoever he may have been, probably with Matthew's account in front of him, selected those parts of the "sermon" that most pleased him and suited his overall purpose, adapting or changing them to suit his theological position and the life situation (in technical terms, the *Sitz im Leben*) of his particular audience or church community.

Add to all of this Matthew's clear aim throughout his Gospel of presenting Jesus as a second Moses, indeed as one "greater than Moses," and it's clear that for him the whole scene is meant to

represent this second Moses, on a mountain—just as first was supposed to have happened at Mount Sinai—handing down a "new
law" for the Christian movement. Papias, the Bishop of Hieropo-
lis in Asia Minor about 120 CE, writes, in a now-famous fragment
on the origins of the Gospels, that Matthew composed "the oracles" (in Greek, *ta logia*) in Hebrew and that "*everyone translated
them as best he could*" (my emphasis).

Notice that Papias, though holding the position of a bishop in
the second century, had not yet seen for himself any written
Gospel at all! He states that, on the authority of one whom he calls
"the Elder," he can say that Mark, having become an interpreter
for Peter, set down accurately—"though not in order"—everything he could remember about the words and actions of the Lord
and that Matthew did as I have already said above. It bears repeat-
ing that Papias makes no claim to have ever seen a Gospel of Mark
himself. Notice also that there's no word in Papias's account of
Luke's or John's Gospel, and clearly no reference whatever to any
supposed eyewitnesses of the purported events themselves. General full recognition of there being four authoritative Gospels—
those of the later official canon, or church law—does not occur
until into the second half of the second century, after 150 CE.

Differing Views

Papias's remark about everybody interpreting Matthew's *logia*
or oracles composed in Hebrew "as best he could" was to prove
strangely prophetic. That is exactly what happened down through
the history of the Church as far as the Sermon on the Mount is
concerned, with astonishing results. What is called the "Absolutist
View" of the Sermon rejects all compromise and "believes that if
obeying the scripture costs the welfare of the believer then that is
a reasonable sacrifice for salvation."[4] On this view every precept
in the Sermon on the Mount must be taken literally and applied

universally. Proponents of this view include St. Francis of Assisi and, in his later life, Leo Tolstoy, the great Russian novelist. According to my own experience and knowledge of the field, no Christian denomination today fully accepts this view, but the early Anabaptists came close, and modern Anabaptist groups such as the Mennonites and the Hutterites, which remain pacifist in outlook, perhaps come closest. The Society of Friends, also known as the Quakers, similarly takes an absolutist position on the issue of non-violence, but not on the Sermon as a whole.

One method of approach, which is more common than might at first be supposed, though not officially or openly endorsed by any denomination, is to simply alter the text to suit one's preference. In earliest times some copyists, for example, changed Matthew 5:22 from "whosoever is angry with his brother shall be in danger of the judgment" to "whosoever is angry with his brother *without a cause* shall be in danger of the judgment." The command to "love your enemies" was changed to "pray for your enemies."[5] The exception for divorce in the case of *porneia* or adultery may well be a Matthean addition (to soften the admonition's bite) since it is not there in Luke 16:18, in the earlier version in Mark 10:11 or in the even earlier view of Paul cited as 1 Corinthians 7:10–11. But in 1 Corinthians 7:12–16, it should be noted, Paul gives his own exception to Jesus' alleged teaching when it involves a non-believing partner who separates. The custom down through history regarding the strictness of the Sermon's stance on divorce has been to paraphrase the text and thus make it far less radical. Today, the Anglican Church of Canada regularly grants a second marriage to divorced persons if certain conditions are met. The Roman Catholic Church holds a superficially much more rigorous position, but the annulment process, called by one prominent cardinal who is a critic "Vatican-style divorce," manages to help members get around it.

A search through the works of almost every major Christian writer shows them at some point to have made this same kind of modification. Even the most extreme literalists find themselves applying an allegorical or other level of meaning to various parts of the Sermon. For example, with respect to chapter 5 of Matthew, where it speaks of the need to remove an offending eye or cut off an offending hand, few congregations have maimed members who have acted on the letter of these admonitions.[6] The so-called "Hyperbole View" makes the argument that portions of what Jesus is made to say need to be "toned down" for use in the "real world"; but the problem, of course, has been to find agreement over what parts are to be taken literally and what are to be seen as somewhat overheated imagery. According to some commentators, closely related to the above is the "General Principles View," which says that Jesus is not giving specifics but general principles of behaviour. Any specific instances given, then, are merely examples of such universal guidelines.

The Two Ways

A two-level approach has been, for many centuries, the traditional position of the Roman Catholic Church. This divides the teachings into general precepts or instructions and specific counsels. Thus, obedience to the general precepts is essential for salvation, but obedience to the counsels is only necessary for those dedicated to attaining total perfection. Accordingly, the great majority of the population need only be concerned about the precepts, while the counsels must be pursued by "a pious few" such as the clergy and monks or nuns. This was the comforting theory initiated by St. Augustine and later further developed by St. Thomas Aquinas, though an earlier version is found in the ancient document called the *Didache* or "Teaching."[7] The official title for this approach is "The Two Ways." "For if you are able to bear the entire yoke of the Lord you will be perfect; but if you are not able to do this, do what you are able."[8,9]

Martin Luther, not content with that view, rejected the Catholic vision and developed his own two-level system, called by some the "Two Realms View." He divided the world into religious and secular realms and argued that the Sermon applied only to the spiritual side of things. In the temporal world, he believed, obligations to employers, family and one's country made it necessary for believers to compromise. Simultaneously, as the Protestant Reformation moved forward, a new movement of Biblical criticism began leading to the "Analogy of Scripture View." Closer reading of the Bible revealed that many of the most rigid precepts collected in the Sermon were explicitly moderated by other parts of the New Testament itself. For example, while the Sermon forbids all oaths, oath taking is quite common in the Hebrew Bible, and we are shown St. Paul boldly using oaths on at least two occasions. So, it was argued, apparently the Sermon—which, of course, was composed later than Paul's writings in any case—did admit of obvious exceptions.

Speaking of double standards or equivocation, it is a source of embarrassment to many Christians all over the world that the United States, the most openly Christian country, led by the most outspoken Christian president in its history—a man who says Jesus Christ is his favourite "philosopher"—has committed itself to the violence of pre-emptive war as a matter of policy. President George W. Bush saw no contradiction between going to war in Iraq and his churchgoing, Bible-reading, "God bless America" style of living. Lip service is paid to the Sermon on the Mount, but horrors such as were committed against prisoners in Abu Ghraib prison in Baghdad and the illegal rendition of suspected terrorists to "third party" countries for "interrogation" appear to raise little more than a minor blip on the American evangelical radar screen. Violence and religion have been and are just as closely linked in Christianity as they currently are in Islam. Consider that American young people now can play with or watch Christian-themed video games where the hero blurts out "Praise the Lord!" after blowing away the bad guys.

There are several other modes of trying to make total sense of the Sermon, but only one more merits brief mention here. That is the view of the renowned thinker and Biblical scholar Dr. Albert Schweitzer. Because Schweitzer had become convinced that the only Jesus that made sense from the Biblical texts was an eschatological (end times) preacher who firmly—and quite mistakenly—thought that the end of the world was about to be ushered in by God, he saw the Sermon on the Mount as an "interim ethic." One could then attempt to keep the Sermon's otherwise impossible demands since in the end times one's own material and physical well-being was not of foremost concern. Such apparent impossibilities as the Sermon demanded—such as to take no anxious thought about tomorrow—were doable in this view inasmuch as the coming end rendered all worldly consequences ultimately irrelevant. Some fundamentalist groups today take the same stance regarding environmental and other critical global issues, such as the AIDS epidemic. Why worry, for example, about global warming when everything will soon go up in a general holocaust anyway? The "saved" will then be "raptured" out of here while the rest of us are "left behind" to perish horribly.

Misquoting Jesus?

Lest any reader be perturbed at the suggestion made above that Luke and Matthew sometimes change the wording of Mark in order to soften or nuance his original intent, and that later hands may have changed other Gospel texts as well, I recommend the 2005 book by New Testament scholar Bart Ehrman, *Misquoting Jesus*. Ehrman's is the simplest yet clearest account to date of how fully human the Bible is as a book. He shows beyond a shadow of a doubt how changes to the texts were made in later attempts to clarify, simplify or emend the original readings. Of course, as he points out, we do not have a single original text of any book in the New Testament. Nor do we have first copies of the originals. We do not even have first copies of first copies. While there are fragments of texts as early as the second century CE, the major Greek versions of the entire New Testament belong to the fourth century. Conservatives are wont to cite the large number of surviving manuscripts of the New Testament compared with other ancient texts. This argument is irrelevant, however. It is not so much quantity as quality, mainly the early dating, that counts here.

In the process of transmission, given the absence of printing presses, it was inevitable not only that some deliberate changes were made, but also that many human errors crept in. While many of them are of little real consequence, there are well over 100,000 variant readings for the total New Testament text. Any good Greek text of the New Testament has a critical apparatus at the bottom of every page with the major variants all duly noted.

How We Can Understand the Sermon on the Mount

Let there be no mistake, however. Trying to see the "sermon" as honestly and clearly as possible is not intended as an attempt to lessen its importance or overall impact. There is no question but that, taken as a whole, the Sermon on the Mount has gathered up within it the sublimest moral teaching of all time, and that it has greatly influenced our moral evolution as a race through its inspiration and its impact upon some of the greatest reformers and leaders of human history, including Mahatma Gandhi and the Reverend Martin Luther King. Clearly the Beatitudes totally challenge and reverse today's prevailing cultural and other values, such as celebrity, power seeking and worldly success. Their placement

in the mouth of Jesus was intended to be understood mythically
and mystically, and the secret of the interpretation lies in a full
awareness of the metaphorical and allegorical nature of all religious language.

I have written at length about the Lord's Prayer in *Prayer—The
Hidden Fire* (1998), so I will not repeat that here. However, because
of their central importance to our theme, let me turn at least
briefly to a fuller interpretation of the Beatitudes.

They are so named after the Latin term *beatus*, "blessed." Both
the King James Version and the NRSV begin with that word
"blessed." This is not a very common mode of speaking today and
really fails to catch the essence of what is being said. As a result,
the entire saying in each case is greatly weakened for contemporary men and women. The word in the original Greek and the
Aramaic behind it give a strong note of congratulation. Hence,
each iteration of this word held for its first hearers or readers a
small explosive charge of surprise.

Suppose we translate them somewhat freely as follows, and
the reader can later check and compare each of them with his or
her own bible in Matthew 5:1–11. (Please excuse the overuse of
exclamation marks here, but they really are needed to underline
just how utterly countercultural and radical all of this was then
and still is today.)

You are poor in spirit? Hearty congratulations. For yours is
the Kingdom of Heaven!

To those who are grieving (or longing deeply for something,
such as release from harmful habits or the next step in inner
growth), hearty congratulations! You will be comforted.

Hearty congratulations to those who are meek! You will
inherit the earth!

For all of you who hunger and thirst—after righteousness—hearty congratulations too, because such will be completely filled!

Congratulations to those who are merciful, for they in turn will receive mercy!

Hearty congratulations to those who are pure in heart, for they will see God!

To all who are peacemakers, heartiest congratulations, for they shall be called the children of God!

Are you being persecuted because of your stand for justice and what is right? You deserve to be congratulated, for yours is the Kingdom of Heaven!

You are to be congratulated heartily also whenever they reproach you and persecute you and utter lies about you on my account. Rejoice and exult, because your reward is great in Heaven. They persecuted the prophets before your time in exactly the same way!

A Fuller Interpretation

When the German philosopher-writer Friedrich Wilhelm Nietzsche (1844–1900) vehemently repudiated the Christian ethic as a "slave morality," he based his criticism largely on the first three Beatitudes. Obviously, he had read them as literally as any fundamentalist could conceive. Since we too are surrounded by a social order in which self-esteem is often encouraged to extremes, and gentleness is mistaken for weakness, we have to look more deeply to discover why it is truly a blessing to be "poor in spirit" and among the mourning or the meek of the earth. None of these terms in the original text suggests for a moment personal weakness of any kind. By poor in spirit, the Sermon doesn't mean lacking in confidence or being a kind of Mr. Milquetoast. It means the true personal humility that lends maturing souls great strength of character. This is the very opposite of arrogance or pride or pushiness. Such a spirit knows well its own inestimable worth and its own limitations as an earthy vehicle for the divine fire. But it is never proud or vain.

The phrase for those who mourn, as already hinted in the above paraphrase, does not mean those who are always "down in the dumps," or even those who cling unduly to loss of friends or loved ones. There is a grief "too deep for tears" that many carry as they long to know new levels of insight or to conquer besetting sins. Those who "knock" at that door sincerely will be comforted because it will be opened to them in due time.

As for being meek, the Greek word is hard to translate adequately. It refers to the quality of inner softness that comes when one has successfully challenged those areas of the heart and mind that are rock hard and rigid in their condemnation or judgments of others. The meek are those who have faced up to all the hardened attitudes we carry on this or that controversial topic or towards one kind, race, colour or character of individuals or groups. They have worked these through one by one and found that, instead of being a closed and negative place, the whole earth is theirs to inherit. As St. Paul says, "All things are yours."

Hungering and thirsting for righteousness is not, on the surface or exoteric reading, all that attractive to modern men and women. We instinctively shrink from righteous people because it seems righteousness so swiftly turns to self-righteousness. But the Greek word used, *dikaiosune*, is the theme of Plato's greatest work, *The Republic*, and is best translated and understood here as "justice." No virtue, no higher rung on the evolutionary ladder, is more urgently needed than this in a world that often seems to have gone mad. There will never, however, be a coming of full justice for the nations until each of us hungers and thirsts for it within. If we truly want it, pray for it and work for it, our own hearts will overflow—"they shall be filled"—and the world in the end will know its blessing.

I believe the remaining "congratulations" are more easily understood, though still a challenge to each of us to apply. Just one word in closing this part, though, about "the pure in heart." This has often been narrowly interpreted to refer to sex alone, but that is a typical anti-body, anti-sexuality ecclesiastical approach. It really means a much wider purity: freedom from ambition that would trample over others, freedom from the lust for control, purity of motive and absence of what is called "attitude" or "side." Really, it fits with another Gospel saying about having "your eye single," being wholly focused upon the divine spirit's presence in the world and especially within. That kind of purity of heart is blessed by "seeing God"—that is, by glimpsing the hand of God in all we attempt or try to be.

Yes, there are contradictions to be found in the Sermon. But the reader should remember that this is true of any collection of wisdom or proverbial sayings ever formulated. A simple example from current folkloric material serves to make the point. We can see the truth of the saying "Look before you leap." But at the same time, it is contradicted by an equally true observation: "He who hesitates is lost." Other examples both modern and ancient could be multiplied. Both sides of the tension involved are true at any given specific time. It depends entirely upon the situation. So it is in the case of many of the precepts of the Sermon.

Sad to say, sheer literalism has made possible the abuse of some of the Beatitudes—about meekness, about being poor in spirit, for example—to oppress the weak and the downtrodden, especially slaves and women. Taken literally, Nietzsche was right.

Or to quote Karl Marx, it affords oppressors a convenient tool for aggression. It acts as a sop or an opiate against throwing off one's economic or other chains. Only a truly spiritual, mythical approach to these texts protects against such wrenching of Holy Writ to serve human selfishness, greed and systemic injustice.

On Being Perfect

Chapter 5, verse 48 of Matthew in the Sermon commands: "Be perfect, therefore, as your heavenly Father is perfect." Though it sums up the entire message, this verse understood literally has caused a huge amount of unnecessary self-hate and psychic suffering among many Christians plagued by an excess of zeal in the form of a rigid perfectionism. In the pastorate years ago, I frequently was consulted by otherwise wonderful people utterly weighed down by this particular form of self-flagellation. Along with general counselling, I tried to help these hypersensitive souls by explaining to them how the word for "perfect" used in the original Greek of Matthew is *teleios*. It is a word commonly found in the Mystery Religions to describe one who has been fully initiated and who is considered to really know the mystery or secret of who he or she really is, a bearer of the divine fire within. There may well be a hint of that spiritual meaning here. The word itself comes from the Greek root *telos*, which refers to a goal or end in the sense of fulfillment.

Aristotle, for example, was a *teleological* thinker. He was interested in studying the goal or purpose for each and every organism or being in Creation. He began his career with a consuming interest in biology; he cared intensely about what each plant or animal had as its ultimate telos or purpose or fulfillment in life. The true telos, for example, of an acorn is the full-grown oak tree. The full telos of any seed is the mature plant. Similarly, we human beings have a telos or goal of full, spiritual maturity. Ultimately, for Aristotle, achieving this goal involved the contemplation of the unmoved mover, God. So, in Aristotelian terms, to be perfect or *teleios* does not mean being a morally perfect, ultra-piously "good," perfectionist type of person, but rather one who aims to become in the very fullest sense what he or she is truly meant to be. That is the real sense here.

In the Sermon, then, this inner meaning is clear. It really sums up the total message: be fully what you are, the child, the bearer, of God within, just as "your heavenly Father is perfect."[10]

8

THE PARABLES

*When you know yourselves, then you will
be known, and you will understand that you
are children of the living father.*

— THE GOSPEL OF THOMAS, Saying #3

A S I SAID when we began, whether or not there ever
was an actual person in history known as Jesus Christ
is really irrelevant to the issue of the importance to us
personally of the teaching ascribed to his "character" in the documents that have come down to us, most specifically in the canonical Gospels and in the Gospel of Thomas. Buddhists and others
face a similar situation with respect to their leaders and teachers.
While I believe each of us must work out his or her own salvation exactly on the same terms as though Jesus had not existed—
clearly, nobody can take our own evolutionary problem and
accomplish the task for us—we have in the teaching and the
example set before us by all the avatars or "saviour" figures of each
successive age or culture the norms and ideals for ever higher
moral attainment. St. Paul applies this lesson when he on more
than one occasion tells the young Christians in his churches to be
"imitators of me as I also am of Christ." This is a vital spiritual
truth to remember.

Three Stories of Our Lost Condition

None can say with certainty who first composed the three parables put into the mouth of Jesus that we are about to examine. They are unique to Luke alone and all deal with a fundamental spiritual problem that inevitably rises to the surface whenever, as has happened so often, groups of religious seekers imagine that they alone have found "the truth" and that any "outsiders" have no place in the kingdom of heaven. Unfortunately, these ancient stories have become so well known to those who consider themselves most truly devout that their true, deeper meaning is seldom well understood or "heard." They only achieve their full aim when you see yourself as the "lost" object of divine love and searching. While, however, on the surface the three mini-stories seem to be about "them" and "us," and about the need for an end to pious yet invidious discrimination against "sinners" by the "saved," the deeper truth is about the universal "lostness" that constitutes our present human condition. The Pharisees and the scribes represent the forces that blind us to the truth of our own "lost" condition and encourage us to busy ourselves with external judgment of others. The more religious we are, the greater the temptation grows. [1]

The Parable of the Lost Sheep

Now all the tax collectors and sinners were coming near to listen to him. And the Pharisees and the scribes were grumbling and saying, "This fellow welcomes sinners and eats with them." So he told them this parable: "Which one of you, having a hundred sheep and losing one of them, does not leave the ninety-nine in the wilderness and go after the one that is lost until he finds it? When he has found it, he lays it on his shoulders and rejoices. And when he comes home, he calls together his friends and neighbours, saying to them, 'Rejoice with me, for I have found my sheep that was lost.' Just so, I tell you, there will be more joy in heaven over one sinner who repents than over ninety-nine righteous persons who need no repentance." (Luke 15:1–7)

The obvious, surface meaning here has great power and needs to be grasped again and again. But, for the philosophers and theologians of the ancient Near East, for example the Gnostics, many of whom were Christians, "lost" was one of the words or terms regularly used to depict the condition of the human soul incarnated in matter. That, for example, is the esoteric explanation behind the bewildered wanderings of the Israelites for forty years in the wilderness. Their fate there, remember, is the stuff of comedy if a literal rendering is forced upon it; but it was in reality a glyph or picture of the fact of Incarnation. We are like wanderers in the wilderness of life in this plane. Thus, the lost sheep in our story is not just the "sinner" and the "tax collector"; it is also the Pharisees, the scribes, and you and I. There is always "joy in heaven" when the Spirit succeeds in "finding," that is, in awakening the individual soul to his or her true being and condition. The divine source is constantly, compassionately, seeking the return of its own.

The Parable of the Lost Coin

The second, briefer parable makes the same two-tiered message clear. Commentators have regularly pointed out that the coin— a silver drachma, perhaps—may have been part of a circlet of jewellery worn by a bride at her wedding or given to her as part of her dowry. In any case, this would explain why it was infinitely precious to her, and she eventually "finds" it by sweeping furiously and eventually bringing it to the light. In the darkness—another potent symbol of our lost state—she "lights a lamp" and begins a diligent searching. Here it is:

> Or what woman having ten silver coins, if she loses one of them, does not light a lamp, sweep the house, and search carefully until she finds it? When she has found it, she calls together her friends and neighbours, saying, 'Rejoice with me, for I have found the coin that I had lost.' Just so, I tell you, there is joy in the presence of the angels of God over one sinner who repents. (Luke 15:8—10)

To be quite personal, as I think of all the wilful ways we take and the devious, evasive tactics we use at different times in our lives to avoid the full challenge of the Spirit finding us and revealing to us who we really are, I am reminded of these haunting lines from the two opening stanzas of Francis Thompson's famous poem "The Hound of Heaven," written in 1890:

> I fled Him, down the nights and down the days;
> I fled Him, down the arches of the years;
> I fled Him, down the labyrinthine ways
>   Of my own mind; and in the mist of tears
> I hid from Him, and under running laughter.
> . . .
>   But with unhurrying chase,
>   And unperturbèd pace,
>   Deliberate speed, majestic instancy,
>   They beat—and a Voice beat
>   More instant than the Feet—
>   "All things betray thee, who betrayest me."

Perhaps you too have felt something of the tug of truth in your heart as you have read these lines.

The Parable of the Prodigal and His Brother

The parable of the lost son is not just the longest of the three stories in this chapter of Luke, but by far the richest in content. In *The Pagan Christ*, I described this parable as "a classic exposition of the incarnational theology" that that book also was focused upon. It illustrates magnificently the total drama of the human-divine soul. Because it is so familiar, it suffers most from being too famil-iar and so the essence of the story too often escapes most tellings. I suggest trying to read what follows with the attention you might give it if you were doing so for the very first time. Pretend to yourself, if need be, that it is a wholly fresh anecdote you have never heard or seen before. It's a sublime example of an event that never happened but whose truth remains and is as lasting and unchanging as the flow of time itself.

> Then Jesus said, "There was a man who had two sons. The younger of them said to his father, 'Father, give me the share of the property that will belong to me.' So he divided his property between them. A few days later the younger son gathered all he had [the Greek word used here means he turned it into "hard cash"] and travelled to a distant country, and there he squandered his property in dissolute living. When he had spent everything, a severe famine took place throughout that country, and he began to be in need.
>
> "So he went and hired himself out to one of the citizens of that country, who sent him to his fields to feed the pigs. He would gladly have filled himself with the pods that the pigs were eating; and no one gave him anything. But when he came to himself he said, 'How many of my father's hired hands have bread enough and to spare, but here I am dying of hunger! I will get up and go to my father, and I will say to him, "Father, I have sinned against heaven and before you;

I am no longer worthy to be called your son; treat me like one of your hired hands.'"

"So he set off and went to his father. But while he was still far off, his father saw him and was filled with compassion; he ran and put his arms around him and kissed him. Then the son said to him, 'Father, I have sinned against heaven and before you; I am no longer worthy to be called your son.' But the father said to his slaves, 'Quickly, bring out a robe—the best one—and put it on him; put a ring on his finger and sandals on his feet. And get the fatted calf and kill it, and let us eat and celebrate; for this son of mine was dead and is alive again; he was lost and is found!' And they began to celebrate.

"Now his elder son was in the field; and when he came and approached the house, he heard music and dancing. He called one of the slaves and asked what was going on. He replied, 'Your brother has come, and your father has killed the fatted calf, because he has got him back safe and sound.' Then he became angry and refused to go in. His father came out and began to plead with him. But he answered his father, 'Listen! For all these years I have been working like a slave for you, and I have never disobeyed your command; yet you have never given me even a young goat so that I might celebrate with my friends. But when this son of yours came back, who has devoured your property with prostitutes, you killed the fatted calf for him!' Then the father said to him, 'Son, you are always with me, and all that is mine is yours. But we had to celebrate and rejoice, because this brother of yours was dead and has come to life; he was lost and has been found.'" (Luke 15:11–32)

In this parable, our "lostness" is expressed by the metaphor of journeying off to a distant land, to foreign soil. The theme is a familiar Bible metaphor of exile from our true home. There, because of the tyranny of the drives from the old, animal self, our Incarnation is expressed in terms of sensuality and excess followed by feeding upon scraps and being starved of the spiritual food our soul once knew in the "father's house" from which we set out so long ago. The familiar esoteric metaphor of death also applies. The father says this son was "dead" and is now alive.

Then there is the coming to one's own higher or truer Self inspired by wistful thoughts of our lost heritage. "He came to himself," that is, to his true or "higher" Self. There are deep in our hearts what Wordsworth so aptly called intimations of our forgotten immortality, our reminiscence or remembering, in Plato's words, of who we really are and whence we have originally come. "The divinity within is recognized, the 'sleeping' Christ is awakened, and we return home" to the anxious and ever-waiting father.[2] This is followed by an allegorical depiction of the "joy in heaven" already cited in the two earlier stories. The feasting and celebration mark the joyous resurrection of the soul in the eternal dimension of the "world to come." I am often asked whether I believe still in a life to come. I do indeed, and this is an expression of that faith for me.

The account at the end of the elder son who was infuriated by the welcome given to his lost brother seems to many to be somewhat anticlimactic and even jarring in tone. Yet it picks up the theme stated at the outset of the three stories, of the inability of the self-styled righteous—those who believe correctly, who belong to the truly "saved," and who firmly hold to all the correct or orthodox dogmas—to accept the bedrock reality that we are all essentially one. We are one in our "lostness" and we remain one in the divinity within that draws us each in our own time ineluctably, with rejoicing, back to the "father's house." We don't have to share John Newton's particular, evangelical theology to know in our own hearts the experience of "amazing grace" he felt

when the former hard-drinking slave trader underwent a sudden
religious conversion on March 10, 1748. Describing this event
later, in 1779, in his now-famous hymn, he tells the whole world:
"I once was lost, but now am found, / Was blind but now I see."

How I wish that every ultra-correct, harsh critic of my work or
that of others who care so deeply for the rebirth of Christianity in
our time (retired Episcopal bishop John Spong's critics, for example) could truly hear that message. Spong and I do not agree at
every point, since he still holds to belief in a historical Jesus, but
our common aim is to communicate the love of God today in a
more meaningful way, and our common goal is a rebirth for Christianity in our time. One thing we certainly agree on is that those
religionists are wrong who argue, some triumphantly, that ultimately some will be "left behind."[3]

The Parable of the Sower

Peel away all the layers of an onion, and at the centre
you will find emptiness; peel away all the layers of a human
being, and at the centre you will find the seed of God.

— DEEPAK CHOPRA, *How to Know God*

The parable of the sower is a very ancient wisdom story and of
pivotal importance in the Gospel records. The fact that this is so is
raised into high relief because not only is it found in Mark, as well
as Matthew and Luke—and Mark has only a bare handful of parables compared with the abundance of them in the latter two—but
it becomes the occasion for an editorial comment by the Evangelist that throws light on our entire understanding of the nature
and use of such imagery in the Gospels. The parable itself is well
known. Significantly, it occurs also in the Gospel of Thomas, a text
or "Good News'" without a crucifixion or resurrection that is
wholly composed of sayings of Yeshua, or Jesus, dating perhaps

from as early as the middle of the first century CE; it could even predate Mark, some scholars say. Here is the Markan or earliest canonical version:

> He began to teach them many things in parables, and in his teaching he said to them: "Listen! A sower went out to sow. And as he sowed, some seed fell on the path, and the birds came and ate it up. Other seed fell on rocky ground, where it did not have much soil, and it sprang up quickly, since it had no depth of soil. And when the sun rose, it was scorched; and since it had no root, it withered away. Other seed fell among thorns, and the thorns grew up and choked it, and it yielded no grain. Other seed fell into good soil and brought forth grain, growing up and increasing and yielding thirty and sixty and a hundredfold." And he said, "Let anyone with ears to hear listen!" (Mark 4:2–9)[4]

At the outset of this book, we saw how this parable was used by Mark as a springboard for launching the fundamental teaching about the purpose served by the exoteric imagery, such as the parables, as an introduction to the deeper esoteric meaning of the "mystery" of the Kingdom of God within us and all around. The text of the long-hidden Gospel of Judas, released by the National Geographic Society just before Easter 2006, makes this concept of secret knowledge—that we are beings of light "trapped" in material bodies of "clothes"—abundantly clear. It was a central tenet of all Gnostic Christianity. But, lest the secret be profaned or trampled upon or otherwise misused, it was to be available only to those who were ready and who were eager and hungering to receive it. Significantly, like most of the other great avatars or saviour figures, Jesus is thus portrayed as teaching at two levels, one for true adepts or initiated, the other for newcomers or outsiders. The reader is reminded especially of verse 33 of this same chapter 4: it says plainly that in public Jesus taught in parables but in private he gave his inner circle the inner significance of it all for the evolution of the soul. All this is the hidden meaning of the otherwise extremely harsh-sounding warning elsewhere in the Gospels about the importance of not casting pearls before swine.

The detailed explanation of the parable of the sower, which accompanies it and which, according to the research of a group of earlier scholars called Form Critics, was not part of the earliest tradition, powerfully illustrates the fundamental "teaching" of the Inner Christ. The "seed" of the divine Logos, or Word of God, is sown in every heart. The ancient Stoics indeed spoke of the *spermatikos* Logos, the "seed" Logos in every person, which makes us all as human beings brothers and sisters at the deepest possible level. The same thinking lies behind the Pagan poets quoted by St. Paul in his speech on the Acropolis at Athens: "For 'in him we live and move and have our being' as even some of your own poets have said, 'For we too arc his offspring.'"[5]

The point of this parable, then, is that, while all have received the gift or seed of the Christ within, there are great differences in how this "mystery" is welcomed and allowed to flourish. "And these are the ones sown on the good soil: they hear the word and accept it and bear fruit, thirty and sixty and a hundredfold" (Mark 4:20). However, it is possible to turn one's back upon the mystery entirely, to let it bear no fruit at all. The Gospel of Thomas (which, unlike the three Synoptics and John, has no miracles, no dying for sins and no Resurrection on Easter morning) gives a similar interpretation.[6]

As we saw in the story of the Temptation, the nurturing of the "seed" within is meant to be understood as an ongoing, lifelong process. In the words of Deepak Chopra, "Two voices are heard in our heads every day, the one believing in the dark and the other in the light. Only one reality can be really real." Redemption, then, he says, "is just another word for calling on your innate ability to see [this light] with the eye of the soul."[7] That is the kind of spiritual language anyone can readily understand.

Being Stewards of the Light Within

Two parables in chapter 25 of Matthew are among the best known and best loved of all the nearly fifty parables of the New Testament. One deals with the foolish virgins and the other deals with a buried talent. To cite familiarity is not, however, the same thing as saying that they are among the best-understood parables or that they resonate with the greatest relevance for our lives today. The secret, I believe, to unlocking both meaning and relevance lies in always keeping the underlying theme of the entire Bible in mind as one reads. It is about the advent into the evolving life of every human being of a degree of consciousness that is not generated automatically in the order of nature itself but is the blossoming to maturity of the conscious potential in a seed of Divine Mind implanted in the order of nature from above.

To change the metaphor, it is about the bestowing of a spark or "sun" of divine fire to crown the former, purely animal level of existence we once knew. Metaphorically speaking, each of us is a solar universe, a planetary system composed of many cells or other systems, and the spiritual light that burns at the centre of our being is the central "sun" of the whole system. The parables often make the point that, if we are able to learn to control this "universe" within, we will one day be put in charge of larger spheres. The constant theme of Bible imagery is that of awakening to this reality within and of stewarding its lambent flame to the glory of God and the furthering of a compassionate, Christly reaching out to those less blessed than ourselves.

Parable of the Foolish Virgins

Thus, in the parable of the ten bridesmaids[8] (five are foolish, five are wise), the oil, as always, is an esoteric symbol of the fire of intelligence and of the Christos or divinity within. Consequently, the wisdom of the five wise virgins who were aware of the preciousness of this endowment and who took its efficacious potency with full seriousness is praised, while those who were foolish and neglected to tend their gift with care and prudence are strongly rebuked. The door to the wedding feast is closed in their faces. The final words, "Keep awake therefore, for you know neither the day nor the hour," echo the same message of so much of the Gnostic and other spiritual wisdom of that period. St. Paul clarions forth the same metaphorical challenge in chapter 13 of Romans where he says: "You know what time it is, how it is now the moment for you to wake from sleep . . ." The same urgency speaks to us today.

The Parable of the Buried Talent

The parable of the talents[9]—note that, according to the New Revised Standard Version of the Bible, a talent "was worth more than fifteen years' wages of a labourer"—is also a very powerful call to each of us to take stock of our spiritual inheritance and invest it to the fullest extent of our varied abilities and opportunities. There are two major thrusts or emphases that strike home to me every time I read this parable. The story tells how a master, before going on a journey, entrusted his property to his servants. To one he gave five talents, and to another two, and to another one.

Central, of course, is the tragedy of the servant (or slave) who, acting out of fear and the other kinds of distorted thinking that so often hinder us in realizing our own best effort, went and buried his talent in the ground. The punishment meted out to him is extreme and obviously influenced by hyperbole in the storyteller's endeavour to really drive his point home as colourfully as possible. But the message even on the surface is one we all need to hear and take to heart. We have all buried our talents in the earth from time to time through fear—fear of failure, fear of offending somebody, fear of success, even.

However, the tragedy is greater when the inner meaning is explored. When we realize that the real gift being entrusted to each for "trading" or for investment in productive living is that of the divine inner presence itself, the stakes are much higher. When and as we awaken to the truly amazing God-given treasure we have been granted stewardship over, there is a debt of gratitude that swells up in our innermost being and we want to do our utmost to make this gift count. There is little gain for the world if we try to save our lives—if we cater to the life of our ego and avoid spending our time and energies for the evolutionary task of building a better, more compassionate world. We are here, ultimately, to help by all possible means the advancement of the Christ spirit or Christ consciousness for all humanity.

Accordingly, rather than a "me-in-my-small-corner" spirituality, we must seek one that is engaged with others for others. That is the only true, future coming of the Messiah or the Messianic Age our world will ever know. The coming of the Messiah is a forlorn hope if people are looking to the skies for a supernatural intervention of some kind. That is never going to happen. We have been given the task, and the responsibility for building the Kingdom of God on earth is fully in our hands.

The second fulcrum of the parable for me lies in the tantalizing promise of the master to those who used their talents profitably: "You have been trustworthy in a few things. I will put you in charge of many things." I believe this should be understood eschatologically. By that I mean I believe the allegorical reference is to some future, as yet wholly unknown and unknowable, state or "place" of being where the glorified soul will be given responsibilities quite beyond our present capacity to imagine. That, of course, is speculation. But I don't believe for a moment that eternity will consist of doing nothing. Or, worse, that it will be anything like the traditional picture of "heaven" given to us in the past. I have tried to do justice to this subject at some length in *Life After Death*. Entering into "the joy of the master" will be, as Carl Jung put it— speaking of a "next life"—"far beyond anything we can ever think or imagine."

The Parable of the Judgment of the Nations

Those who allow long custom or excessive piety to dull their senses as they read the Gospels are often afraid to acknowledge their real feelings or to think clearly when certain scriptures are read either in church or in private. Frequently, a misleading sense of "respect" dulls or dampens down their normal rational processes. The truth is that while there is much to inspire one in the Jesus Story, there is, and it must be faced squarely, a lot that is intellectually or even at times morally offensive. For example, if you read chapters 23 to 25 of Matthew with an alert mind, you will find a side of Jesus' teaching set out there that is dark, judgmental and at times vividly apocalyptic. It seems in places to stand in sharp contradiction to certain specific teachings described by Matthew in the Sermon on the Mount, for example the injunctions not to judge others and to show love to one's enemies or opponents.

While filled with symbolism, such passages, taken together with the Book of Revelation and construed literally, form the basis for the highly popular but scary "end times" theology of many ultra-fundamentalist groups today. Eloquent testimony to the success of this simplistic and sometimes crude approach is found in the fact, among other signs, that the Left Behind series of novels by the American evangelicals Tim LaHaye and Jerry B. Jenkins have now sold well over 60 million copies—more even than *The Da Vinci Code*—and are currently spawning a spate of films to follow.

There is a huge irony to all of this. It is one we have witnessed and stressed before. In chapter 24, Matthew interrupts his vivid word-pictures of the end of the age with a verse that should jolt every literalistic enthusiast for the alleged Rapture to his or her very foundations. In verse 34, Matthew writes: "Truly I tell you, this generation will not pass away until all these things have taken place. Heaven and earth will pass away, but my words will not pass away."

Think about it. Nothing could be clearer. No literal understanding of these words can escape the conclusion that on that level the speaker was and remained utterly mistaken. The sentence about heaven and earth passing away before his words are proven false shows a monumental error. Several prominent New Testament scholars today hold a similar view, based upon such passages as these, to that of Albert Schweitzer already commented upon. They take the view that a historical Jesus expected an end of the age and that he was sadly mistaken. This issue has enormous significance today because of the near hysteria in some ultra-evangelical circles over the conviction that the "end times" are now upon us. The various calamities or dangers surrounding us, instead of being viewed as urgent problems to be addressed and solved—for example, the crisis of global warming, the risk of lethal pandemics, or nuclear proliferation to rogue states—are heralded with enthusiasm as sure "signs" of Bible fulfillment. Fundamentalist chat room sites on the Internet are filled with shameful glee over current tensions in the Middle East and calamities of all kinds.

The first two parables of Matthew 25 are straightforward enough, with their call to constant watchfulness and the emphasis upon responsible stewardship of the various gifts or talents given to each of us; after all, nobody knows when the next moment of life may be his or her last. We live daily, each of us, in the uncertainty

of life's vicissitudes. But it is the final story as follows, the one that
brings to a close all of the store of parables Matthew unpacks for
us, that has always held the strongest attraction for me:

> When the Son of Man comes in his glory, and all the angels
> with him, then he will sit on the throne of his glory. All the
> nations will be gathered before him, and he will separate
> people one from another as a shepherd separates the sheep
> from the goats, and he will put the sheep at his right hand and
> the goats at the left. Then the king will say to those at his right
> hand, "Come, you that are blessed by my Father, inherit the
> kingdom prepared for you from the foundation of the world;
> for I was hungry and you gave me food, I was thirsty and you
> gave me something to drink, I was a stranger and you wel-
> comed me, I was naked and you gave me clothing, I was sick
> and you took care of me, I was in prison and you visited me."
> Then the righteous will answer him, "Lord, when was it
> that we saw you hungry and gave you food, or thirsty and
> gave you something to drink? And when was it that we saw
> you a stranger and welcomed you, or naked and gave you
> clothing? And when was it that we saw you sick or in prison
> and visited you?" And the king will answer them, "Truly I tell
> you, just as you did it to one of the least of these who are
> members of my family, you did it to me." Then he will say to
> those at his left hand, "You that are accursed, depart from
> me into the eternal fire prepared for the devil and his angels;
> for I was hungry and you gave me no food, I was thirsty and
> you gave me nothing to drink, I was a stranger and you did
> not welcome me, naked and you did not give me clothing,
> sick and in prison and you did not visit me."
> Then they also will answer, "Lord, when was it that we
> saw you hungry or thirsty or a stranger or naked or sick or in
> prison, and did not take care of you?" Then he will answer

them, "Truly I tell you, just as you did not do it to one of the
least of these, you did not do it to me." And these will go away
into eternal punishment, but the righteous into eternal life.
(Matthew 25:31–46)[10]

Under the powerful metaphor of the sheep and the goats, the
king, representing God, separates all the members of humanity
and destines them for either the punishment of the age to come
or the life of the age to come. (Notice that the translation of the
NRSV here—"eternal punishment" and "eternal life"—is highly
misleading. The adjective in Greek here translated as "eternal" is
aionios and it is qualitative; it means "belonging to the kind of life
in the age to come." It is not, thank God, a description of dreary,
boring, unending time.)

What impressed me most the first time I read this parable as a
very young boy, and what has stayed with me about it down all the
years ever since, is the basis on which the judgment is said to be
going to be made. It struck me as quite at variance with the crite-
ria for salvation being preached every Sunday by the evangelical
clergy I was forced to listen to. Like in the Egyptian judgment hall
scenes of old, the standard is a highly practical, ethical one—a
matter not of correct belief or dogma or ritual. No questions are
asked here about church attendance, about having had the correct religious experience—all the way from being "born again"
to "speaking in tongues" or being a minister-cum-evangelist. It's
purely and completely a matter of what a Buddhist would call "right
action," of compassionate conduct—feeding the hungry, giving
drink to the thirsty, hospitality to the stranger, clothes to the
naked, care to the sick and personal presence to those in prison.
This cuts across all false, human-constructed barriers, all divisive
creeds and all other forms of discrimination to the universal
"Christ" or divinity in every living man, woman and child on
earth. Remember, as we sow so shall we reap.

The culmination of it all resounds in what for me is perhaps the key to everything else, about how to understand and live our lives. The central character of the drama says: "Truly I tell you, just as you did it to one of the least of these who are members of my family, you did it to me." There can be no clearer, no more absolute statement of the truth of the Christ or divine presence in the hearts and lives of every human alive than this. It is the unique key to peace and to human solidarity. There is no more potentially transformative affirmation in the whole world than this, I'm convinced. It could revolutionize human relationships on our planet in an instant: the "other" is, in a deep sense, yourself. What a powerful vision!

The Parable of the Two Sons

There is, as we have seen, a famous parable about two sons in chapter 15 of Luke. It takes its name from one of these young men, the well-known Prodigal Son. However, there is another, much less well-known parable about two sons found in chapter 21 of Matthew that, in spite of its brevity, has always appealed very much to me personally. I suppose the reason is that, in its terse and biting wisdom, it seems so aptly to put the spotlight on what has to be recognized as the major problem facing any religion—the issue of the huge gap between the ideal and the reality, the talk versus the walk; the great gulf that seems perennially to emerge between saying and doing, between creed and deed. All the horrors that can be laid at religion's door, as well as all the sacrifices and all the saintly virtues that can be heaped in praise upon it, are conjured up by this brief but brilliant word-picture, this cameo from the Christos. We forget what Ralph Waldo Emerson said so well: "Go put your creed into your deed,/Nor speak with double tongue."[11]

The parable reads simply enough. It tells about a certain man (of no name, time or place, because what is at stake here is not history but timeless truth) who had two sons. He went to the first of them and told him to go and work in the vineyard "today." Again we are not told what vineyard, or whose vineyard, or where— because none of that matters one iota. The son immediately said he wouldn't go. But, later on the same day, he had a change of heart "and went." The father, meanwhile, went to his second son and made the same request. This young man instantly said, "I go, sir," but he never went at all. You can almost hear his heels clicking and then the sound of him marching off to the job. But he never arrived. He went through some of the motions, but nothing got done. Jesus then says to the priests and temple elders who were hassling him to give an account of his authority for teaching and healing, "Which of the two did the will of his father?" They have little choice but to answer, "The first." That is why, Jesus then tells them, the tax collectors and the prostitutes "are going into the kingdom of God ahead of you."

The point couldn't be any clearer. Yet organized religion and too many adherents constantly fall into the obvious trap. It has proven over and over again all too easy for the pious to profess "I go," that is, to make a profession of discipleship or of obedience, and then to turn wholly in the opposite direction. One has only to think with shame not just of the horrendous cruelties in the past wrought by Christians—or Muslims, for example—where all that the religion preaches and proclaims has been bloodily denied, but also of things much closer to home. From years of covering all religions in Canada and around the globe, I have come to know not just the glories but the terribly dark shadow side of the major faiths as well. Too often, looking for genuine honesty, compassion or even tolerance, one has not found it where the religiously minded say "I go" but then don't. Instead, it is frequently where one least expects it, among the so-called unchurched or those who may seem intellectually or even morally to have said "no" to God or the Divine within, that one has to turn to discover acceptance of "the least of these my brethren" or a true integrity of heart.

I think particularly in this regard of two Canadian young people I once met who were working as volunteers in the House of the Dying in Calcutta, when I visited Mother Teresa's crude hospice in the porch of the Temple of Kali in December 1979, just after she had been awarded the Nobel Prize. These two, who told me they were atheists, were serving in the most menial of ways in one of the most daunting places on earth. As I spoke with them, it became evident that not only were they not being paid, but they were in Calcutta at their own expense and accounted it a privilege to be allowed to minister to the destitute and dying patients there. One thing has stayed with me about them down the years. While most people whom one interviews for a newspaper feature are anxious to see that their names are correctly spelled and their photos properly posed, these young people resisted both completely. In fact they would speak of their beliefs and their motives only on the condition that they received no personal publicity whatever. I can't remember a believer of any other faith or sect throughout a long career in journalism who took that stand—except perhaps once or twice where I was on an investigative story and there was something to hide.

If I were preaching regularly to a congregation today, I would make it a habit to preach a sermon on this brief parable of the two sons once a year, not only for others' benefit, but for my own as well. We are all at times guilty of hypocrisy. This parable is eloquent instruction on the need to pray daily—and then see to it that it happens—that our actions come ever more closely in sync with what it is we often are so very quick to say.

9

PALM SUNDAY

The letter kills, but the Spirit gives life.

—ST. PAUL, 2 CORINTHIANS 3:6

The Triumphal Entry into Jerusalem

Palm Sunday, the Sunday before Easter, was one of the annual markers or festivals of the church year that made the deepest impression upon me as a young child. For some years, until I was around twelve or thirteen, my father saw to it that we attended an Anglican church in Toronto's east end. That was before he decided it was not sufficiently evangelical and moved us to a Gospel Hall on the city's outskirts.

This Anglican church was anything but "high church," and didn't even provide token palms for the Sunday celebration. My father (who was raised in the Church of Ireland in County Tyrone, where they were so "low church" that, as some wit exclaimed, they even "said" the hymns) would have regarded that as "popery" or the edge of a slippery slope headed in that direction. However, as I sang in the choir as a boy chorister complete with a starched surplice and the traditional gleaming white collar, I relished the special hymns of Palm Sunday, the general sense of pomp and circumstance, and the packed church.

In particular, I was fascinated by the regular, yearly ritual in which we—the children of the congregation, led of course by those of us who were somehow special because of our robes and prominent position in the front choir stalls—took our little pyramid-shaped cardboard Lenten boxes and proceeded up to the chancel to deposit them in a similar-shaped but much larger container. The individual boxes were actually small savings "banks" into which we had put pennies and the odd nickel all through the weeks of Lent since Ash Wednesday. There were pictures of brown- and black-skinned children on the little pyramids and the idea was to help promote missionary work in distant lands. Each one dropped into the larger pyramid made a deeply satisfying clank that enhanced our sense of self-importance.

It was not until many years later, when I was already in training for ministry in the Anglican Church, that Palm Sunday caused a metaphorical "clank" in my mind as I listened in a church to a reading of the earliest account of it, from the Gospel of Mark. As the reader began with the traditional Anglican phrasing "Here beginneth the first verse of the eleventh chapter of the Gospel according to St. Mark," I opened a pew bible and read along silently. You need to see the text for yourself to get the full impact, so here is the earliest version as Mark narrates it:

> When they were approaching Jerusalem, at Bethphage and Bethany, near the Mount of Olives, he sent two of his disciples and said to them, "Go into the village ahead of you, and immediately as you enter it, you will find tied there a colt that has never been ridden; untie it and bring it. If anyone says to you, 'Why are you doing this?' just say this, 'The Lord needs it and will send it back here immediately.'"
>
> They went away and found a colt tied near a door, outside in the street. As they were untying it, some of the bystanders said to them, "What are you doing, untying the colt?" They

told them what Jesus had said; and they allowed them to take it. Then they brought the colt to Jesus and threw their cloaks on it; and he sat on it. Many people spread their cloaks on the road, and others spread leafy branches that they had cut in the fields. Then those who went ahead and those who followed were shouting, "Hosanna! Blessed is the one who comes in the name of the Lord! Blessed is the coming kingdom of our ancestor David! Hosanna in the highest heaven!" (Mark 11:1–10)

There were two things that leaped out at me then as never before. The first was that, in his telling of the story, Mark makes it seem that it was all prearranged. The two disciples are told where to find the donkey colt and are given a kind of password to clear their action in taking it. Lovers of conspiracies, for example Hugh Schonfield's *Passover Plot*, have taken this as evidence for an actual staging by Jesus of the eventual denouement of the tale. Personally, I believe that the writers and editors of Mark were aware that the ancient myth they were retelling required a donkey as an important element and that its acquisition had to somehow sound plausible. It could not be made to come, so to speak, out of thin air. We will see the muddle Matthew makes of it all in a moment.

The second, and far more important, aspect of this passage that struck me is the way it ends. In the narrative there is a vivid sense of growing intrigue, excitement and tension, and then a mounting crescendo of praise and triumph as the humble procession turns into a joyous, victorious parade. The crowds surge ahead and behind shouting "Hosanna!" and then we read: "Then he entered Jerusalem and went into the temple; and when he had looked around at everything, as it was already late, he went out to Bethany [a village a short distance east of the Holy City] with the twelve." And there the Markan Palm Sunday story abruptly ends.

I was struck forcibly as I listened and read along that this is one of the greatest anticlimaxes of almost any story I have ever heard. It falls and lies there like some huge dead animal in the middle of a room. Mark simply leaves the thread of the narrative there and moves on to the following day, when Jesus curses the fig tree for not having fruit on it even though "it was not the season for figs" and in spite of the warnings given about oaths and curses in Matthew's Sermon on the Mount. The symbolism, of course, is all that really matters here. The fig tree is Israel, and God's people should "bear fruit" at all seasons.

As I reflected on all of this, it was obvious to me that Matthew and Luke, as well as John, were aware of the extraordinary awkwardness of Mark's handling of the "Palm Sunday" incident and did their best to smooth it over. In the case of Matthew and Luke in particular, the anticlimax is avoided by having Jesus proceed directly from the triumphant procession to the cleansing of the temple.[1] John, who has Jesus cleanse the temple at the very outset of his ministry, in chapter 2 of his Gospel, manages more or less to smooth the whole matter out by having a group of Greeks come and surround Jesus and initiate a situation where he gives some of his deepest teachings.[2]

Nevertheless, certain glaring problems remain. None of the Gospels really makes a success of harmonizing the triumphal entry into a logical whole with the rest of the drama. The sudden shift from adoring, exulting crowds hailing their Messiah-king as the blessed one of God, and ready to virtually crown him as their leader, to the raucous, cruel mob crying out for Jesus to be crucified is nowhere given an adequate explanation. The old, pious clichés about the general fickleness or sinfulness of human nature, provided by my seminary professors, no longer made real sense to me. Then there was the obvious misunderstanding of Matthew, who, in his anxiety to prove that everything is happening "as it was foretold" by prophet X or Y, actually has Jesus throw his leg over two donkeys at the same time!

Matthew quotes Zechariah: "Tell the daughter of Zion, 'Look, your king is coming to you, humble and mounted on a donkey, and on a colt, the foal of a donkey,'"[3] and then, taking it quite literally, says: "The disciples did as Jesus had directed them; they brought the donkey and the colt, and put their cloaks *on them* and he sat *on them*" (my emphasis). In reality, the prophecy was expressed simply in terms of Hebrew parallelism: a thing is stated one way and then emphasized by being restated in a slightly different but parallel fashion. The Psalms are filled with this kind of idiom, for example "The Lord is a light unto my feet, and a lamp unto my path." But Matthew, as inevitably happens when literalism is forced upon allegorical texts, presents a grotesque manoeuvre: Jesus rides on the backs of both.

Reincarnation?

Having said that, however, esoteric theology has seized on the presence of the two animals (without insisting Jesus rode both!) as symbolic of something deeply rooted in ancient spiritual thinking: that the soul's evolution up into full divinity cannot be consummated in a single cycle of experience in the flesh but must proceed through a succession of lives, always passing continuously from the older phase of one generation to the succeeding younger phase. Each younger generation of animal bodily life took up the labour of carrying the soul onwards through its progression; hence the symbolism of the adult with its colt. For many ancient theologians, from Pythagoras to Plato and beyond into early Christianity—Origen, for example—this meant reincarnation. There is a certain compelling logic about this aspect of the doctrine.

I discuss reincarnation more fully in the forthcoming updated
version of *Life After Death*. However, since I have raised the subject
here, as well as previously in the discussion of the healing of the
man who was blind from birth in chapter 5, and since reincarnation is widely believed to be an answer to the problem of how
souls actually evolve, it is important to look at it briefly here. The
idea that we return to the earth plane repeatedly over a vast cycle
of time according to the laws of karma is very ancient and was
held by several key theologians in the early Church—Origen
in particular comes to mind. The belief persisted until repeated
church councils finally repudiated it as heretical in the sixth century CE. It was held—wrongly, I believe—to be contrary to orthodox dogma about the resurrection of the body. Since none of us
is as yet spiritually perfect, and since there are gross injustices in
the world, the theory that we must "pay off" our karmic debts,
and that the soul needs the widest possible experience in order to
grow to full maturity, is highly attractive to many. For them, any
belief in the immortality of the soul demands it.

I believe, however, that there is another possibility to consider.
Yes, we all need to learn more, for example, about perseverance
in the face of suffering, about truly loving both ourselves and
others, about vast ranges of human possibilities and failings. There
are a myriad of inequalities in life to be balanced out. But why
should all of this be limited to this one planet and to our physical
existence on it? I would like to postulate an entirely different scenario—one that may take place over eons of time on utterly different planes or on other planets far beyond our knowing. With
physicists today talking about parallel universes and astrophysi-
cists describing trillions upon trillions of teeming galaxies beyond
our wildest imagination, surely it is time the old doctrine of reincarnation was interpreted anew? There is a verse in the Gospel
of John where Jesus, talking about life after death, says, "In my
father's house are many mansions." The Greek word means "rest-

ing places" or "temporary lodgings." I take this to signify that death does indeed not bring the end of all our journeying or the sudden miraculous perfecting of our soul. It is but the doorway to untold experiences of further unfoldment in other spiritual realms, until at last we are ready for what St. Paul called the moment of "knowing even as I am known." Meanwhile, we see "through a glass darkly," but one day "face to face."[4]

Summing Up

In any case, what has become crystal clear about the triumphal "Palm Sunday" procession story is that:

a) it is in reality an allegory of the soul's victory over the material, animal nature (imaged by the donkey) and its final triumphant entry into the place of holy peace—which is what the word *Jerusalem* actually means; and

b) the reason the story in the Gospels falls so flat in Mark and is only somewhat more smoothly cobbled into the flow of the other Gospels is that it is entirely out of place where we now find it.

Let me explain. Because this is the mythical or allegorical way of picturing the soul's final, victorious entry into the realms of peaceful bliss, it really belongs not just after the Crucifixion but after the passages about the Resurrection—close to, or immediately followed by, the Transfiguration, where its true, innate glory is finally revealed. Mark is to blame for misplacing it in the first instance, and the others, finding it that way in his work and the growing tradition, made of it the best they could. There seems little room for dispute over the fact that Mark used a cut-and-paste approach to the Old Testament as he framed his story and, in addition to the Greek version of the Old Testament (already

influenced by Egyptian mythology), used snippets from the surrounding culture as well. For example, Yale professor Dennis
MacDonald, in his controversial 2000 book *The Homeric Epics and
the Gospel of Mark*, draws many telling parallels between Mark's
account and the *Odyssey*, the best-known and most often allegorically interpreted textbook in the entire culture of the first-
century Mediterranean world.

Certainly we know that Dionysus or Bacchus, a god heavily
influenced by the prototypical Horus of Egypt (who was also, as
noted already, a god of abundant wine), was carried at times
astride a donkey. Writing very early in the first century (around
4 CE), Hyginus (Book II, "Cancer") says that when Dionysus had
come to a certain great marsh that he was unable to cross, having
come upon two young donkeys, he is said to have caught one of
them "and so in this way was carried across so that he did not touch
the water at all."[5] In this connection, to show further that in the
Jesus Story we are dealing with myth based upon astronomical,
zodiacal imagery, it is worth noting that the ancient Greek sign
for the constellation Cancer, the Crab, was usually "an ass and its
foal."[6] The scholar Thomas Thorburn, whose aim was to discredit
any mythical interpretation of the Gospels, nevertheless describes
how the astronomer Ptolemy named two stars in the body of
the Crab, or Cancer, as "the two asses" and the luminous patch
between these two as the "Manger." Thus, when the sun was in
the midst of the zodiacal sign Cancer, it was said by the old Greek
astronomers to be "riding upon two asses."

In their book *The Jesus Mysteries*, British authors Timothy Freke
and Peter Gandy document how, when the crowd of pilgrims at
Athens walked the Sacred Way to Eleusis to celebrate the famous
mysteries, there was a donkey carrying a basket containing the
sacred "paraphernalia" that would be used to create the idol of
Dionysus. As they journeyed in procession, the crowds shouted

out their praises of Dionysus and waved bunches of branches in the air. The similarities are extraordinarily striking.

So, by this point we have reached a new understanding of this story. The donkey, as we have seen, was associated with various deities in antiquity, both in Egypt and around the Mediterranean basin. In the Greek mysteries of Dionysus, the animal was a common symbol of the lower animal nature in all of us. It thus typified, for example, lust (there is at least one ancient vase with art depicting a donkey with an erect phallus dancing with the devotees of Dionysus), greed and the other baser instincts. The figure of the god-man riding on a donkey in a victory parade was the ultimate symbol of the final mastery of each of us over our lower, animal self. The Roman writer Lucius Apuleius wrote a now-famous story called *The Golden Ass*. In it, Lucius is transformed into a donkey through his own folly and weaknesses. However, he endures a succession of "stages of initiation" adventures through which he is finally brought to recognize who and what he really is. The tale is an allegory of what the Pagan mysteries were all about.[7]

In the light of all of the above, today the lessons and hymns on Palm Sunday, the Sunday before Easter, resonate with a wholly transformed meaning. It's not about a short-lived moment of celebration in the life of a far-off saviour figure in the past. It's about the final entering into glory of your soul and mine.

10

THE PASSION

*If we had not been taught how to interpret the
story of the Passion, would we have been able to say
from their actions alone whether it was the jealous
Judas or the cowardly Peter who loved Christ?*

— GRAHAM GREENE, *The End of the Affair*

Betrayal—The Judas Story

*Then Judas Iscariot, who was one of the twelve, went to the chief
priests in order to betray him to them. When they heard it,
they were greatly pleased, and promised to give him money.
So he began to look for an opportunity to betray him.*

— MARK 14:10—11

THE THEME OF BETRAYAL looms large in the final denouement of the Jesus Story precisely because it is such a crucial and universal element in the drama of human life itself. No mythos of the soul's journey could be complete without it. Betrayal of one sort or another is enacted in every major work of literature from every age and every culture known to us. What is more, every one of us has experienced, or one day most probably will, the pangs of disappointment, bitterness or sheer dismay and panic at finding ourselves either the betrayer or the betrayed.

In one of the most widely known stories of the ancient Mediterranean world, that of the death of Osiris, he is betrayed by his own
brother Seth. In the Hebrew Bible, the mythic story of how the
children of Israel came to be the slaves of Pharoah in Egypt began,
it should be remembered, with a notorious betrayal: Joseph, the
dreamer with the multicoloured coat, was betrayed and sold into
slavery by his own jealous brothers. King Arthur, who like Jesus
had his twelve followers, the Knights of the Round Table, is
betrayed by his close friend Sir Lancelot's adultery with Queen
Guinevere. In the North American Indian lore, there is the Sioux
legend of Black Crow, who was betrayed by his lifelong friend
Brave Eagle when both men fell in love with the same beautiful
woman. Betrayal is a frequent refrain in the sonnets of Shakespeare, and in his plays no three words have been so immortalized
as those of Julius Caesar to Brutus—"Et tu, Brute?"—as his closest friend adds his dagger to the assassins' onslaught.[1] In reports
of the death of al Qaeda leader Abu Musat al-Zarqawi from an
American air strike on January 8, 2006, Iraq's "most wanted ter-
rorist" was said to have been betrayed ultimately by "tips from
within his own network."[2]

But for Mark and the other Evangelists, keen as they were to
present their story as built upon and as a fulfillment of the only
Bible they knew, the Scriptures known to us as the Old Testament, one verse and one betrayal tradition stood out as precedent
and symbol of betrayal above all others. In Psalm 41, the Psalmist
laments that his enemies plot and "imagine the worst for me."
Then, he goes on to say, the lowest blow comes from the one
who is closest to him: "Even my bosom friend in whom I trusted,
who ate of my bread, has lifted the heel against me."[3] It cannot
be emphasized too strongly that this is the very scene that many
centuries later is deliberately and allegorically dramatized for us
as we read in Mark and the other Evangelists of Jesus predicting
at the Last Supper that one of those eating with him was about to

betray him. "He said to them, 'It is one of the twelve, one who is dipping bread into the bowl with me.'"4

Real soul-wrenching betrayal in life, then, comes not from our enemies but, by definition, from very close friends. There's deep truth in the otherwise seemingly offhand saying "God protect me from my friends; I'll take care of my enemies myself." Reading the Gospel accounts of Judas' betrayal with keen attention, you have to be struck by the dramatic repetition of the ominous-sounding phrase describing the traitor: "He was one of the twelve," indeed a close, familiar friend.

Significantly, the earliest Gospel, Mark, supplies us with no motive whatever for the plotting on Judas' part aside from the mention of an offer of silver after the proposal had already been made; the betrayal was simply a necessary part of the timeless, ancient mythos. But Matthew obviously felt the need to make Judas' actions more credible—and more blameworthy—and so has him ask the authorities more explicitly ahead of time what they will give him "if I betray him to you." They paid thirty pieces of silver—and this detail is again pregnant with meaning. As Matthew points out later, after Judas tried to give the money back when he saw that Jesus had been condemned, this sum was already part of an ancient tradition. He quotes Scripture to prove it. The chief priests took the silver back, and since it was "blood money" they took it, we are told, to buy a potter's field as a place to bury foreigners, that is, non-Jews. At this juncture we get one of Matthew's frequent "then was fulfilled" formulaic quotes: "Then was fulfilled what had been spoken through the prophet Jeremiah, 'And they took the thirty pieces of silver, the price of the one on whom a price had been set . . . and they gave them for the potter's field, as the Lord commanded me.'"

It is to many intelligent inquirers obvious that the whole of the Gospels' story of the Passion is written and structured around the "skeleton" of such passages already centuries old in the Judaism of the day—and for much longer indebted to the religious writings of ancient Egypt before that. Readers of Plato will, of course, be aware that when Socrates—who also was guilty of no crime—was about to suffer death at the hands of the state, his followers offered thirty pieces of silver (*minae*) to obtain a reprieve for him. They were turned down. The sum of thirty pieces of silver is quite common in other books of the Old Testament, for example in a well-known passage in chapter 11 of Zechariah, or in chapter 21 of Exodus. In the latter, it is the exact sum required to be paid to a slave's owner if one of his slaves is gored by the ox of someone else. So, the thirty pieces of silver was a stock element in ancient mythmaking and other forms of storytelling. Some authorities believe that the number appears with such frequency because there are thirty days in a solar month. That certainly lies behind the fact that various sun gods begin their adult lives at that age.

Interestingly, Judas has been given a much kindlier treatment of late by some Biblical scholars. Shunning the tendency of the Gospels to paint him as avaricious and full of all manner of other evils (John, for example, heaping up the vilification, pegs him as a common thief), they have postulated a much higher vision of his scheming. Putting forward the thesis that his treachery arose not from lack of belief but an excess of it, they have theorized that he was secretly a member of, or sympathetic to, the zealots. He fully believed in Jesus' claims and powers on this view, and so, determined as it were to force his master's hand, he agreed to lead the authorities to the hidden rendezvous—the "garden"—and did so believing that, when push came to shove, Jesus would act decisively. He would summon down legions of angels, overthrow the hated Roman oppressors and usher in the Kingdom of God on earth. When, however, Jesus was led out passively to be executed, Judas realized too late his colossal misunderstanding, and so went out and hanged himself.

This, of course, is all speculation. Mark's simpler account states that Jesus' death was an inevitable and necessary fulfillment of prophecy—"For the Son of Man goes [to death] as it is written of him," Jesus says. The paradox is boldly stated. There had to be a betrayer, "but woe to that one by whom the Son of Man is betrayed! It would have been better for that one not to have been born."[5] In other words, evil deeds may be inevitable, given the human condition, and yet, even so, some ultimate good may be drawn forth from them. Nevertheless, a price must be paid. There is an inexorable karmic consequence to all action. Paul states it in chapter 6 of Galatians: "You reap whatever you sow."

Judas and Judaism

The whole Judas narrative is plagued by truly insuperable logical and moral difficulties if one insists on forcing a literal interpretation upon it. He gets blamed for doing what God had planned in any case! Jesus told him: "What thou doest, do quickly." What's most tragic about such literalizing is the sheer enormity of the very real evil that has flowed from it all down the centuries since. Harold Bloom, the distinguished American literary critic and author of several authoritative books on religious themes, comments trenchantly on the Gospel's Judas as "a transparently malevolent fiction that has helped to justify the murder of Jews for 2000 years."[6] The fact that he was called Judas itself shows he is being used as a stand-in for all of Judaism in its rejection of Jesus. He becomes the stereotype used to justify all manner of contempt and violence.

Most people, even devout churchgoers, are not aware that the New Testament itself gives a different, alternative account of how Judas died, not by suicide, as the Gospels say, but by a "headlong" fall upon which "all his bowels gushed out." Notice again, however, that he was actually held to be fulfilling God's plan by what he did. It says in Acts:

> In those days Peter stood up among the believers (together the crowd numbered about one hundred twenty persons) and said, "Friends, the scripture had to be fulfilled, which the Holy Spirit through David foretold concerning Judas, who became a guide for those who arrested Jesus—for he was numbered among us and was allotted his share in this ministry." (Now this man acquired a field with the reward of his wickedness; and falling headlong, he burst open in the middle and all his bowels gushed out. This became known to all the residents of Jerusalem, so that the field was called in their language Hakeldama, that is, Field of Blood.) "For it is written in the book of Psalms, 'Let his homestead become desolate, and let there be no one to live in it'; and 'Let another take his position of overseer.'" (Acts 1:15–20)

In the spring of 2006, *National Geographic* magazine released a never-before-seen manuscript, *The Gospel of Judas*, a Gnostic text dating originally from the second century CE, in which a wholly different picture of Judas was given. It was found in Egypt in 1970. In the new gospel, Judas is the one to whom Jesus reveals the secret of the kingdom of heaven—that we are each of us beings of light temporarily trapped in fleshly bodies. (That, in essence, is the message of *The Pagan Christ*.) Jesus in this gospel takes Judas into his confidence and plots the betrayal in the garden with him as the means whereby he, Jesus, will be "unclothed" from the burden of the physical body and enabled thus to return to the glory of the realms of light. Conservatives predictably have discounted the find as the heretical document it was first described as by the arch heresy-hunter Irenaeus, the Bishop of Lyons, in what is now

France *circa* 170 to 200 CE. But it is further evidence, along with about twenty other gospels discovered at Nag Hammadi in Upper Egypt in 1945, that originally there were many "lost Christianities" and not just the one monolithic establishment that from the fourth century onwards became the orthodox version of what I have elsewhere called Christianism. These gospels were buried to escape the flames of the heavy-handed victorious side following Constantine's "conversion" to Christianity and the subsequent Council of Nicaea in 325 CE. They reveal for the most part a kind of spirituality much closer to that of this book than traditional church teaching. Hierarchies were not important. Personal experience was. Women were looked upon as fully equal.

Significantly, it is only in very recent times that some Christians have shown themselves willing to grapple with the enormity of the crimes involved in the Gospel portrayal of Judas specifically and Jesus in general. In 2004, for example, director Celia Lowenstein's bitingly satirical look at the tragic issues surrounding Judas' role—*Sorry, Judas*, produced for and shown on British television's Channel 4—shocked sedate viewers all over the U.K. It showed how all the negative images of Jews as corrupt, ugly, greedy, traitorous and so on derive from a literally interpreted understanding of specific Gospel passages, especially regarding Judas. Consider, for example, the way John's Gospel further demonizes Iscariot by saying that the reason he was upset by Mary, the sister of Lazarus, using expensive ointment to anoint Jesus' feet was not because, as he said, it should have been sold and the money given to the poor. Rather, "He said this not because he cared about the poor but because he was a thief; he kept the common purse and used to steal what was put in it."[7]

The hour-long film has not yet been aired by any North American television network; they have lacked the courage to face the wrath of the powerful "religious right." But, in the final week of

Lent, 2006, it was shown at a special session of the congregation of the very progressively minded Grace Episcopal Cathedral in San Francisco, followed by a lively panel discussion led by several clergy. It is to be hoped that many more congregations in North America and elsewhere will follow this example.

Our Shadow Side

The Christos figure is both the universal model or ideal for humanity and the symbolical divine core of our own individual being. Judas, seen allegorically as an essential part of the drama, is a powerful metaphor for a shadow aspect of our personal spiritual experience. Try as we will, nobody can wholly escape or avoid it. The world in which we live, with all its glories and joys, is filled with deep disappointments and betrayals of every kind. The Judas we experience takes many forms. Nor is this limited solely to friends or close associates in some organization or common task. Frequently, we betray ourselves. This can be the closest and thus the worst betrayal of them all. As Lord Byron says, "One lies to oneself more than to anyone else." Then too, as we grow older, our body or even our mind can fail and hand us over to the dark powers of chaos.

My wife, Susan, and I have intimate knowledge of this latter dimension of reality. At sixty-three, my wife's mother, Joan, suffered a severe stroke during heart valve surgery. The former loving, vigorous, youthful-looking mother was suddenly impaired cruelly by left-side paralysis and memory loss, and she remained this way for the rest of her life. Her hands, which all her life had never ceased from her love of knitting, sewing, ironing and baking her own bread, would no longer do her bidding. She could not walk or remember the most recent things said or done. Left with awareness of these losses but powerless to remedy them, she endured for twelve years, as cheerfully as possible, what for most of us might well seem a kind of hell.

As Scott Peck argued in *The Road Less Traveled*, life is ultimately about "giving up things," usually against our will. At the end, we must surrender life on this plane entirely. The material body "betrays" us. The meaning through it all, however, is that even in the hour of deepest betrayal and of darkest despair the Christ presence within us never fails, never forsakes us. No matter where the path of life may take us, there is a brightly shining victory ahead. The overall spiritual meaning of the Jesus Story makes that triumphantly clear. That was the faith that kept us full of hope for Joan even as her suffering brought such sadness in its wake for all who loved her.

Simone Weil, the French mystic who died in 1943 at age thirty-four and who never knew a day free from terrible pain as an adult, writes movingly of this theme. She says:

> The outward results of true affliction are nearly always bad. We lie when we try to disguise this. It is in affliction itself that the splendour of God's mercy shines, from its very depths, in the heart of its inconsolable bitterness. If still persevering in our love, we fall to the point where the soul cannot keep back the cry, "My God, My God, why hast thou forsaken me?" . . . if we remain . . . without ceasing to love, we end by touching something that is not affliction, not joy, something not of the senses, common to joy and sorrow: the very love of God.

In itself, she says, the knowledge of the presence of God even in suffering does not afford consolation, but "we know quite certainly that God's love for us is the very substance of this bitterness and this mutilation."[8]

The Crucifixion and Death of Jesus

*The mythologies . . . referred to were of the dead and
resurrected god: Attis, Adonis, Osiris / Horus, one after the
other. The death and resurrection of the god is everywhere
associated with the moon, which dies and is resurrected every
month. It is for two nights and three days dark, and we
have Christ for two nights or three days in the tomb.*

— JOSEPH CAMPBELL, *The Power of Myth*

Regarding Joseph Campbell's reference to the moon and its connection with the death and Resurrection of Jesus, it is important
to recall that Easter each year still falls on the first Sunday *after the
first full moon* following the spring equinox. Both the sun and the
moon thus play a significant part. This is a total clothing of Pagan
realities and symbols in Christian dress. The Jewish Passover is
similarly linked with solar-lunar mythology.

Now, in *For Christ's Sake*, published in 1986, I took what was
for me a bold step, after much study, thought and heart searching.
I had finally acquired the gift of the courage to state clearly what
I had for some years come to believe about the true meaning and
nature of the Crucifixion as described in the Gospel drama. At a
much earlier age, I had for some years accepted and subscribed to
the orthodox dogma that only his blood "cleanseth us from all
sins" and that believing Jesus died for me personally (that I was
indeed "there when they crucified my Lord") was an essential step
in "becoming a real Christian." Nevertheless, I had always felt
strangely ill at ease over this dogma on both moral and intellectual
grounds. I used to cringe inwardly upon hearing such gospel
hymns as:

Would you be free from your burden of sin?
There's power in the blood, power in the blood . . .

or:

> Wash me in the blood of the lamb
> And I shall be whiter than snow . . .

or:

> There is a fountain filled with blood
> Drawn from Immanuel's veins;
> And sinners plunged beneath that flood
> Lose all their guilty stains.

The kind of gorefest so graphically depicted in Mel Gibson's 2004 film *The Passion of the Christ* was implicit in all the evangelical thinking of my youth. Virtually every preacher I had ever heard was gripped by this kind of theology. Unitarians, for example, were scorned because they "didn't preach the blood." Everything depended on an Atonement for sin by the substitutionary role of Jesus as the "Lamb of God" in the place of sacrifice where you and I should really be. As I matured, the more I thought about it, the more education I received, and the more I realized, for example, the sheer horror of the evil wrought upon the Jews as a people because of an overly literal understanding of the suffering and death on a cross of Jesus, the more I was led to a total rejection of this entire mode of exegesis, or interpretation. As I wrote at length in *For Christ's Sake*, none of this any longer made any sense to me. For example, God could not have a "son" in any literal sense—the anthropomorphism was too clumsy to bear more than a few moments of rational thought.

Supposing, though, that he actually did send "his only son into the world to save sinners," how and by what possible stretch of human imagination could such a stratagem work? I realized that I had never really understood how the death of one innocent person, be he ever so holy, even divine, could for one instant eradicate and annul the entire sins of all humanity—including such outrages as the excesses of the Crusades, the tortures of the Inquisition and the nightmare of the Holocaust of six million Jews. It still staggers the mind to realize that there are millions upon millions of Christians today who cling to this tragic and, to me, utterly incomprehensible line of blind faith based upon a crude literalism. What of all the unjust wars in the name of religion? What of the unnumbered crimes of sexual abuse of children by the very priests who also preach this seeming folly?

And then, supposing even for a moment that the gargantuan load of all sins past and present was somehow forgiven through what is said to have happened at Calvary, is such a transaction truly moral in any case? Is it in any way explicable in acceptable terms of normal ethical reasoning that one person should—supposing it were possible—pay the penalty or price of somebody else's deliberate misdeeds and crimes? To give it a more cosmic dimension, how does it advance by one iota the moral growth or evolution of the race as a whole if the entire burden of responsibility and opportunity for progress through experience is lifted from the shoulders of all others through the power of one? Small wonder St. Paul cries out for the Christians at Philippi to "work out your own salvation for it is God who works along with you" (my translation).

Added to this is the sheer mind-numbing incomprehensibility of a loving Father who would deliberately demand the death of his "beloved Son" in order to achieve satisfaction for his offended sense of righteousness and justice. No loving human father would behave like that, but we are asked (told) to believe that the God of love did.

This mode of thinking does not and cannot work for a growing number of people today. It is too reminiscent of the idea of God probed by Tennessee Williams in his well-known 1964 play

The Night of the Iguana. In act 2, Shannon, a defrocked Episcopalian priest who leads tours of Central America for a living, describes his total loss of faith. He says he got fired for telling his congregation that the Christian concept of God was "a senile delinquent," and that he could no longer conduct services in praise and worship of this "angry, petulant old man." He told them he could no longer accept the cruelty implied in "blaming the world and brutally punishing all he created [including his own Son] for his own faults in construction." It is not difficult to see why he lost his pulpit and his job, but his logic is to my mind unassailable.

I have come now to see even more fully why Carl Jung had such little use for theories of substitutionary or vicarious Atonement that referred to a far-off event in which Jesus endured suffering once and for all of time for the whole world. Jung's view of Christ's suffering is rather that it symbolizes or exemplifies "the suffering that anyone must undergo in the process of maturation." Moreover, it had come to me forcibly that taking such vicarious forgiveness literally or historically could, as Jung believed, serve to hinder or block one's growth and maturing by "alleviating the suffering that can only be lived through by the individual in the process of becoming whole."[9]

Finally, since in the Gospel accounts, taken literally, it is clear that the entire death of Jesus was planned and preordained—he was "the lamb slain from the foundation of the world"—the whole idea that the Jews, the Romans or anybody else, including you and I, were to blame is made by literalism itself to appear wholly unjust. John's Gospel in particular seems on the surface to underline this aspect, since in it Jesus appears not at all as the helpless victim in the Passion story, but as the one who is wholly in charge. He can lay down his life or preserve it; no man, he is given to say, can take it from him. A number of passages make this fully evident. For example, in John 14:30–31, in one of the final discourses, Jesus is given this line to say: "I will no longer talk much with you, for the ruler of this world [Satan] is coming. He has no power over me; but I do as the Father has commanded me."

Still, in spite of all of this, on recently rereading the chapter called "The Death of Jesus" in *For Christ's Sake*, I realized how far my journey has led me in the intervening years. Viewed as symbolism, I can still rest content with the summing-up I gave there: ". . . the death of Jesus on the cross is not a matter of an angry deity requiring a perfect offering or sacrifice, a case of one of the Persons of God dying to appease the other; nor does it represent some kind of transaction between God and Satan as was at one time believed by the church. The Cross is at the centre of Christian faith now and unto eternity because it is a window into the heart of reality. It reveals the height, depth and breadth of never-ending divine love and pardon . . . it trumpets forth the Resurrection in which we shall all one day share . . ."[10] But in the more than twenty years which have passed since I wrote that, and especially after the depth of research leading to *The Pagan Christ* and then for this present work, the entire meaning of the Gospels has been transformed for me.

Nowhere is this more true than in my understanding and interpretation of the role of Jesus in the story as a whole and of the final events in the timeless drama. I say timeless here advisedly, because once you see the fully symbolical significance of these Gospels you realize that the few historical references there are simply irrelevant to the overall inner meaning.

Pontius Pilate

The apparently historical references, on the other hand, can at times be seen to have their own symbolical meaning to enrich the story. This seems most obviously true in the case of Pontius Pilate. The words "suffered under Pontius Pilate, was crucified, dead and buried" are the only reference to a historical event or personage in the Creed. And there is no doubt that Pilate was indeed the Roman governor or prefect of Judea from 26 to 36 CE under Emperor Tiberius. He was known to be a cruel man. Even Rome itself had to rebuke him for this on at least one occasion we know about. However, the sole piece of secular evidence for linking him to the death of Jesus comes from a brief passage in the *Annals* of the Roman historian Tacitus, about 115 CE. For a full discussion of the flimsiness of this as a reliable source of Tacitus's account, I refer readers to a chapter devoted to the subject in *Living Waters*.[11]

In brief, Tacitus was relying not on any official records or personal research but on hearsay from Christians in Rome. He even manages to get Pilate's official title as Praefectus (Prefect) wrong; he calls him the Procurator of Judea. But closer examination reveals why Pilate was singled out by the mythmakers as the one to play a key role in the divine drama. The secret lies in his name, Pontius Pilatus. The two terms are from two Greek words: the adjective, which translates into Latin as *Pontius*, means "having to do with the ocean or water in general"; *Piletos*, from the Greek verb *pileo*, "to pack together in a dense form," as in felt cloth, for example, carries the meaning of "thick" or "dense." Since water esoterically often denotes matter, the hidden or symbolic significance of the name is that of dense matter. The Christos principle, in other words, was made to endure a sort of suffocation or "death" under the weight of full immersion in the depths of the material realm. He suffered under dense matter. It looks like history but plays out fully as sublime myth, the myth of the soul in matter.

Significantly, the whole Pontius Pilate aspect of the Crucifixion ignited a firestorm of forgeries in the second century. "Documentary proof," especially forged letters (by Christians), was purported to have been written by those responsible for the execution of Jesus. Of these letters, the forged correspondence allegedly between Pilate and Emperor Tiberius is no doubt the most notorious.[12]

Incidentally, there is one glaring contradiction in the orthodox approach to the Crucifixion that church theologians seem simply to ignore or try to cover up. The death of Christ, it is argued, was an act of God in history to save humanity from the penalty of sin, make Atonement (literally, at-one-ment) or reconciliation with God, and open the way to eternal life. The original sin or cause of this supposed alienation, however, took place in a mythical garden, with a talking serpent and a lot of other aspects already well known in Sumerian and Babylonian lore from a more distant past.

Nearly every educated person today, including all but the most extreme of fundamentalists, knows that the entire story of the "Fall" in Genesis is pure myth. Yet the total non sequitur—that the remedy for something that was wholly mythical must necessarily be historical—is swallowed and proclaimed from pulpits without a blush. Both poles or phases of this drama of salvation are mythical, filled with metaphors and symbols, and are not based upon history at all. That's why, for St. Paul, the death of Christ takes place on an entirely different, spiritual plane than this good earth. Insisting upon the historicity of the Crucifixion devalues the symbolism. It attempts to make literal and concrete what belongs to the eternal realm of the Spirit. The suffering and death of all the gods symbolizes the cost of the divine love and energy outpoured upon us all.

Barabbas

There is another intriguing feature of the Crucifixion story that lends an exterior texture of historicity while actually being quite the opposite. I am referring to the extremely curious story within a story about a criminal called Barabbas. Mark, who like other New Testament authors does his best to downplay Roman responsibility—in this case Pilate's—for the death of Jesus, tells us in chapter 15 that there was a custom of Pilate's releasing a prisoner "at the festival," that is, Passover. Notice that there isn't a single strand of historical evidence anywhere available from Jewish or Roman writers that this alleged routine was ever followed. In any case, we are told that the crowd (miraculously gathered in what was now the middle of the night) called on Pilate to honour this "custom" and release Barabbas, a rebel and convicted murderer, and to crucify Jesus. Mark says the "chief priests stirred up the crowd" to get their way. Then the crowd cried again, "Crucify him." So Pilate, wishing to satisfy the crowds, released Barabbas for them; and, after flogging Jesus, handed him over to be crucified.

Where the rub lies is in the highly symbolic name of the man the priests want to see released. The words that combine to compose it are from Aramaic: *bar* means "son of" and *abba(s)* means "father." In other words, they are asking that a son of a father, or of "the" father, be freed while the Son of the Father—Jesus—is crucified. This piece of doublespeak irony is pure invention by Mark or his sources. Indeed, there are some very ancient manuscripts in which Barabbas is actually called "Jesus Barabbas" in Matthew's version.[13] Apart from dramatic irony, and apart from the attempt to paper over myth with false trappings of historicity, there is a deeper meaning here. At moments of crisis, of extreme testing, there will always be "voices" or influences calling for the destruction of what is authentic and real in us and the substitution for it of what is fake and even grossly destructive. The true "son of the father" is rejected in favour of the popular but treacherous "other."[14]

The "Death" of the Gods

As we know, there are many other stories of the Christos or other bearers of Christ consciousness in the great mythologies of the world, and each in its way is a call to become aware of the Christ principle and presence dwelling in our own hearts. As Carl Jung once said, "The general idea of Christ the Redeemer belongs to the worldwide and pre-Christ theme of the hero and rescuer . . . this hero figure is an archetype which has existed from time immemorial."[15] The huge question, however, that presents itself from each of these stories is one put to me quite recently by a well-read woman who came to the front following a presentation I had just made in an author series at the main Toronto Reference Library. Speaking of the range of various avatars or saviour figures I had mentioned—Jesus, Horus, Attis, Orpheus, Adonis, Tammuz and several others—she asked, "Why did they all have to die? If the death on the Cross was not to remove 'the sin of the world,' what is it all about?"

To comprehend that, one has to understand how ancient theology viewed God's participation in the drama of human evolution. As the ancient Greeks put it, "The gods distribute divinity." We must always remember that, for the ancient sages of the world's great religious traditions, human beings were given a tremendous "forward lift" on the evolutionary path at a point far back in our long journey from the slime of the ocean to humanoid creatures suddenly possessed of self-reflective consciousness. Each human being became a "God in an animal's body" by an act whereby God stooped or "emptied himself," to quote an ancient hymn in Paul's Letter to the Philippians. In the creation myth of chapter 3 of Genesis, the moment in our evolutionary history where we became self-reflective beings is symbolized, as we have seen earlier, by Adam and Eve eating of the fruit of the forbidden tree. "Then the eyes of both were opened and they knew . . ." This had nothing whatever to do with sex, and everything to do with the joining of spirit with flesh in the great adventure of becoming and being human.

Changing the metaphor of divine self-emptying, ancient sages believed that the divine Source (God) chose to be torn apart, divided up or distributed into the lives of humans. In this breaking up of the one into many we see the zeal of eternity for Incarnation in time and the joyful acceptance of suffering this involves. One analogy was that of a large jar of water poured from a great height. We know that, as it falls, the water meets resistance from the air and begins to break up into ever-smaller parts. If it falls far enough, it will seem like rain. So too, then, the unity of the deity, in part, was thought of as being poured out and distributed to us all. The point, however, is that this act of divine compassion and self-giving was and is in philosophical or theological terms enormously costly—hence the allegory of mutilation of some kind or of violent death, often by crucifixion. The fate of Prometheus, who brought down fire and paid a price, is a case in point. The Cross, then, is seen in its true luminosity only when it is understood as the sign and symbol of this gift of Incarnation. The vertical of God's love plunges into and through the horizontal dimension of matter—our bodies. God cannot die, whatever the literalizers keep saying. That's why many of the early Gnostics denied the actual death of a historical Jesus on the Cross. They were far too intelligent to accept the logical contradiction such an affront to the very meaning of the term "god" would involve. All of this, then, was heralded and symbolized through various repeated, cyclical astronomical events, as described in *The Pagan Christ*. But once you carefully read the Passion accounts in all four canonical Gospels with this allegorical interpretation in mind, the story no longer implodes upon itself, but radiates with fresh meaning and power. The entire concept of the Cross has been transformed for me by seeing it thus with new eyes. It symbolizes the suffering involved in our evolving human experience, but it also is a potent sign of the final victory of our higher Self.

Agony in Gethsemane

Incidentally, one of the reasons the allegorical and symbolic nature of the Passion narrative is not instantly recognized by the majority of people—churchgoers and non-churchgoers alike— is that the very familiarity of the "old, old story" lulls their normal, waking intelligence into a kind of pious or indifferent stupor as the church lessons are read. The words simply wash over them and there is no thought at all about whether what is being repeated (or, worse, acted out in a film version touted as "authentic" and complete with the usual ultra-conservative Biblical "experts") is indeed logical or credible.

Otherwise, for example, it would instantly strike home that the moving description of Jesus' agony in the garden on the night of his betrayal is clearly fictional from the terms of the story itself. Even a non-Biblical scholar such as popular doctor-writer Deepak Chopra sees what is happening and comments on it. In *How to Know God*, he writes: "The story of Jesus reaches its poignant climax in the garden of Gethsemane, when he prays that the cup be taken from his hands.[16] He knows the Romans are going to capture and kill him, and the prospect gives rise to a terrible moment of doubt. It is one of the loneliest and most wrenching moments in the New Testament—and it is utterly imaginary."

Chopra goes on to say why. The text itself expressly says Jesus had drawn apart from everyone else—even Peter and James and John—and adds that they were asleep. In fact, twice he draws apart to pray and twice discovers they are fast asleep. "Therefore no one could have overheard what he said, particularly as he was praying. I think this . . . was projected on him by writers of the gospel."[17] So too would anyone who really pays attention. It is all wholly imaginary, but it is a transcendent, empowering truth that is being imagined throughout. We need to be constantly reminded when reading any ancient sacred literature that it is chiefly allegorical, and that an allegory is a dramatization of a phenomenon that has its real existence only in the subjective world, not the world of surface event or presumed history. In this case it is our own very real struggle and wrestling with doing what is right that is being depicted.

The same is true when in the Gospels Jesus tells those who would be his disciples to pick up their cross and follow him. This is not about shouldering either a literal or a metaphorical wooden instrument of torture. It's about facing up to and accepting the real cost of living a spiritual life in a physical body. It's a call to embrace fully our incarnational reality and then to move on ahead. The ancients, as we know, spoke of our life here in the body as a "death," a "sleep," an arduous gaining of experience, from which, eventually, physical death would actually be a tremendous release, a real bursting out of the prison of mere physicality into the life of true spirit.

This, I believe, is what Mozart had in mind when, in 1786, on hearing the news of his father's final illness, he wrote his famous letter describing death as "the true goal of our existence," as "the best and truest friend of mankind" and as "the key which unlocks the door to our true happiness." Mozart's biographer, Maynard Solomon, comments, "Thus Mozart was one of those for whom death was an ontological opportunity, an affirmation of faith, a release from pain."[18] Solomon there quotes Herbert Marcuse as saying that Mozart thought that "a brute biological fact, permeated with pain, horror and despair, is transformed into an existential privilege."[19] Death need not be permeated with suffering, fear and hopelessness—particularly when seen as Mozart, with the ancients, believed it to be. Though in his all too brief, creativity-packed existence Mozart lived life to its fullest intensity, like St. Paul he also knew what it was like to feel, at times, "Who will rid me of the body of this death?"

Significantly, the recently published Gospel of Judas, alluded to previously, expounds precisely the view of life in the body, and the "resurrection" to true existence wrought by death, that I have just described. It was the Gnostic view; it was St. Paul's understanding; it is closer in many ways, I believe, to the core mythos than orthodoxy has ever been. When we read of the Gnostics being spoken of disparagingly by either ancient or modern critics, it is well to remember that they had the ill fortune of being on the losing side. But as the great historian Edward Gibbon stated quite plainly, they were the brightest and the best that early Christianity could claim. When the wife of an Anglican vicar in a rural parish told me that, from what she had heard (not read herself) about *The Pagan Christ*, it was clear that I was a Gnostic, I thanked her for the compliment. She seemed surprised.

The Universality of the Cross as Symbol

In *The Pagan Christ* the widespread use of the cross as a potent symbol in Egyptian and other ancient religions was carefully documented. Both Alvin Boyd Kuhn and Joseph Campbell in their writings cite the remarkable Mayan temple at Palenque, in the jungles on the border of Mexico and Guatemala, called the Temple of the Cross. There is a shrine there exhibiting a cross that is associated in Mayan mythology with a saviour figure called Kukulcan. He was known also to the Aztecs as Quetzalcoatl. The sacred writings associated with the figure tell of his being born of a virgin, how he died and was resurrected, and how he is revered "as some sort of saviour who will return at a Second Coming."[20] Campbell says there is a bird sitting on top of the Mayan cross, and at the base there is "a curious mask, a kind of death mask." He goes on to note that a number of paintings of the Crucifixion from late medieval times and the early Renaissance show the Holy Spirit above in the form of a dove. We are reminded by the death mask that the hill of the Crucifixion was called Golgotha, in Aramaic "the place of the skull." In Latin, the word from which *Calvary* comes means the very same thing.[21] In the Icelandic sagas (the Edda) there is a story of the "All-Father" Othin who hung for nine days upon the "world tree" called Yggdrasil. Christ was three hours on the Cross. The nine days (3 x 3 = 9) echoes the same mythic theme.

Ancient, Sacred Ground

There is really no way that any description could ever exhaust all the depths and nuances of subtle meaning surrounding the story of the Passion of the Christ. We are here treading upon hallowed, very ancient, sacred ground. The echoes of our walking here sound forth from the farthest recesses of the human psyche. Anyone who has ever read and pondered the deeply moving words of Psalm 22 knows that this story was already ages upon ages old before the Gospels were ever formed or even thought of. The compilers of the Gospels knew this archetypal imagery of both the soul's agony and its eternal hope like the back of their own hand. So it is not mere chance or pure invention that has Jesus utter that haunting cry from the Cross, an exact quote from verse 1 of the Psalm: "My God, my God, why have you forsaken me?" Anyone who has ever known the depths of depression, the torments of great grief or the throbbing bite of unendurable physical pain will recognize that cry of dereliction intimately. It comes from the heart of the human condition. And as you read on in the same Psalm, the mocking, the taunts to come down from the Cross, the dividing of the clothes and the casting of lots for them—the entire narrative is all there. But notice that the struggle and the pain are not the whole of it. The Psalm ends on a crescendo of hope, of confidence and of final, victorious resurrection: "To him [God] shall all who sleep in the earth bow down . . . and I shall live for him."

11

ENTERING
INTO GLORY

*The blazing evidence of immortality is our
dissatisfaction with any other solution.*

—RALPH WALDO EMERSON, *Journal* (July 1855)

The Resurrection

HAROLD BLOOM makes a powerful point in his book
Jesus and Yahweh—The Names Divine when he comments
on the Gospels' portrayal of the death and Resurrection
of Jesus. He states quite categorically—and correctly—that there
is nothing less Jewish than the "artificial theological construct" of
Jesus Christ as a dying and reviving God. He says: "It shatters both
the written and the oral [Jewish] tradition."[1] Bloom, who is quite
emphatic that "from the start Jesus Christ was not Yeshua [i.e., a
Jewish Messianic claimant] but a theological rather than a human
God," doubts everything that is said or written about the Resurrection because everything that was truly important in the story
"reaches me from texts I cannot trust."[2]

You begin to get an immediate feel for the problems Bloom
has with the Easter texts in particular if you take the time and
trouble—which few if any lay people ever do—to put the four

Gospel accounts of the Resurrection side by side and compare them. They simply do not agree about anything except that there was an empty tomb. Paul, who wrote much earlier, of course, never mentions an empty tomb at all. Nor does the Gospel of Thomas, which is completely silent about the Resurrection.

In Matthew, who says there was one angel at the tomb—so does Mark, but Luke and John both have two—the disciples are told to go to Galilee because "he is going ahead" (Matthew) and "There you will see him" (Mark). But in Luke nothing whatever is said about Galilee. Indeed, in Luke the risen Lord himself expressly contradicts Matthew's and Mark's accounts and tells the disciples to "stay in the city" (Jerusalem) until the giving of "power from above." John too, we find, has the Resurrection appearances located in Jerusalem. Chapter 21 of John, which does move the action to the Galilee, is agreed by most scholars to be a later addition or "second ending" to the Gospel by another editorial hand.[3] There is so very much more, but this gives at least a glimpse of the conflicts and difficulties involved here for scholars.

There was a time, however, when I trusted one particular New Testament text on the Resurrection, and I want to begin this discussion by referring back to it—only in a fresh light. Just over twenty years ago, Oxford University Press in Canada published my "manifesto" and the already cited *For Christ's Sake*. It was considered quite radical in its day (1986) and generated considerable controversy. Sermons were preached condemning it as rank heresy; there were attempts by some fundamentalists, mainly on the west coast, to have me dismissed from a lectureship I held on the theology and praxis of mass media at the Toronto School of Theology (they waged a phone-in campaign); and the book was banned from the great majority of "Christian bookstores" across the country. Such ideas in *For Christ's Sake* as the view of Jesus as fully human, and the repudiation of the outworn ideas already discussed about being "saved by the shed blood" at Calvary, seem very tame in today's theological climate. But I refer to the book again here because in it I did defend the concept—since rejected in *The Pagan Christ*—of a historical Jesus and, in particular, the basis in history of his Resurrection. I said there that I felt "wholly at one" with the tradition of there having been actual eyewitnesses to a risen Christ. I nevertheless rejected the doctrine—untenable to me—of a so-called "physical" Resurrection (I held it to have been purely spiritual) and also any idea that the fact that God had apparently raised him from the dead was "proof" that he too was God. But I clung like a drowning man to there having been some sort of near-death-type "appearances" upon which early Christian faith was based.

Most scholars in the middle today, between the conservatives on the one hand and those who follow views similar to those of the roughly one hundred members of the California-based Jesus Seminar on the other, believe that it all started with visions of one sort or another in the Galilee, where the Jesus movement is believed by many to have originated. Some indeed refer to all of this as the "Big Bang" which explains all that allegedly followed. It's worth noticing here, however, that religious traditions, particularly in their initial birth pangs, have almost always been marked by dreams and visions that have acted as the basic raw material for significant future developments. Carl Jung's exploration of the creative power of the unconscious in forming religious archetypes has greatly increased our understanding of such phenomena. In any case, what was originally one or more visionary experiences later assumed the character of history, according to liberal scholars. They have in mind, for example, the kind of presumed "encounters" described by Luke in a passage about the risen Jesus, disguised as a stranger, meeting two disciples on the road to Emmaeus, or the various visions described by Paul in his well-known list in chapter 15 of 1 Corinthians.[4] Rudolph Bultmann, for example, wrote that the Resurrection is not an event of past history: "It is nothing else than the rise of faith in the risen Lord . . ."[5]

A key passage for me then (as it remains for conservative Christian apologists today) was 1 Corinthians, chapter 15, beginning at verse 1. Here Paul, writing about twenty years at least before Mark's account, followed by the other Gospels, gives the earliest known testimony to the Resurrection. It is very important to keep in mind always that Paul's letters are prior in time to anything else in the New Testament. He writes to remind the young Christians at Corinth of the contents of the "Good News" that he had proclaimed to them on his first missionary visit there. He states clearly that he handed on to them a tradition that he himself had received: "that Christ died for our sins in accordance with the scriptures, and that he was buried, and that he was raised [by God] on the third day in accordance with the scriptures."

Paul, it must again be noticed, makes no mention whatever here or anywhere else in any of his letters of an empty tomb, nor does he follow the specific witness of Matthew, Luke and John in stating that it was the women disciples who first saw the risen Lord. Instead, he says that he first "appeared to Cephas [Peter], then to the twelve. Then he appeared to more than five hundred brothers and sisters at one time, most of whom are still alive, though some have died. Then he appeared to James, then to all the apostles." Then, last of all, by a sort of aberration—Paul says "as to one untimely born"—he "appeared also to me." Faced with this, I wrote in *For Christ's Sake* that I was convinced that something historical had occurred at the Resurrection because of Paul's apparent ability to cite eyewitnesses, some of whom were putatively still around to back him up.

Obviously, I no longer find this the firmly convincing piece of evidence it once seemed to be, and it is of considerable importance here to explain why not. I now realize, after much further research and a closer analysis of this key passage, that its value as solid "historical" evidence falls apart upon a fuller examination. In the first place, there is no way to square this obviously earlier account with the later, conflicting versions given in the Gospels. The lack of any reference to Mary Magdalene and the other women already mentioned is in itself quite striking. Then there is the fact that the whole list given by Paul of what he had "received" (that is, it had already become a kind of repeated formula or second-hand "tradition") is utterly devoid of any specific reference to times and places. There is a total vagueness where one wants something solid if he was, as is generally supposed, intent on claiming this as in any way "historical." The passage lacks any basic information about two key elements in the five Ws—where and when. A third element, the "who," is ambiguous as well. Paul's account offers no context whatever. Furthermore, it would have been quite easy to tell people living far away in Corinth in a formulaic way that they could check out the facts for themselves, when the likelihood of any of them ever going to Palestine and searching around for these alleged and unnamed "witnesses," some of whom had reportedly died in the meanwhile, was virtually nil.

However, there is more. Anyone who reads this Corinthians testimony in the original Greek will notice at once that St. Paul uses the same Greek verb—translated "he appeared to" in the New Revised Standard Version—every time he lists a witness. And he does not vary this in any detail when he comes to what he admits was an unusual appearance to himself, on the road to Damascus, after the Ascension, long after the post-Easter appearances are said to have taken place. The same Greek word used throughout is *opthe*, "he was seen." Now, we know from his own description elsewhere that Paul's experience was clearly a vision, not a historical encounter. He says in Galatians, possibly his earliest letter, "When it pleased God to reveal his son in me." What's more, and this was the clincher for me, the word *opthe* is precisely

the word used in the contemporary Mystery Religions and elsewhere for seeing a vision.

Finally, there is one more bit of evidence that Paul was reciting
a kind of "set piece" and not laying down an objective or independently based case. He says Jesus appeared to Cephas "and then to
the twelve." However, because of the death of Judas and the fact
that Acts tells how his replacement was chosen much later than
the events that Paul is supposed to be here describing, there were
no longer at that point in time twelve apostles, as he says, but only
eleven. Acts 1, verse 15 to the end, describes how Judas was later
replaced by Matthias, chosen by lot.

From all of this, plus some other subtleties of language too
obscure for general consumption, my conclusion now, following
many other contemporary scholars, is that Paul's recital provides
no solid linkage to any historic Jesus of Nazareth, but is sheer
mysticism throughout. The one thing that is absolutely certain
about St. Paul is that he was a deeply mystical, intuitive person
open to a whole range of paranormal experiences and phenomena. No New Testament authority can deny that. Indeed, Paul
bears eloquent testimony to his far-ranging psychic capacities in
a fascinating account in his Second Letter to the Corinthians. He
says:

> It is necessary to boast; nothing is to be gained by it, but I
> will go on to visions and revelations of the Lord. I know a
> person in Christ [himself] who fourteen years ago was
> caught up to the third heaven—whether in the body or out
> of the body I do not know; God knows. And I know that
> such a person—whether in the body or out of the body I do
> not know; God knows—was caught up into Paradise and
> heard things that are not to be told, that no mortal is per-
> mitted to repeat. (2 Corinthians 12:1–4)

We never are told what he saw and heard. Other passages in his letters show that his entire understanding of his faith was—as was the case with many of the Gnostics—based mystically upon personal, private "revelations." For example, in his Epistle to the Galatians he says plainly that the Good News he preached was "not of human origin" because he neither received it from "a human source" nor was taught it, he says, "but I received it through a revelation of Jesus Christ." What Paul goes on to say in the remainder of his famous chapter 15 of 1 Corinthians about the wholly "spiritual" nature of the Resurrection—both of Jesus Christ and of us as well—fully, to my mind, confirms the understanding of this particular passage that I have set out above. He says there that there is a physical body and a spiritual body. Only the spiritual one can ever enter into immortality with the soul.

Modern New Testament scholarship has quite literally sliced and diced the Resurrection stories in the Gospels from every conceivable angle and point of view. The keenest of Bible students would be hard put to master even a small portion of the burgeoning bulk of books, monographs and articles about the subject, never mind the ordinary layperson. Even as distinguished a scholar as the Most Reverend Rowan Williams, Archbishop of Canterbury, agrees that there are "difficulties" with Paul's list, as outlined above, and goes on to say that what the Gospels contribute is "a monumentally confused jumble of incompatible stories." The Archbishop, who by his calling is intended to be a leading guardian of the ancient Anglican tradition, says the conflict between them has yet to be sorted out satisfactorily, and that all of them "bear the mark of extremely sophisticated literary editing."

According to the Archbishop, what the Easter texts present to the reader are "imaginative approaches" in the form of stories or "narratives" to the question of what it means to say that Jesus, who was executed, is now alive with God and somehow "present to his followers."[6] He calls the appended chapter 21 in John's Gospel "a Galilean fantasy" and an obvious second ending added later. Read the last verses of chapter 20 and see this for yourself. Most if not all of the members of the Jesus Seminar, it should be remembered, do not believe in the historicity of the Resurrection stories. As one member said at a recent meeting that I attended of Snowstar, the Canadian affiliate organization of the Jesus Seminar: after the Crucifixion "Jesus was seriously dead." By this somewhat glib remark he indicated his conviction that this was the earthly end of the story.[7]

The Meaning

The Christ in you doesn't die—it resurrects.

— JOSEPH CAMPBELL, *The Power of Myth*

If none of these narratives about Jesus as a dying and resurrected god—a theme so widespread and common in the ancient Near East as well as in the mythologies of other cultures in other parts of the world—are historical, what is the real meaning of this story for us today? That's the authentic question for us. I can honestly say again that Good Friday and Easter are far more meaningful for me now than they ever were before I had the "scales removed from my inner eyes" and was given a fuller glimpse of their true spiritual intent. Let me explain why.

Certainly, what two thousand years of church history have proven to me beyond doubt is that the restricting and focusing of all the Church's attention upon the supposedly historical death and rising of one single individual long ago has unfortunately robbed all the rest of humanity of its own divinity. The death that was seen as overcome at each Eastertide is the death of the soul—not of one man's soul only, but the souls of all who have ever lived or ever will live. It is this universal reality that the Easter stories symbolize or typify. That is what the Jesus mythos is all about.

What is more, if we can only let the light shine through the opacity of the literal narratives in the Gospels, with all their contradictions and problems, we can realize that Christ's Resurrection had nothing whatever to do with the rising of a corpse and its bursting the barrier of a rock tomb on a Judean hillside on some distant morn. We can see instead that it is a powerful testimony to the daily Resurrection that can take place moment by moment in our own lives if we allow the inner Christ, the divine fragment or "spark" that dwells in every heart, to quicken us again to newness of living. The big question arising from the story of the death and Resurrection of Jesus Christ is not, What can we make of events that happened nearly two thousand millennia ago? but rather, Are you and I constantly experiencing right now what it is to die to the past and to rise again to what the Anglican prayer book, following Paul, calls "newness of life"? That is really the paradigm for a truly spiritual life, whatever our personal faith or religion (or lack of one) may be.

But there is an even deeper meaning behind the Easter texts than what is directly aimed at the here and now. There is no question that the ancient authors of these narratives had more than one layer of significance in their minds. The Easter story at this point is at the same time a profound allegorism aimed at depicting the truth of every soul's eventual bursting through this "tomb" of imprisonment in our earthly body and winging its way in the full glory of celestial light back to its source in God. The "victory of the grave" and the curse of "the sting of death" have been overcome.

For those who die, Resurrection and the life of the age to come are immediate, today. That's the meaning behind Jesus' words to the dying thief: "Today you will be with me in Paradise." Or, to quote from Paul, to be absent from the body is to be forever present with the Lord. It is high time, I believe, to stop the futile, endless attempt to rationalize the Easter story in literal terms and instead to see it in all its glory as a resplendent myth bearing eternal truth from beginning to end. If it is true, as those who originally told this story believed—that is, that we are all the bearers of an immortal soul—then physical death is but the door or gateway or transition to a different plane of being, where the great adventure of our journey continues and untold experiences of growth and of illumination yet await. Easter is not just a yearly but a constant reminder of that glorious reality. It is a celebration of the immortality of the soul and its triumphant destiny with God. As Carl Jung once wrote, "What happens after death is so unspeakably glorious that our imaginations and our feelings do not suffice to form even an approximate conception of it." Or, to quote a famous scripture, "Eye has not seen nor ear heard, neither has it entered into the heart of human beings such good things as God has prepared for all who love him."[8]

The Ascension

It is to this future state of higher consciousness and transfigured form—the new, spiritual body of which St. Paul writes in chapter 15 of 1 Corinthians—that the two "authentic" accounts of Jesus' "Ascension into heaven" bear witness. Both of them occur in the writings ascribed to Luke.[9]

The first of Luke's stories of the Ascension, in the final verses of his Gospel, tells how the risen Jesus led the disciples to the village of Bethany, just east of Jerusalem, and lifted his hands in blessing on them. "While he was blessing them, he withdrew from them and was carried up into heaven." Some early manuscripts omit the words "and was carried up into heaven." But the overall sense is clear.

However, when Luke describes the same "moment" in the drama at the outset of the Acts of the Apostles, the story has already expanded considerably. Acts 1:9–11 says nothing whatever about going to Bethany or any particular blessing. Instead, Jesus tells the Apostles that they will receive the Holy Spirit shortly and be witnesses even to "the ends of the earth." Then, as they watched, "he was lifted up, and a cloud took him out of their sight." As he was going up, two men in white robes, angels in Luke's view, asked them why they were standing there looking heavenwards: "This Jesus . . . will come in the same way as you saw him go into heaven."

This occurred, according to Luke, a symbolic "forty days" after the Crucifixion. In a composite of Jewish and Christian writing, an apocalypse-type document from the second century known as the Ascension of Isaiah, the forty-day period becomes eighteen months, and in the *Pistis Sophia* ("Faith Wisdom"), a third-century document reflecting Gnostic Egyptian Christianity, the time from the Resurrection to the Ascension is described as eleven years in all! Clearly, in all three versions, the number of days, months or years is purely arbitrary and dependent upon the theology of the writer. Behind all the imagery of the myth (as Bishop Spong has said, literalists have a problem with where exactly in the heavens Jesus was headed as he went straight up from a particular spot in the Middle East!) is the glorification that is being symbolized.

Joseph Campbell has a timely warning against taking any of this as historical fact. Noting that the Roman Catholic Church teaches that not only Jesus but, sometime later, also his mother Mary are taken up into heaven (the Assumption of the Virgin), he comments that the tendency to literalize the meaning here "simply devalues the symbol" and misses the whole point. Campbell says that what is described as being in outer space is intended to connote what ought to happen in inner space. "The heaven to which these bodies . . . supposedly ascended physically is really that to which you descend if you go into yourself, which is the place . . . out of which you came. And within which you are. And where you indeed are."[10]

Our bodies, then, are "vehicles" of consciousness or soul, and Jesus' Ascension symbolizes the truth that ultimately, when we die, the present physical body departs but our real Self moves on into greater glory. Campbell sums up the story of Jesus' Resurrection and Ascension thus:

> Jesus dies, is resurrected, and goes to Heaven. This metaphor expresses something religiously mysterious. Jesus could not literally have gone to Heaven because there is no geographical place to go. Elijah went up into the heavens in a chariot, we are told, but we are not to take this statement as a description of a literal journey. These are spiritual events described in a metaphor.[11]

Indeed.

12

REACHING FOR TRANSCENDENCE

One thing that comes out in myth is that at the bottom of the abyss comes the voice of salvation. The black moment is the moment when the real message of transformation is going to come. At the darkest moment comes the light."

— JOSEPH CAMPBELL, *The Power of Myth*

Allegory and Literalism

NOBODY in recent times, in my view, has done more to encourage people to seek, through an understanding of the centrality of myth and metaphor, the meaning of the sacred—the glory of the transcendence for which we were made—than the late Joseph Campbell. His little posthumous book titled *Thou Art That* sparkles with spiritual insight and inspiration. It is a classic of its kind. However, sad to say, some of his fellow intellectuals waged a campaign after his death in 1987 to try to diminish the lustre of his gift of illumination. I am reminded in this of some trenchant words from Robert Funk, founder and spokesperson for the Jesus Seminar until his sudden death in 2005. Funk once wrote: "The worst enemy for all scholars of the Bible—indeed for all scholars—is elitism. In the academic

world, penalties are severe for the author who writes a book that
sells well, or for sponsors of the lucid sentence, or for teachers
who can teach but fail to publish." The academics as a group, he
said, look askance at success and argue that if a work elicits a
broad readership, if a sentence is understandable, if students
learn and enjoy it, "that scholarship cannot be very profound."[1]

I must say, as we near the end of this exploration, that Campbell's work, especially his PBS interviews with Bill Moyers and
Thou Art That, has had a deep impact on how I have learned to
interpret the ancient scriptures. No one understood the need to
emphasize the difference between allegory and history, metaphor
and literalism, better than he. Like him, I long that we may all
come to a deeper understanding of the mystery of our own being
and in doing so know more of God.

There is no one correct way in which anyone should be told
he or she *must* read the Bible as a whole, or the four Gospels in
particular. In the end, each must follow his or her own path, and
God's spirit will give him or her his special gift in his own time.
My own reading of the Bible and prolonged study over the years
have led me inexorably to the mythological and allegorical interpretation I have just laid out. I strongly believe that this is the
way in which the Bible was written and the way in which it was
intended to be understood. This approach is made even firmer in
my mind by the works of such respected academics as Dr. Carl
Jung, Professor Northrop Frye, Joseph Campbell and Dr. Alvin
Boyd Kuhn, to name a few.

Of this, however, I am most certain: there is one way *not* to
read sacred scriptures, and that is the road of unnuanced literalism and historicism. This path makes void the richer layers of
meaning behind the text. It worships what St. Paul called the dead
"letter" of the text and ignores the Spirit which alone "brings life."
Sam Harris, in his 2005 book *End of Faith*, is right when he says
that if, God forbid, this earth ends up one day as an incinerated

planet, it will be because of some words inscribed in the sacred scriptures of ultra-literalists.

Apart from very real and harrowing risks such as that, the Bible, when pressed too literally, can be farcical, for example the wanderings of the children of Israel in the wilderness for forty years. We note again that the number forty signals the mythological nature of what is being described. But imagine six or seven hundred thousand people on a trek within what is after all a fairly limited territory, for forty years, trying to find the Promised Land. (A *Toronto Star* photographer and I once took five days to walk the 165 kilometres from Nazareth in northern Galilee to Bethlehem, via Jericho and Jerusalem.) Surely some bright-eyed lad would have cried out at some point: "Hey, Moses, I think we passed that same pile of white bones this time last week!" "The wilderness" is not meant literally. It represents this world in which we wander as incarnate spirits. It signifies our alienation from our true home. The "Promised Land" is not a piece of territory that has to be taken by pillage and mass murder. It is a special region of the heart where God abides. [2]

Fact or Fiction?

There are dozens of familiar Bible tales that quite obviously "ain't necessarily so" as events. They are quite incredible, in fact. Take the story of Noah's Ark, or the dividing of the waters of the Red or "Reed" Sea for the Israelites, or the parting of the waters of the river Jordan for Joshua. None of these incidents happened historically—they are metaphor and symbolism. Water, as we have seen, always symbolizes either the depths of our unconscious or, most often, matter itself. All of this Biblical passing through water, including Noah and the Deluge, is eloquent witness to humanity's dual nature of spirit and animal. We must pass through the waters of this physical life until one day we are reunited with our source. As the Ark story shows, God will see us safely through it all.

Take the Old Testament story of David and Goliath. On one level it makes an interesting, heroic tale. I loved reading about it as a boy at a boy's level. But, properly understood in its mythic nature, the giant represents all the unruly forces and passions that the God in us has to educate and control. Notice that David's slingshot drives the stone, not into Goliath's belly or his chest, but deeply into his forehead. The message is clear: the way to deal with the brute animal passions is through the divine gift of mind, intellect and reason. This is part of the Christ in us. Though there has not been space here to speak of all the other wonderful, symbolic stories in the Hebrew Bible—the iron axe head that was made to float, Daniel in the lion's den, the sun standing still in the heavens for Joshua, Jonah and the whale, and dozens of others—they all in their various ways deal with the same truth of Incarnation.

Another example of a humorous result from a purely literal interpretation, this time from the New Testament, is a passage where two disciples of John the Baptist are said to have asked Jesus whether he was indeed the Messiah or not. He tells them to go and tell John "what you have seen and heard: the blind receive their sight, the lame walk, the lepers are cleansed, the deaf hear, the dead are raised, the poor have Good News brought to them."[3] The King James Version, the standard translation from 1611 to the modern era, says "to the poor the Gospel is preached." Some comfort for the poor! On a simply literal reading, their fate, it seems, is to be endlessly sermonized or harangued by preachers. However, from this and other passages, by "poor" is meant those who have not yet recognized the treasure within, or the "pearl of great price." Clearly, people in such a state do need to hear the Good News of who they really are. There is a passage in the Gospel of Thomas that confirms this interpretation for me. In saying #3, Yeshua explains: "When you know yourselves [who you really are], then you will be known, and you will understand that you are children of the living father. But, if you do not know yourselves, then you dwell in poverty and you are poverty."[4]

Reading the Bible Literally Has Sometimes Led to Disaster

There is a passage in the Epistle to the Hebrews that speaks of God as having "subjected" or placed all things "under the feet" of us human beings. The words deliberately echo Genesis, where the mythical creation of *Homo sapiens* is first described. (There is a second version of this same event from a different source in chapter 2 of Genesis.) What the story says is of great significance, especially when one reflects on how deleteriously the fallout of a literal understanding of it has affected our relationship to the natural world—the environment—and to all other living organisms on the face of the earth. It reads:

> And God said, "Let the earth bring forth living creatures of every kind: cattle and creeping things and wild animals of the earth of every kind." And it was so . . . and God saw that it was good: Then God said, "Let us make humankind to our likeness; *and let them have dominion over the fish of the sea, and over the birds of the air, and over the cattle, and over all the wild animals of the earth, and over every creeping thing that creeps upon the earth.*" (my emphasis) (Genesis 1:24–26)

A few lines later, humans are told to "fill the earth and subdue it" (!) and the command to have dominion over the fish, the birds and every other living thing "that moves upon the earth" is repeated and underlined. The obtuse and literal interpretation of this has played a devastating role in shaping fundamental attitudes throughout the development of Western culture. It accounts, among other things, for the view that nature is simply there for us to rape and plunder as well as for the speciesism by which all other life forms are regarded as the legitimate raw materials for our use and pleasure. Direct opposition to concern for and action on behalf of the environment from some religiously ultra-conservative lobbies in the U.S.A. today flows immediately from this kind of reading of the above-cited Bible texts.

The literal rendering, pushed to conclusion, leads to total anthropocentrism—human above everything else. It would mean that we are to go and establish our control over everything from elephants and whales to scorpions, lizards and fleas. The meaning plainly is to be found not in literalizing but in the allegory depicted of our inner destiny. The myth here is not concerned about externals but uses them for its single purpose, the imparting of wisdom for our evolutionary task. The animal nature that we are to control and subdue is the lower half of our own constitution. The tiger, the scorpion, the stinging gnat or even the full matter of the earth itself all stand for our animal natures. That is why Noah was told to take the animals into the Ark. We are to take dominion over and put into subjection the animal in ourselves. No more and certainly no less.

The Gift of Compassion

There is one gift that we all must get from our reading of the Gospels or of any scriptures, and from any religion worthy of the name, and that is compassion. Philosophers and theologians, and indeed all ordinary people of good sense, know in their hearts that the core of any true religion is to be found in compassion. All the great faiths agree on that. Each has its own version of the golden rule, as do many secular philosophies. Yet, as we know, no evil has been more violent or disruptive or cruel than religion down through history. Of the more than 150 serious conflicts raging around the globe today, the vast majority are either rooted in or coloured by a religious component. It's important, therefore, before concluding this discussion, that we examine this crucial value and seek to understand how it can be more fully embraced. We badly need a universal ethic upon which to build a global peace. To help us in this task, we will finally look at what is perhaps the greatest parable in the Gospels.

The Good Samaritan

The parable of the man who was set upon by robbers on the lonely Jericho road and left for dead is surely familiar to us all, perhaps again too much so, thereby stripping it of its punch. But we tend to remember at least the other main actor in the drama, the Samaritan. Others—a priest and a Levite, people who should have known better—felt nothing but contempt for this mugged, bleeding stranger lying by the road and passed him by on the other side. The Samaritan, on the other hand, a man hated by the audience to whom this story was told (for the Jews had no dealings with Samaritans because of bitter and long-standing religious differences), stopped, gave him first aid, took the man on his own mount to an inn and even left money to pay for future expenses. Anybody can see that the Samaritan was "the good neighbour" and that the others were not. By the way, Simone Weil, in writing about love of neighbour in her powerful little book *Waiting Upon God*, says that being a good neighbour has nothing to do with sentimental feelings but with truly "paying attention" to the other person. But what was the secret of the Samaritan's compassion?

This reminds me of a question raised by the great philosopher Schopenhauer in his essay *On the Foundations of Morality*:

> How is it possible that suffering that is neither my own nor of my concern should immediately affect me as though it were my own, and with such force that it moves me to

action? . . . This is something really mysterious, something for which Reason can provide no explanation, and for
which no basis can be found in practical experience. It is not
unknown even to the most hard-hearted and self-interested.
Examples appear every day . . . of instant responses of this
kind, without reflection, one person helping another, coming to his aid, even setting his own life in clear danger for
someone whom he has seen for the first time, having nothing more in mind than that the other is in need and in peril
of his life.[5]

Schopenhauer's answer was that the immediate reaction and response represented the breakthrough of a spiritual or metaphysical realization best rendered (in terms of Hindu religion) as "thou
art that." The German philosopher wrote that this represented
a penetration of the barrier between persons so that the "other"
was no longer seen as an indifferent stranger but as a person "in
whom I suffer in spite of the fact his skin does not enfold my
nerves." He concluded that what is revealed in such an act is that
our own true inner being actually exists in every living creature.
This is the true ground of that compassion on which all unselfish
virtue rests, he said. By our paying full attention, this truth comes
home to us with power.

When you realize the truth about the divinity within us all,
you know that you are in the other and the other is in you. This is
what Jesus means when he is presented in chapter 25 of Matthew
as saying: "Just as you did it to one of the least of these . . . you
did it to me." We will never have true compassion in the religions
of the world until we acknowledge this common bond—the
divinity, the Atman or Christ that is in everyone on earth. We need
to expand our understanding of this truth until we see the divinity
in other species and throughout the natural world as well. That is
a spiritual or metaphysical foundation on which an all-embracing

global harmony will one day rest. When it does, the "Messiah" will truly have come.

Moving Ahead

I feel a deep compassion and pastoral concern here myself, as we come to the close of our "exploration into God," for the untold thousands right now who want to express the new ways in which they are experiencing God today. They long to be able to worship and to unite in common concern for the welfare of others in a community where reason is respected, where they are not compelled to recite outworn creeds or sing theologically offensive hymns, and where nobody need ever feel excluded. Many no longer feel comfortable in a church at all—except perhaps for a musical event or for meditation when the building is silent and empty. Countless readers have asked, "Where can I go to find others who believe and think as you and I now do?"

What is needed, I believe, is not more "renewal." There is really little or no time left for that, and in any case, in my experience, what church "renewal" means when translated is simply, to use an expression drawn from bells, "ringing the changes" on the old. The time has come for a radical rebirth of the Church. (I have suggested one approach along the lines of the seven points outlined in the conclusion to *The Pagan Christ*.) But births or rebirths can be extremely difficult and painful. There are many with vested interests who have too much to lose to even consider what is contained in these pages. According to Carl Jung, "For many, the rewards of clinging to spiritual infancy in the name of fidelity or commitment to a final revelation are too great to be abandoned. The security of certitude, of possessing the final truth as a member of the chosen people, a people set apart, simply outweighs the pain of disorientation that invariably accompanies the risk of growth."[6]

For those who are still loosely connected with a church or who are thinking of leaving, I would counsel this: Go with others, or if necessary alone, to see the clergy of the parish or congregation and explain what and how you are thinking and feeling. See whether they would consider at least having a study group to examine the possibilities for genuine, radical change. One of the first things I would do myself today if I were to find myself back as leader in a parish is to form a parallel "congregation" that would hold separate sessions open to all where seekers and those more interested in the journey than in fixed answers could feel free to question, to experiment with worship, and to find fresh ways of reaching out to include, to help and to share their journey.

If you find that you are rebuffed and rejected, or politely put on an indefinite hold, find two or three others who have read what you have, or who are also thirsty for the "living waters" that the local church or temple or mosque may not seem able to offer, and meet with them in one of your homes. Recent polls show that more than half of all adult Canadians have their spiritual needs met either by private devotions, or meditation, or (and this is by far the largest number) by meeting in small groups to study the books of those theological writers who are keen on exploring new ideas and new paths. Like the first Christians at the very beginning, they get together in a member's living room or recreation room and, though many would prefer not to call it by that name, they become "a house church." Two points are important to remember:

1) No major change for the better in history was ever brought about by a majority. It is always, initially at any rate, the hard work of a few. It takes courage and it takes great determination. That is the whole point of the sayings about our being "salt" or "yeast" or "the light of the world" in the Gospels.

2) If there is to be a rebirth of Christianity in our time, it will not come from the top down to the pews. Granted, church and other religious leaders can surprise us at times. We all can cite as an example Pope John XXIII suddenly calling for the Second Vatican Council in 1962. But, even for him, the institutional overburden, the ecclesiastical entropy, proved in the end much more powerful than any one individual. The reforms promised by Vatican II that Pope John thought would open a window to the world—the *aggiornamento*—have now been mostly forgotten or ignored. There has been a huge sagging of morale in many parts of the Roman Catholic world as a result. Change can only come, it is clear, from the bottom up. My prayer is that this book may play some part in helping you to assist in bringing it about. Make a beginning. The Spirit will help find a way.

Let me remind you of a life-changing moment in the career of the greatest thinker in the early Church, St. Augustine. Augustine was in his early thirties, a brilliant rhetorician and professor who was agonizing over intellectual problems, as well as moral, associated with becoming a Christian. The major hurdle before his conversion was overcome because of a unique experience he had in Italy. A friend invited him to hear the great theologian and preacher Ambrose, preaching in Milan. Enraptured, the young man went to hear the bishop many times. In his *Confessions*, written later, he tells how "with joy I heard Ambrose in his sermons to the people, oftentimes most diligently recommend this text for a rule, *the letter killeth, but the Spirit giveth life*; whilst he drew aside the mystic veil, laying open spiritually what, according to the letter, seemed to teach something unsound . . ."[7] That's what this book has attempted to do, to "draw aside the mystic veil" to reveal the spiritual truth within.

Transformation

We come finally, then, to this. The basic question today is not what church or religion you belong to, what are your creedal beliefs or what religious leaders you follow. Instead, the burning question is: what is happening inside you right now? In other words, spiritual life today—being awake and aware in the eternal now—is not about events long ago and doctrines built around them, but about your own experience, in this present moment, of the dimension known as the "numinous"—the place where one becomes fully alert and alive to the awesome, radiant mystery shining behind, and in, and through the whole of life. I am thinking here of that ineffable, mysterious, indefinable presence we call God. But not the God of any specific system, ism or creed. Rather, God as the ultimate metaphor for the dynamism, the glory and the mystery of life or being itself. Once words too closely define that ultimate reality, what you have is only an idol or a kind of cosmic black hole. I know it is not popular today to speak of a personal God. But while I do not believe God is a person, a large being "out there," I do experience God in a very personal way through his/her presence within my life and the lives of all those around me, in nature, in art and literature and music—in beauty as well as in suffering everywhere. The God within us is not an "it" but profoundly, and however mysteriously, always a *Thou* in Martin Buber's sense of Thou, to whom and with whom we can "pray without ceasing." We are entirely responsible for our own life and our own destiny, but there is an inner power or Spirit upon which we can always draw for fresh strength and courage on our journey. This is what I call the Christ within.

The quest of the human, thus, is for transcendence, an experience that carries us beyond the purely animal or the purely materialistic, the purely selfish, to that for which we yearn—a deep sense of oneness with the core of our own authentic selves and with the whole of the cosmos. We have an intuition down inside that knowing this transcendence ever more fully will transform our lives, not all at once but, as St. Paul says, steadily "from glory to glory." Joseph Campbell once put it this way: we all have a great yearning for something that has never yet been seen in this world. "What can it be that has never yet been seen?" he asks. The answer can be life-changing: "What has never been seen is your own un-precedented life fulfilled. Your life is what has yet to be brought into being."[8] That is the true "hero's journey." And it is yours and mine to make.

In my boyhood years, as a young seminarian and later as a parish priest—even beyond that, as a professor of the New Testament and Greek at the Toronto School of Theology—I believed what the Church had been teaching ever since the fourth century, that is, that there was and is but one unique true-God-and-true-man, Jesus Christ. That dogma, tragically, for a very long time blocked for me the road leading to the discovery of the divinity that lies within us all. What a release and sense of sheer joy it brought when, through much study, as well as travels to other regions of the world than those once dominated by the Church, I discovered that in the ancient world of Egypt and Greece, in the Gnostic and other communities of the very first Christians—the so-called "lost Christianities"—and throughout the Orient, a very different truth held sway. There, each person was called and challenged to recognize the reality of the Incarnation in his or her own life. Such incarnations as Horus, Krishna, Rama, the Buddha or the Jesus of the Gospels were or still are simply models through which each of us is to realize the mystery of the Incarnation in ourselves. As Pauline mysticism so eloquently puts it: "This is the mystery; Christ in you, the hope of glory."

Two brief parables from Matthew bring home the message of this whole exploration as nothing else can do. Both are from chapter 13, beginning at verse 44. The first says the kingdom of heaven—God's presence in our hearts and lives and all about us—is like buried treasure in a field. Someone finds it suddenly, hides it and then sells everything he has to buy that field in order to possess it utterly. The second parable likens the kingdom to a merchant searching for fine pearls. He finds one of rare value and sells all that he has in order to buy it. Nothing could be more beautifully put. Nothing could be clearer. The discovery of the Divine within yourself is that unique treasure offered in the Gospels; it is that extraordinary "pearl of great price."

My hope and prayer is that every reader will know the joy and the reward of this, our God-given inheritance and birthright.

A Vision

Together with the above-mentioned hope and prayer, I wish to share in conclusion a vision for the future that was first written by a great but—at least at the popular level—not sufficiently well-known Canadian, Dr. Richard Maurice Bucke. It comes from the introduction to his groundbreaking work *Cosmic Consciousness*, first published in 1901 and, amazingly, never since out of print. *Cosmic Consciousness* is a study of enlightened individuals throughout history who have all experienced a visionary moment or state of consciousness, which brought a unique sense of being at one with the whole of the cosmos and with God. Bucke, who was a friend of Walt Whitman, was not to know that his vision would be—as I discovered for myself quite by accident—reproduced verbatim by the Russian philosopher Peter Ouspensky (1878–1947) in his widely acclaimed book *Tertium Organum*. The plagiarized passage became known as the "jewel" of *Tertium Organum*, which was published in Russian in 1912 and in English in 1920.[9]

Here, then, is Bucke's "jewel":

- In contact with the flux of cosmic consciousness all religions known and named today will be melted down.
- The human soul will be revolutionized.
- Religion will absolutely dominate the human race.
- It will not depend on tradition.
- It will not be believed and disbelieved.
- It will not be a part of life, belonging to certain hours, times, occasions.
- It will not be in sacred books nor in the mouths of priests.
- It will not dwell in churches and meetings and forms and days.
- Its life will not be in prayers, hymns nor discourses.
- It will not depend on special revelations, on the words of gods who came down to teach, nor on any bible or bibles.
- It will have no mission to save men from their sins or to secure them entrance to heaven.
- It will not teach a future immortality nor future glories, for immortality and all glory will exist in the here and now. The evidence of immortality will live in every heart as sight in every eye.
- Doubt of God and of eternal life will be as impossible as is now doubt of existence; the evidence of each will be the same.
- Religion will govern every minute of every day of all life.
- Churches, priests, forms, creeds, prayers, all agents, all intermediaries between the individual man and God will be permanently replaced by direct unmistakable intercourse.
- Sin will no longer exist nor will salvation be desired.
- Men will not worry about death or a future, about the kingdom of heaven, about what may come with and after the cessation of the life of the present body.
- Each soul will feel and know itself to be immortal, will feel and know that the entire universe with all its good and with all its beauty is for it and belongs to it forever.

- The world peopled by man [humans] possessing cosmic consciousness will be as far removed from the world of today as
  this is from the world as it was before the advent of self-
  consciousness.

  —Dr. Richard Maurice Bucke (1837–1902)

This "jewel," envisioned over a century ago, still awaits its universal fulfillment. But I remain confident that a vast movement
towards it is already under way in our time. A major change of
consciousness has already begun in spite of "wars and rumours of
wars." The growing awareness of an immanent divinity, the divine
spark or "Christ" in the inner being of every human being on the
planet, is central to this seismic shift. So too is the returning realization that religious literalism kills while the Spirit leads to life.

As our exploration closes, some famous words of Phillips
Brooks, the American Episcopal Bishop of Massachusetts (1891)
who preached the sermon at Abraham Lincoln's funeral and wrote
the well-loved carol "O Little Town of Bethlehem," resonate
through my mind. Brooks said that the sacred scriptures, the
Bible, are like a telescope. If you look through your telescope,
you see worlds beyond. But if you look only *at* the telescope, you
see nothing else. The Bible, he said—and this applies particularly
to the Gospels—is "a thing to be looked through to see more
clearly that which is beyond." The world today cries out as never
before for that which is beyond, without realizing it is already
here in our midst, waiting to be claimed.

APPENDIX A

Differences between John's Gospel and the Synoptic Gospels

Here, in summary, are some of the major differences between John's account on the one hand and that of the Synoptics on the other.

- While Matthew and Luke describe a virgin birth, John's Jesus has, as it were, a cosmic conception. With words reminiscent (deliberately) of the first verse of Genesis, the author's prologue says: "In the beginning was the Word . . ." Notice that this Word or Logos passage probably originated independently as a "Hymn to the Logos"—Philo Judaeus, whom we have already met, wrote extensively about the Logos—and was then adapted for an introduction here. Scholars have noted that, after using the Logos theme in this way, the author or editors of John never refer to it again throughout the rest of the account. But what is important for our study is that the real meaning of the Word being made flesh is that it refers to the Christ or divine presence incarnated in the life and heart of every one of us. The huge failure of the Church down the ages to grasp this momentous truth and instead to have supplanted it with a literal reading that has restricted it to one particular individual—a historical Jesus—has in the process robbed all the rest of humanity of the awareness of its divinity.

- This Gospel, often designated by scholars simply as the Fourth Gospel, has no parables.

- There is no Transfiguration or Ascension of Jesus.

- There are—unlike, for example, in Mark, where as we have seen they abound—no exorcisms of demons or evil spirits.

- There is no mention of Gehenna, Hades or "hell."

- The style of Jesus' teaching, his utterances, is 180 degrees different from the Synoptic tradition. Readers have to sample a couple of chapters of Luke, Matthew or Mark and then read John to catch the full significance of this contrast for themselves. In the former, Jesus is made to speak for the most part in short, pithy aphorisms, apart from the parables. This closely resembles the style of that much earlier work, the Gospel of Thomas, or the hypothetical sayings source Q (if it really existed). In John, however, Jesus delivers lengthy, spiralling discourses in the style of contemporary Hellenistic orators. To be utterly candid, even back in my student days in seminary, I have always found many of these to be ponderously self-conscious and at times, dare one confess it, more than a little repetitive and even tedious. Think about it for a moment. Anyone who made such involved and self-expanding soliloquies today would find himself or herself either being ignored

entirely or in danger of becoming the object of ridicule and
scorn.

- There are miracles in John, but they are presented in a very
precise, edited and schematic way. The author or redactor
calls them "signs" (*semeia* in Greek, the same word root from
which our word *semantics* comes) because they point to the
power and glory of the indwelling Christos. They are seven in
number, beginning with the changing of water into wine and
concluding with the raising of Lazarus from the dead.[1] It has
been suggested that John chose seven to carry on the notion
mooted by the opening words of the Gospel—"In the beginning . . ."—of a second Genesis or recapitulation of divine
action; the seven "signs" would then echo the seven days of
Creation. However, one thing is certain: the number seven
was a sacred number absolutely fundamental to the whole
building up of the universe. There were seven stars for each
of several major constellations important in the ancient astronomical theology (Orion, the Great Bear or Big Dipper,
and many others); there were seven notes to the scale in
music, seven colours in the spectrum, and much more. In the
iconography of early Christianity the infant Jesus is portrayed
in the Virgin's arms or in her womb surrounded by seven
doves symbolizing the Holy Spirit. There seemed to the
ancient sages to be a law that the Holy Spirit, or a divine, working efficacy of spirit in matter, must always fall into the sevenfold segmentation that force inevitably undergoes when it
energizes matter. Seven, in short, spelled out a dynamic perfection. Each of the "signs" in John, as we have seen in the chapters on miracles and healings, speaks in eloquent allegory of
the power of the Christ within us to provoke divine ferment of
soul, to turn the water of life into wine, to heal our sicknesses
by making our inner "lameness" fit to walk again, by feeding

us with the "bread" of the divine presence, and by opening our eyes so that we may truly see the fullness and beauty of our real nature, the path ahead and the needs of those all around us. Finally, this power will ever raise us from our spiritual "death" to newness of life (the Lazarus story) and one day will raise us up in the Resurrection to the life of the age to come.

- The chronology is quite different. As already pointed out, John makes it a three-year public ministry rather than the roughly one year of the Synoptics. Also, he places the cleansing of the temple right at the outset of the ministry instead of immediately before the betrayal and Crucifixion, i.e., at the end. Furthermore, John gives a totally different time sequence for the betrayal, the trials and the Crucifixion. He moves it all one day ahead, presumably for the symbolism of synchronizing the killing of the lambs for the Passover with the night of Jesus' arrest.

- Finally, while there is more, it is enough to add here that, curiously enough, John entirely omits the institution of the Last Supper. Leonardo da Vinci did not get his inspiration for his famous painting from John's stylus or pen. Instead, on that final night, John has something unique inserted in his narrative, the story of Jesus' washing of the disciples' feet. The symbolism of that very moving passage needs little comment here. It is a parable of how in Christly love we are to behave towards one another. As Albert Einstein once said, ultimately we are here to serve each other and the common good.

For more on the distinctiveness of John's Gospel and especially on its similarities to the Gnostic gospels found at Nag Hammadi in 1945, see the Gospel of John in Barnstone and Meyer's *The Gnostic Bible*.

APPENDIX B

Mystical Parallels between the Gospels and the Vedic Scriptures

Elsewhere I have endeavoured to set out the close parallels between Osiris/Horus of Egypt and the mythical story of Jesus. But it is of critical importance to establish an even wider basis for this kind of religious understanding by looking at some parallel ideas from the ancient East itself.

The Upanishads— "The Breath of the Eternal"

Many years ago, as a student at Oxford, I came across a copy of the Upanishads, known to India for untold ages as *The Breath of the Eternal*. These storied ancient accounts of mystical revelations to the ancient Rishis of the Himalayas made an indelible impression upon me with their profundity of spiritual insights and with their astounding similarity at so many points to the Christianity I was studying in preparation for the Anglican priesthood. They spoke movingly of the supreme God, Brahman, as "the ancient, effulgent being, the indwelling Spirit, deep-hidden in the lotus of the heart . . ."[1]

They spoke also of the true Self within us as none other than the one, as the Book of Acts has it, "in whom we live and move and have our being." Time and again as I read the Upanishads verses such as the following would literally jump out at me, since they described so vividly the same reality I was finding in the New Testament. For example, "The highest knowledge, the knowledge of Brahman, having drunk of which one never thirsts . . ." closely parallels Jesus' words in chapter 4 of John about how "those who drink of the water that I will give them will never be thirsty."[2] Jesus, who in the Gospels represents the Christ within each of us, says, "I am the light of the world." In the opening or prologue of John's Gospel he is called "the true light, which enlightens everyone." Hear, then, the Upanishads as Brahman, who dwells in every heart as the Atman or true Self (corresponding to the Christian's Christ within), is addressed as follows:

Thou alone art—thou the Light
Imperishable, adorable;
Great glory is thy name.
No one is there beside thee,
No one is equal to thee.[3]

and these Sutras or sayings:

- "The secret of immortality is to be found in purification of the heart, in meditation, in realization of the identity of the Self within and Brahman without. For immortality is union with God."[4] Jesus said in John: "I and the father are one."

- "Smaller than the smallest, greater than the greatest, this Self forever dwells within the hearts of all . . . the Self is not known through study of the Scriptures nor through subtlety of the intellect, nor through much learning; but by him [or her] who longs for him is he known. Verily unto him does the Self reveal his true being . . . Know that the Self is the rider, and the body the chariot; that the intellect is the charioteer, and the mind the reins . . . Like the sharp edge of a razor, the sages say, is the path. Narrow it is and difficult to tread!"[5] In the Sermon on the Mount in Matthew, Jesus says: "For the gate is narrow and the road is hard that leads to life . . ."

- Paul says, "If you sow to your own flesh [live the life of the animal self], you will reap corruption from the flesh; but if you sow to the Spirit, you will reap eternal life from the Spirit."[6] Compare that with the following from the Upanishads: "Fools follow the desires of the flesh and fall into the snare of all-encompassing death; but the wise, knowing the Self as eternal, seek not the things that pass away."[7]

- The New Testament says that perfect love casts out fear. Here's the Vedic or Hindu version of that: "He who knows that the individual soul . . . is the Self—ever present within, lord of time, past and future—casts out all fear. For this Self is the immortal Self."[8]

- In a saying that is almost an identical replica of a saying from the Gospel of Thomas, the ancient Vedic sage says: "What is within us is also without. What is without is also within." And speaking of the Self, he says also: "He is the lord of time, past and future, the same today and tomorrow."[9] In the New Testament's Hebrews it says: "Jesus Christ, the same yesterday, today, and forever."

- In the Gospels, Jesus says: "Seek and ye shall find." The Upanishads say: "But by him who longs for him is he known. Verily
  unto him does the Self [God within] reveal his true being."[10]

- In the Gospels, Jesus says: "In this world you will have tribu-
  lations. Fear not, I have overcome the world." In the Upanishads, the divine Self says: "I am life immortal! I overcome
  the world . . . Those who know me achieve Reality."[11]

The Bhagavad-Gita— "The Song of God"

Inspired and thrilled as I was by this, to me, new body of revealed
scripture, there was an even greater surprise and treasure store
of spiritual nourishment ahead. One day many years later, while
on assignment in Rome at a synod of bishops for the *Toronto Star*,
I wandered into a bookstore on the Corso and found a slim
paperback volume titled *The Song of God, The Bhagavad-Gita*. Published by the Vedanta Society of Southern California in 1948, it
had a fascinating introduction by one of my favourite novelists
at that time, Aldous Huxley. His opening essay on the Perennial
Philosophy was alone more than worth the price of the book.

The Perennial Philosophy

The understanding or philosophy there described by Huxley has
long been one of my deepest convictions, after a lifetime devoted
to the study and communication of spiritual and religious truths
and values. Just as there is a "monomyth" underlying all other
mythologies, so too there is a "perennial philosophy" behind all
the major faiths. Grasping it is, I believe, of urgent importance to
global harmony. There are, he says, four fundamental doctrines
at the core.

First: The phenomenal world of matter and of individualized consciousness—the world of things and animals and people and everything else—is the manifestation of "a Divine Ground or essence within which all partial realities have their being, and apart from which they would be non-existent." All things emanate or flow from this one Source of being.

Second: "Human beings are capable not merely of knowing *about* this Divine Ground by inference; they can also realize its existence by a direct intuition, superior to discursive or ordinary reasoning. This immediate knowledge unites the knower with that which is known." This is the kind of knowing of which the early Gnostics spoke and wrote.

Third: Humans possess a twofold nature, a phenomenal ego and an eternal Self, which is the inner person, the Spirit, "the spark of divinity within the soul." It is possible for a person, if he or she so desires, "to identify himself or herself with this inner spirit and therefore with the Divine Ground, which is of the same or like nature with the Spirit." I discuss techniques for learning to do this in *Finding the Still Point*.

Fourth: Human life on earth "has only one end and purpose: to identify one's self with the eternal Self [in Christian terms, the Christ within] and so to come to unitive knowledge of the Divine Ground."

As Huxley goes on to point out, these and similar ideas are wholly compatible with Christianity and indeed have always been in play by most Roman Catholic, Orthodox and Protestant mystics when describing or outlining a theology to fit facts observed by super- or non-rational intuitive awareness. He cites as paramount examples the two Christian mystics Meister Eckhart

(1260–1327) and John of Ruysbroeck (1293–1381). Both men
held that there is an "Abyss of Godhead" or, as I call it, "the God
beyond God" underlying the Christian Trinity, just as Brahman
underlies the Hindu Trinity of Brahma, Vishnu and Shiva.

> *"Part of myself is the God within every creature."*
> — SRI KRISHNA, *The Bhagavad-Gita*

After reading about the Perennial Philosophy, I went on to read
the brief essay at the back of *The Song of God*, by Louis Fischer,
about the impact of the Bhagavad-Gita on the life and work of
Mahatma Gandhi, and how he compared it in many ways to the
Sermon on the Mount and other Gospel sayings. I was fully hooked
and entranced. Gandhi had not read the Gita until 1888–89, during his second year as a law student in London. It had an enormous impact upon him, which remained throughout his whole
life. Much later, in his weekly magazine *Young India*, on August 6,
1925, he wrote the following: "When doubts haunt me, when
disappointments stare me in the face, and I see not one ray of hope
on the horizon, I turn to the *Bhagavad-Gita*, and find a verse to
comfort me; and I immediately begin to smile in the midst of over-
whelming sorrow." His secretary over many years, Mahadev Desai,
has testified that every moment of Gandhi's life was a conscious effort to live the message of the Gita. He called it "his spiritual reference book."[12] He also read daily from the Sermon on the Mount.

The Gita is a poem of some seven hundred stanzas, originally
written in Sanskrit. I believe it should be read by everyone seriously concerned with leading a spiritual life. Every minister-
to-be should be compelled to read it as an integral part of preparation for a life devoted to what was once called "the cure [care]
of souls."

While it takes the form of a discourse between the distinguished warrior Arjuna and his charioteer Sri, or Lord, Krishna,

"the Hindu Christ," on a high ground between two opposing armies on the very eve of battle, Gandhi (and many others since, including myself) understood it as an allegory. The "battlefield" is life itself, and the struggle is that between the lower impulses of our animal nature, together with the forces outside us that oppose our higher development, and Krishna or the Christ Spirit within us, which constitutes the true, divine Self. It is not necessary to believe in reincarnation to be illumined and challenged by the Gita, but it should be said that the doctrine is very much a part of it, and the Indian disciple's highest reward in following it is to be so firmly united with God after death that he need never return again to the cycle of rebirth. Gandhi himself expressed the hope more than once during his life not to have to be born anew. Significantly, in Buddhism there is the belief that some may become truly enlightened "saints" or Bodhisattvas, who choose to be reborn so that they can return to earth and help others attain liberation also.

Jesus and Krishna

I believe it is important at this point for you to see for yourself how striking the parallels between Krishna and Jesus Christ really are.[13] These correspondences are with sayings from each of the Gospels, but the most potent from the Christian perspective are those found in the Fourth Gospel, that of John.

Jesus' words in chapter 14 of John, "I am the way, and the truth, and the life," are well known, but relatively few Christians have ever read where Krishna says to Arjuna:

> For I am Brahman
> Within this body,
> Life Immortal
> That shall not perish:

I am the Truth
And the Joy forever.[14]

Churchgoers have often heard the lesson from the Bible where Jesus says: "I am the same yesterday, today and forever"; and also, "I am alpha and omega, the beginning and the end" (of the alphabet). But most have not heard these words from the Bhagavad-Gita: "In the alphabet, I am the A: among compounds, the copulative; I am time without end; I am the sustainer: my face is everywhere."[15]

Conservative Christians are fond of pointing to the great "I am" statements made by Jesus in John's Gospel as "proof" that he was the unique Son of God—such sayings as "I am the way, and the truth, and the life," already referred to, "I am the door" (to the sheepfold of the faithful), "I am the light of the world," "I am the bread of life," "I am the vine, you are the branches" and "I and the Father are one." However, the claim of many Christian apologists that other religious figures never dared to speak like this is abundantly refuted by the facts. Inscriptions have been found in several places around the Mediterranean basin in which the Egyptian goddess Isis makes a series of "I am" claims similar to those of her son, Horus. But the "I am" statements of Krishna in the Bhagavad-Gita are more numerous and more powerful in scope even than those assigned to Jesus himself. Here are some:

- "I am the Atman [divine presence] that dwells in the heart of every mortal creature: I am the beginning, the life-span and the end of all."[16]

- "I am Vishnu [second person of the Hindu Trinity of Brahma, Shiva and Vishnu]: I am the radiant sun among the light-givers."[17]

- "I am Indra, king of heaven: of sense organs, I am the mind: I am consciousness in the living."[18]

- "I am Shiva: I am the Lord of all riches: I am the Spirit of fire."[19]

- "I am the knowledge of things spiritual: I am the logic of those who debate."[20]

- "Oh Arjuna, I am the divine seed of all lives. In this world, nothing animate or inanimate exists without me. There is no limit to my manifestations, nor can they be numbered . . ."[21]

Clearly here, in chapter 11 of the Gita, as Krishna fully shows forth the true glory of his being, i.e., is transfigured, like Jesus, for his disciples' instruction, what is being said is that he is that divine essence by which the cosmos was made and by which it all coheres and lives. One is instantly reminded of what the author of the Letter to the Colossians says in the very first chapter, speaking of the exalted Christ principle or energy: "He is the image of the invisible God, the firstborn of all creation; for in him all things . . . were created . . . all things have been created through him and for him. He himself is before all things, and in him all things hold together."[22]

One is reminded as well of the often-quoted saying from the Gospel of Thomas: "Yeshua said,

I am the light over all things.
I am all.
From me all has come forth,
and to me all has reached.
Split a piece of wood.
I am there.

Lift up the stone
and you will find me there."²³

Conclusion

Finally, then, in completing this mini-review of the intimate parallels between ancient Vedic or Hindu wisdom and the Christian
texts, we read from an ancient scripture known as the Rik Veda:
"In the beginning was Brahman, with whom was the Word; and
the Word was truly the supreme Brahman." It seems almost word
for word a translation of the first verse of John's Gospel. Indeed,
some scholars believe the philosophy behind the concept of the
Logos, or Word, may be traced in various forms and modifica-
tions down from the ancient Hindu scriptures, through the teachings of Plato and the Stoics, to Philo of Alexandria, in Egypt, to
the author of the Johannine Prologue.²⁴ This is not an attempt to
argue for complete dependence of the Greek thinking upon Vedic
tradition, for there is also a "word of God" theology to be found in
ancient Egyptian thought as well. The point is that we are dealing
here with profound, universal, archetypal ideas common to many
different cultures and times. We appear to be "wired" for them by
the divine Source of all that is.

APPENDIX C

The Egyptian Theological
and Philosophical Roots
of Christianity

This section is specifically for those of a scholarly bent, and who wanted more about Egypt after reading *The Pagan Christ*.

The Legacy of Egypt

In an essay entitled "Mystery, Myth, and Magic," A. A. Barb points out that in Egyptian theology there are "trinities of gods which are at one and the same time three distinct persons."[1] This, he correctly observes, is "a concept which for the logic of Western Christianity is still an inaccessible, if accepted, mystery." At the same time, he says, we find many expressions that definitely sound "monotheistic."

Barb then cites the Roman historian Ammianus Marcellinus as an authority for ancient Egypt as the "cradle" of ancient religion.[2] The fourth-century writer describes how Pythagoras, Anaxagoras, Solon and Plato all visited Egypt and learned much of their wisdom from the priests there. Herodotus, of course, much earlier testifies also to this. In addition Barb states: "The Isis cult and its esoteric mysteries very soon conquered the ancient Graeco-Roman world."

On Jesus and Horus, he has this to say: "It can hardly be doubted that the innumerable figures of the enthroned Isis nursing her son Horus prepared the way for . . . the later images of the virgin Mary, just as occasionally we find on early Christian monuments Horus, the young sun-god and conqueror of evil, identified with Christ."[3]

When it comes to the widespread first-century cult of Serapis, Barb explains: "Serapis is fundamentally Osiris/Horus . . . and he serves as the expression of monotheistic tendencies: [there is] one god, Serapis," it says on numerous monuments in Greek.[4]

Barb says, "We find in Egypt large numbers of . . . stelae (stone pillars) of Horus, reliefs showing the young sun-god Horus holding serpents, scorpions, lions . . . and treading down two crocodiles under his feet."[5] This is definitely a "saviour" figure with clear connections to Christianity.

In the Renaissance, there was great interest in Osiris (and hence Isis and Horus), Barb says. "Plutarch's story of the suffering god, unjustly killed, his resurrection as 'king of the dead' and 'saviour,' and his relationship with his loving wife Isis and his son Horus contained a profusion of elements which were considered mythical anticipations of the Christian passion."[6]

Barb adds that Diodorus's account of all of this inspired the scenes from the life of Osiris that were painted by Pintoricchio as ceiling decorations for the Borgia Apartments of the Vatican Palace, where privileged visitors can still see them today. I was once shown them by a bishop whose major function at the Vatican was safeguarding sacred relics, pieces of which were sent out to every new church in the Roman Catholic world to be kept in a compartment in the altar.

The Black Madonna

On June 11, 1979, *Time* magazine reported on Pope John Paul II's visit to Poland's holiest shrine, the Black Madonna icon of Czestochowa. He made several return visits there during his lengthy pontificate. The Polish Catholic Church encourages its members to pray to this Black Madonna every morning before rising.

What is important here is that statues and paintings of the Egyptian goddess Isis with her child Horus in her arms were the prototypical madonna and child. They were frequently renamed Mary and Jesus when Europe was forcibly Christianized. The worship of Isis and Horus was, as we know, very popular in ancient Rome, and Roman legions carried this madonna figure all over Europe, where shrines were set up for her. They were considered so holy and venerable that the figures of black Isis holding her black child became the black madonnas that still today are in the holiest Marian shrines. There are dozens of black madonnas in Russia (see *Russian Icons* by Vladimir Ivanov), Germany, Poland, Italy, Spain, Belgium, Portugal and France.

In some cases iconoclasts wishing to destroy traces of the original Theotokas or Mother of God have altered the African features to look more European. Often the black figures were replaced with white ones but the originals were not destroyed, just hidden in church crypts and elsewhere. In the case of the Black Madonna of Czestochowa, the official church reason that she and her child are black is because of centuries of soot from votive candles of the faithful.

Theologian Karl W. Luckert

An important source for confirmation of the thesis that Christianity owes most of its substance to ancient Egyptian theology—quite apart from the conclusions of Gerald Massey and Alvin

Boyd Kuhn as outlined in *The Pagan Christ*—is the 1991 book by
Karl W. Luckert, Ph.D. (Chicago), *Egyptian Light and Hebrew
Fire*.[7] Luckert, an expert on the history of religions, is a professor
emeritus at Missouri State University. The following citations are
from this 367-page work. (It may be helpful to provide a brief
explanation of three terms: *emanationalism* is the flowing forth
of the Divine from one original source; *ontology* is the branch of
metaphysics dealing with being or ultimate reality; *soteriology* is
the doctrine of salvation.)

- Chapter 19, titled "Bequest of the Mother Religion," begins
  with a reference to a verse from Hosea also quoted in *The
  Pagan Christ*: "Out of Egypt have I called my son." Noting
  that this sentence from Hosea 11:1 was quoted in Matthew
  2:13–15 to support the story about the flight of the Holy
  Family into Egypt, Luckert asks: "Has this brief addendum
  to the nativity tradition of Christ Jesus been intended to hint
  at the broader nativity of Christian theology in Egypt? Did
  some of the first Christians . . . sense the Egyptian direction into which their theologizing tended to move?" He goes
  on to say that a turning point, an "Exodus in reverse from
  Palestine to Egypt," is implied even in the surface meaning
  of the story. "Subsequently, there in Egypt . . . Isis as the
  Egyptian divine madonna with her Horus child as a representative of the Ennedean 'Tefnut-Nut-Isis' lineage, passed
  on her mantle to the unsuspecting mother of Jesus."[8]

- Luckert notes the well-known fact that, with few exceptions, Paul in his letters drops all mention of the kingdom
  of God theology of the Gospels, preferring a form of "mysticism" instead. He says that this provided Christians with
  an opportunity to participate more intimately in the death
  and Resurrection of Christ, and "*in Christianized Egyptian*

soteriology. The kerygma of god having begotten a son, of that son having been born, having died, risen, and ascended to the Father is what has an encouraging resonance from the broad spectrum of ancient Egyptian ontology" (my emphasis).[9] Luckert develops Paul's "Christian Egyptianness" at considerable length.[10] His theology, he argues, is a "spin-off from Egyptian theology." What is more, this history of religions expert says that "there is no better summary of ancient orthodox Egyptian theology than the Prologue to the Gospel of John: 'In the beginning was the Word . . .'" Again he says that "the total pattern of divine activity"—of God's creation by Logos, of God begetting his Son, and his presentation of eternal life to wayward humankind—"are Egyptian soteriology throughout."[11]

- Furthermore, in this scholar's view, as the Holy Roman Empire later evolved, Christendom's reliance on proven ancient Egyptian theological structures became even more obvious. "The Egyptian theological heritage, as philosophized by Neoplatonism, provided the emerging Christian Church organization and the Holy Roman Empire with much-needed doctrinal structure and ontological substance." Following the lead of earlier Alexandrian theologians (Origen, Clement and Dionysius the Great), Augustine of Hippo, he says, infused Egyptian ontology into Christian soteriology "to a point where its presence no longer can be overlooked."[12] In fact, according to Luckert, the entire struggle to build a comprehensive Christian theology in the first five centuries "in Christology, Mariology, and numenology all demonstrate the intrusion of ancient Egyptian emanationalism among Mediterranean peoples . . ."[13] Thus, in short, he concludes that Egypt provided "Christendom's mother religion." For Egypt, Christ had come to be the saviour, "the new Horus-Osiris, expressly for all the people" and not just for the ruling elite. [14]

- On Gnosticism: (Here we remember Elaine Pagels's dictum about how we are left only with what the winners in that ancient struggle have to say about events and beliefs.) Luckert writes that it is no longer necessary to define Gnosticism vaguely as a general milieu of thought or "syncretism" that somehow, coming from nowhere, permeated the Greco-Roman mixture of Hellenistic culture. He says that Gnosticism's root notions hereby reveal themselves not merely as having belonged to a larger family of Near Eastern religions; *we now know that ancient Egyptian religion was the matriarch of that family*" (my emphasis). By the way, in the past, scholars such as Kurt Rudolph in 1669 (*Unparteiische Ketzer und Kirchen-historie*) listed a host of tributaries and multiple syncretisms behind Gnosticism—traits of Jewish monotheism, Jewish apocalyptic, Qumran, Jewish Wisdom teaching, Jewish skepticism, Iranian Zoroastrian ideas, Greek philosophical enlightenment, the Hermetica, Hellenistic Mystery Religions, Orphism, Greco-Roman syncretism, individualism and esoterism, spiritualization, economic conditions, the spread of oriental cults (Cybele, Isis, the unconquered sun god, Mithras, etc.). But, Luckert comments, "it seems remarkable that the primary stream, ancient Egyptian orthodoxy, has not yet been recognized among these tributaries. *Indeed that stream is so wide it can easily be mistaken for the ocean itself*" (my emphasis). [15]

- Luckert, in a section titled "Egyptian Christianity," notes how Helmut Koester (*History and Literature of Early Christianity*) remarks upon the fact that early Christian writings in Egypt were destroyed because the growing orthodox party deemed them "heretical." He goes on to say that, fortunately for historians, copies of some of these early "heretical" Egyptian documents have since come to light. "The Nag Hammadi library (discovered 1945 in Upper Egypt) contains a number of them. . . . As a result of the new oblique 'Egyptian light' streaming from those directions much of traditional Christian theology stands better illuminated as well," he believes. "The distances between ancient Egypt, Christendom, and gnostic doctrines have been lessened in the process."[16] Significantly, Dr. Luckert argues that the Nag Hammadi gospels and other such writings must all now be re-examined in the light of "possible Egyptian antecedents." He writes: "In addition to some specific Nag Hammadi texts that allude *directly* to Egypt—for example, *On the Origin of the World*, *The Exegesis on the Soul*, *The Gospel of the Egyptians*, *The Thunder*, *Perfect Mind*, *Asclepius*, and *Discourse on the Eighth and Ninth*—at least another dozen or so treatises contained in this 'gnostic' library *clearly are indebted to ancient Egyptian theology*" (my emphasis).[17]

- While appreciative of Hans Jonas's *The Gnostic Religion* (Boston, 1963), Luckert is critical of Jonas's insistence that Gnosticism was marked by a "radical dualism." Specifically, Luckert quotes the famous saying of the Christian Gnostic—later deemed heretical—Valentinus, where he states: "What liberates us is the knowledge of who we were, what we became, where we were, whereinto we have been thrown, whereto we speed, wherefrom we are redeemed; what birth is, and what rebirth."[18] Luckert in my view rightly contends that this bit of Gnostic advice reveals to us no truly "dualistic" worries on the part of its author. "That person was concerned merely with getting from here to there within a rationally coherent dimension of reality."[19]

This, it should be said, was a specifically Egyptian mode of thought regarding the Incarnation of spirit or the Divine in every human being.

Importantly, Luckert maintains that ancient Egyptian soteri-ology—the theology of salvation—was genuinely monistic and can best be expressed in Kurt Rudolph's summary, in *Gnosis*, of the central myth of Gnosticism: "the idea of the presence in man of a divine 'spark' . . . which has proceeded from the divine world and has fallen into this world of destiny, birth and death, and which must be reawakened through its own divine counter-part in order to be finally restored."[20] Rudolph thus, in Luckert's view, has beautifully summed up "the basic emanational unity of ancient Heliopolitan [Egyptian sun-god worship] religion in gnostic teachings."[21]

- Luckert then moves to the subject of Isis. He states unequiv-ocally that Isis, as mother of Horus and a member of the He-liopolitan Ennead (the nine great deities), "represented divine womanhood in Egypt like no other goddess." She was the goddess closest to humankind and was, in some tradi-tions, self-sufficient even in conceiving and giving Horus birth.[22] Regarding the fact that Gnostics in general, includ-ing Christian Gnostics, reserved their most strenuous objec-tions to the emerging orthodoxy for the literal proclamation of Christ's death and not his Resurrection, Luckert has this to say: "The resurrection of an incarnate God posed no prob-lem to minds who already reasoned on the basis of orthodox Egyptian theology. Such resurrection (i.e. a spiritual event) was self-evident and a matter of common sense."

Finally, for an overall appreciation of the extent to which the Isis–Osiris–Horus cult was a presence everywhere throughout the ancient Mediterranean world—including Palestine and at Sepphoris, a Roman city about three miles from Nazareth where daily worship was conducted to the Egyptian deities—see *Jesus the Egyptian* by Richard A. Gabriel.

While Dr. Luckert strongly confirms that Egyptian theology had a profound effect upon early Christian beliefs and rituals, nevertheless he and I disagree over the historicity of Jesus. He holds a more traditional view.

Egyptologist Erik Hornung

Lest anyone think that Dr. Luckert is a lone voice, here are some relevant observations by one of the world's leading Egyptologists today, the German scholar Erik Hornung, in his latest book *The Secret Lore of Egypt and Its Impact on the West*.

- On Gnosticism: "With its origins at least in part on Egyptian soil—Simon Magus, one of its founding fathers, was supposed to have acquired his learning in Egypt—and with Alexandria as one of its most important centres—it also incorporated concepts from Pharaonic Egypt."[23]

- "Especially well-known, and cited by a number of writers, including Augustine, is the passage in the Asclepius in which Egypt is praised as the 'temple of the world' . . ."[24]

- "In the Christian Gnosis, Jesus became a messenger and saviour from the realm of light," i.e., the sun.[25]

- "There was an obvious analogy between the Horus child and the baby Jesus and the care they received from their sacred mothers; long before Christianity, Isis [as mother of Horus] had borne the epithet 'Mother of God.'"[26]

- "Notwithstanding its superficial rejection of everything pagan, early Christianity was deeply indebted to ancient Egypt. In particular, the lively picture of the Egyptian afterlife left traces in Christian texts . . . the descensus (into Hades or hell) by Jesus which played *no role in the early church* was adopted into the official Credo (creed) after 359 thanks to apocryphal legends that again involved Egypt. Christ became the sun in the realm of the dead, for his descent into the netherworld had its ultimate precursor in the nightly journey of the ancient Egyptian sun God Re . . ."[27] "The Christian slayer of the dragon had its model in the triumph of Horus over Seth, and there was a smooth transition from the image of the nursing Isis, Isis lactans, to that of Maria lactans. The miraculous birth of Jesus could be viewed as analogous to that of Horus, whom Isis conceived posthumously from Osiris, and Mary was closely associated with Isis by many other shared characteristics."[28]

GLOSSARY

Allegory

A word, based upon two Greek words, meaning "to say one thing by means of another."

Metaphor

A figure of speech that comes from two Greek words meaning "beyond" and "to carry." A metaphor carries you beyond the ordinary meaning to fresh connotations.

Myth

A sacred story that is fictional in respect to history but eternal in the meaning it contains.

Parable

A fictional story in which one situation is compared to another. It comes from two Greek words meaning "alongside" and "to throw" or "to put." Parables usually have one key point to make, whereas allegories may touch upon many.

Notes

Except where otherwise indicated, all Biblical quotations are from the New Revised Standard Version.

All epigraphs from the Gospel of Thomas are taken from *The Gnostic Bible*.

1: OUR JOURNEY BEGINS

1. Carl Jung, *The Undiscovered Self* (Princeton, NJ: Princeton University Press, 1990), 119.

2. Harold Bloom, *Jesus and Yahweh—The Names Divine* (New York: Riverhead Books, 2005), 19.

3. Ibid., 22.

4. Ibid., 19.

5. See Robert M. Price, *Deconstructing Jesus* (New York: Prometheus Books, 2000).

2: THE MYTH AND YOU

1. Egypt (c. 150–215), *Stromateis* 6.15.126.

2. See Bart Ehrman, *Lost Christianities* (San Francisco: HarperCollins, 2005).

3. Eusebius lived c. 260–c. 340 CE; *Ecclesiastical History* 2:17.

4. *Anacalypsis* 1:747. See also Timothy Freke and Peter Gandy, *The Jesus Mysteries: Was the "Original Jesus" a Pagan God?* (New York: Random House, 1999), 184–88.

5. The Reverend Dr. Giles, in *Hebrew and Christian Records* vol. II, page 86 (London, 1877), says that Emperor Hadrian, who reigned 117–138 CE,

recorded that he could see no difference between Christians and wor-
shippers, also called Therapeutae, of the ancient Egyptian god Serapis.
In a letter to the Consul Servianus, Hadrian reportedly says: "There are
[in Egypt] Christians who worship Serapis and devoted to Serapis are
those who call themselves 'Bishops of Christ.'" I was unable, however,
to confirm the authenticity of the letter for myself. What is certain is
that the term *Christos* translated the Hebrew word for "Messiah" or
"anointed" and *Iesous* translated the Hebrew for "Joshua" in the Septuagint over two hundred years before the first century CE.

6. Tom Harpur, *Living Waters* (Toronto: Thomas Allen, 2006), 86–88.

7. See Tom Harpur, *The Pagan Christ* (Toronto: Thomas Allen, 2004), ch. 9.

8. For a modern collection and translation of all of the others, and related
    literature, see Willis Barnstone and Marvin Meyer, eds., *The Gnostic Bible:
    Gnostic Texts of Mystical Wisdom* (Boston: Shambhala Publications, 2003).

9. Goulder's critique first appeared in *The Journal of Biblical Literature* 115
    (1996). It can be downloaded from the Internet.

10. See www.sacredtexts.com/cla/pr/prc10/htm.

11. See G.A. Wells, *Did Jesus Exist?* (London: Pemberton, 1986), 29ff.; and
    for fuller treatment of the 1 Cor. 15 passage about the Resurrection,
    see Wells, 32–34. It simply does not agree with the accounts in the
    Gospels.

12. Rom. 1:3.

13. Rom. 9:5 and 15:12.

14. Rom. 12:3.

15. Rom. 8:26.

16. 1 Cor. 1:22.

17. Matt. 28:19 and 1 Cor. 1:17.

18. 1 Cor. 7.

19. 1 Cor. 2:8.

20. Gal. 1:19 and 1 Cor. 9:5.

21. See Ephesians 1:9 where the writer, probably a follower of Paul, speaks
    of the "mystery of his will" as what has been made known to the Chris-
    tian community. In Ephesians 3:10 we read that there are things in
    heavenly places—"principalities and powers"—that need to be recon-
    ciled. See Col. 1:25–26.

22. ***Words of the Lord quoted by Paul:*** 1 Corinthians 11:23–25 describes the institution of the Lord's Supper. Since this happened after Jesus' death and Resurrection, clearly Paul is talking about a revelation directly "from the Lord"—i.e., some supernatural or visionary experience. But there are many un-Pauline words in the verses. These have thus suggested to scholars that this is a tradition handed on to Paul as a "cult-legend" already in the Christian community. The drinking of blood would have been anathema to Orthodox Jews and seems to belong to a wholly pagan origin. Freke and Gandy in *The Jesus Mysteries* argue that the passage is in fact a Mystery Religion formula. Note also that Paul's "do this in remembrance of me" is wholly missing from the Gospel accounts. "To suggest that an ordinance of such importance was made by Jesus but was forgotten by the Evangelists is tantamount to abandoning all confidence in the gospels," Wells concludes. A relevant context for the Eucharist, or Lord's Supper, is provided by a range of the Mystery Religions, especially the celebrations in the cult of Mithras.

  The Lord's "command" for preachers to get support: 1 Corinthians 9:14—As Bultmann has pointed out with respect to the sayings on marriage and on ministerial finances, these were customs becoming standard in the early community and they were most likely secured by being attached to the Lord's name. Wells comments: "It was the risen (not the earthly) Jesus who proclaimed these rules to his community." We know that there were many Christian prophets who used the name of Christ even in the first person to "encourage, admonish, and censure" the early Christians. Thus, the earthly Jesus was made to say things only possible for the risen Christ. See, for example, Matthew 28:20: wherever two or three are gathered in my name "there am I in their midst." This presupposes a Jesus not limited by time or space, i.e. by history. He is a purely spiritual being.

3: THE VIRGIN BIRTH AND JESUS' CHILDHOOD

1. John Hick, ed., *The Myth of God Incarnate* (London: SCM Press, 1977), 89.
2. Matt. 1:1ff.
3. Luke 3:23–38.
4. This tradition is based upon two references in the Gospels, the earliest in Mark 6:3 and the other in Matthew 13:55.

5. In the King James Version and also the NRSV.

6. For discussion of the textual variants for Mark 6:3, see Bart Ehrman, *Misquoting Jesus* (San Francisco: HarperCollins, 2005), 203.

7. Joseph Campbell, *Thou Art That* (Novato, CA: New World Library, 2001), 63.

8. Sermons and Collations LXXXXVIII.

9. Campbell, *Thou Art That*, 29.

10. Luke 2:47.

11. See the chapter "Transformation."

12. 2 Cor. 3:18.

4: TRANSFORMATIVE STAGES IN THE JESUS STORY

1. Excerpts from Theodotus 78.2. Quoted in Karl W. Luckert, *Egyptian Light and Hebrew Fire* (Albany: State University of New York Press, 1991), 297.

2. Mark 1:14–15.

3. Luke 1:36.

4. Gen. 18:12.

5. John 3:30.

6. See the fuller discussion in my book *Finding the Still Point*.

7. Barnstone and Meyer, *The Gnostic Bible*, Gospel of Thomas Saying #10, 47.

8. Ibid., Saying #82, 64.

9. Wells, *Did Jesus Exist?*, 146ff.

10. In the Book of Acts, some angry Jews call Paul the "ringleader of the sect of the Nazoreans," that is, the Christians. (The King James Version uses the term Nazarenes.) Indeed, there is some evidence that there was a pre-Christian group of Jewish sectarians, most probably Essenes, by this same name. The word probably derives from the Hebrew *NZR*, meaning "a branch" and then "consecrated" or "separated off," i.e., by specific vows and lifestyle. For example, in Judges 13:7 the angel tells Samson's mother-to-be that he is to be dedicated or "holy to God from the womb." In verse 5 it says, "No razor is to come on his head, for the boy shall be a Nazirite to God from birth." The term "Nazorean,", as we know from Epiphanius, denoted at first a pre-Christian pious Jewish

sect similar to the Essenes, and then for a time it was used to describe Jewish Christians. For example, see Acts 24:5.

11. Lawrence H. Schiffman, *The Encyclopedia of the Dead Sea Scrolls* (New York: Oxford University Press, 2000), 2:605.

12. Harold Leidner, *The Fabrication of the Christ Myth* (Tampa, FL: Survey Books, 1999), 184–85.

13. See relevant articles on "Nazarene" and "Nazareth" in *The Anchor Bible Dictionary* (New York: Doubleday, 1992).

14. See Harpur, *Living Waters*, ch. 5.

15. Carl G. Jung, *Man and His Symbols* (New York: Dell Publishing, 1968), 75.

16. Lord Raglan, *The Hero: A Study in Tradition, Myth and Drama* (Mineola, NY: Dover, 2003), 215.

17. Ibid, 111.

18. See Deut. 8:3.

19. See Ps. 91:11, 12.

20. Deut. 6:16.

21. Compare Matt. 4:18–22 and Luke 5:11.

22. I am not arguing that there was no leader in the Jesus movement in Jerusalem called Peter. In the story, however, he is part of the larger myth. Paul writes in Galatians about once spending two weeks with him in Jerusalem but he never once referred to anything Peter told him about Jesus, his teachings, his miracles, his death or resurrection.

23. A form of oracle, see Lev. 8:8 and Exod. 25:30.

24. Barnstone and Meyer, *The Gnostic Bible*, 5.

25. To compare these various texts, see Matt. 21:1–22, Luke 19:28–38 and John 2:13–17.

26. For examples of this, see www.apologeticspress.org.

27. Megillah 29a–b.

28. The names Matthew, Mark, Luke and John were not originally given to the Gospels that later came to bear these names. The truth is, we do not really know for certain who wrote the Gospels in their present form.

29. Campbell, *Thou Art That*, 36–37.

30. See my discussion of hell and purgatory in *Life After Death*.

31. Campbell, *Thou Art That*, xx.

32. Freke and Gandy, *The Jesus Mysteries*, 52.

33. Professor Geering is the author of several books, including *Christian Faith at the Crossroads* (2001). In 1966 he published a highly controversial article on "The Resurrection of Jesus," and in 1967 another on "The Immortality of the Soul," which sparked a lengthy theological debate culminating in charges of heresy and "disturbing the peace of the Church" by the Presbyterian Church of New Zealand and a publicly televised trial. After two days of hearing evidence and Geering's defence, the Assembly's court decided that "no doctrinal error" had been proved. See also his 1998 article "How Did Jesus Become God and Why?" in *The Fourth Hour*, the magazine of the Jesus Seminar (September–October issue).

5: MIRACLES OF WHOLENESS

1. Origen, *Contra Celsum* 2:48.

2. Sarah Iles Johnson, *Religions of the Ancient World* (Cambridge, MA: Harvard University Press, 2004), 460.

3. See "leprosy" on Medline Plus, by the U.S. National Library Institute, on the Internet.

4. Matt. 8:28.

5. A short recap of the story: To appear important, a miller lied to the king that his daughter could spin straw into gold. The king called for the girl, shut her in a tower room with straw and a spinning wheel, and demanded that she spin the straw into gold by morning. Failure to do so would result in her execution. She had given up hope when a dwarf appeared and spun straw into gold for her in return for her necklace; then again the following night for her ring. But on the third night, the dwarf spun straw into gold for a promise that the girl's first-born child would become his. The king was so impressed that he married the miller's daughter, but when their first child was born, the dwarf returned to claim payment. The queen offered him all the wealth she had if she could keep the child. The dwarf refused, but finally agreed to give up his claim if the queen could guess his name in three days. At first she failed, but before the second night her messenger overheard the dwarf hopping about his fire and singing:

> "Today I brew, today I bake,
> And then the child away I'll take;
> For little deems my royal dame
> That Rumpelstiltskin is my name!"

When the dwarf came to the queen on the third day and she revealed his name, Rumpelstiltskin lost his bargain. In the Brothers Grimm version, he then tore himself apart in his rage.

6. See Freke and Gandy, *The Jesus Mysteries*, 41, and the references cited there, especially W. Burkert, *Ancient Mystery Cults* (Cambridge, MA: Harvard University Press, 1987).

7. In Matt. 12:24ff. and Luke 11:14ff.

8. John 9:1–34.

9. Mark 5:21ff.

10. 2 Cor. 4:6.

11. Irenaeus, *Adversus Haereses* [Against Heresies], Book 1, ch. 7.

6: NATURE MIRACLES

1. Joseph Campbell with Fraser Boa, *This Business of the Gods* (Caledon East, ON: Windrose Films, 1989), 39.

2. Matt. 14:22–33.

3. John 6:33.

4. Matt. 17:27.

5. Mark 9:2.

6. From the translation by the famous Greek writer/film director Michael Cacoyannis (New York: Penguin Books, 1982).

7: THE SERMON ON THE MOUNT

1. Anybody with time to spare can find contradictions of varying degrees of importance throughout the books of the Bible. Since there are still total literalists and Biblical "inerrancy" champions on all sides today, it may be helpful to point out just a few such problems relevant to the Sermon on the Mount. This list is merely a sample and not in any specific order of occurrence. In Matthew 5:5, meekness is praised, but Jesus in the Gospels is at times anything but meek himself. One can refer not only to the cleansing of the temple but to many passages in John's Gospel where he makes very strong claims for himself, for example John 10:30–33, and others where he denounces various groups in the strongest possible language. For example, Matthew 5:21–22 gives firm

teaching against being angry with a brother or sister, and saying "thou fool" to them makes one "liable to the hell of fire," yet in Matthew 23:17 Jesus calls the Pharisees "blind fools," and the entire chapter is taken up with some of the harshest insults ever uttered against another religious sect. In 23:33 we read: "You snakes, you brood of vipers! How can you escape being sentenced to hell?" So much, then, for "blessed are the merciful for they will receive mercy." In Luke 24:25, the risen Lord is made to call the two disciples on the road to Emmaus *anoetoi* in Greek, which means "foolish ones" or, more plainly, "fools." The NRSV translates: "Oh, how foolish you are . . ." In Matthew 11:20–24, whole cities are consigned to Hades, or hell in the King James Version, because of their lack of response to the miracles and preaching. In Matthew 5:9 the peacemakers are counted as blessed, but in 10:34 Jesus says, "Do not think that I have come to bring peace but a sword."

The U.S.-based Focus on the Family and most other American faith-initiative efforts to promote the well-being of family life seem utterly unaware that this saying about a sword is followed by some of the most seemingly anti-family sentiments ever expressed by anyone of note: "For I have come to set a man against his father, and a daughter against her mother, and a daughter-in-law against her mother-in-law, and one's foes will be members of one's own household." Matthew 5:17–18 says that not one tiniest stroke of a letter in the law will be changed or altered "until all is accomplished." Yet Jesus quite plainly broke the Jewish law on several occasions (see John 8:1–11, Mark 7:18–19) and in Mark 2:27–28 challenged even the law concerning the Sabbath itself, saying the Sabbath was made for humanity and not humankind for the Sabbath. In Matthew 21:19 he curses a fig tree for not bearing fruit even though it was not the right season for figs. This directly contradicts Deuteronomy 20:19–20, which prohibits injuring any tree that is fruit-bearing. And much, much more.

2. Celsus, "On the True Doctrine," in *A Discourse Against the Christians*, vii:i. See *Celsus on the True Doctrine*, trans. R.J. Hoffman (New York: Oxford University Press, 1987), 94.

3. For many years now scholars have argued that there is a sayings source behind the material that Matthew and Luke have in common but which is not found in Mark. Whole careers have been built and many doctorates decided on the basis of this hypothesis. However, the most recent scholarship is now challenging this entire concept. See especially the

article by Michael D. Goulder from the University of Birmingham, "Is Q a Juggernaut?" *Journal of Biblical Literature* 115 (1996), 667–81. It can be read online at www.ntgateway.com/Q/goulder.htm. Goulder states that Q is "now hardly defended in the University of Oxford."

4. *Wikipedia*, s.v. "Sermon on the Mount" (Interpretation), http://en. wikipedia.org/wiki/Sermon_on_the_mount. There are literally hundreds of scholarly books and articles on the subject. I recommend *Sermon on the Mount*, by Hans Dieter Betz, Minneapolis, Fortress Press, 1995; and *The Setting of the Sermon on the Mount* by W.D. Davies, Cambridge University Press, 1976.

5. The Didache, *c*. 100 CE, 1:3.

6. Matt. 5:29ff.

7. www.earlychristianwritings.com/didache.html.

8. Hans Kung in his 1984 book, *On Being a Christain* (Doubleday, New York), notes that traditional Catholic teaching has held a "two-class ethic." There was a righteousness based upon the Ten Commandments for the laity and a "higher righteousness" or "perfection" for a chosen few (pp. 244–247).

9. As Harper's Bible Commentary put it (Harper & Row, San Francisco, 1988), "When church and state entered into a partnership [with the conversion of Emperor Constantine] a double standard ethic evolved. Only monastic communities practised the absolute ethic of the Sermon on the Mount. Christians in the world were expected to live only according to the Decalogue [the Ten Commandments]" (p. 961).

10. Matt. 5:48.

8: THE PARABLES

1. Scholars of the New Testament are fond of pointing out that a parable differs from an allegory because in the former only one central point is being made by the story whereas in an allegory all the details have a symbolic reference. This is a valid distinction, but it is not always necessarily so. Some parables have various "layers" and not simply one single theme.

2. Harpur, *The Pagan Christ*, 127.

3. For a detailed examination of all the Biblical and other evidence for

universalism, the belief that God will ultimately bring everyone to "heaven" or full salvation, see Ken Vincent's *The Golden Thread, God's Promise of Universal Salvation.*

4. The account in Matthew is found in 13:1–9 and in Luke in 8:4–8.

5. According to Acts 17:28.

6. Barnstone and Meyer, *The Gnostic Bible.*

7. Chopra, *How to Know God,* 24.

8. Matt. 25:1–13.

9. Matt. 25:14–30.

10. This judgment scene is no doubt firmly based upon the stories and scenes of the final judgment most familiar to educated people all over the ancient Mediterranean world, those of the ancient Egyptians as depicted on tomb walls and in the various copies of *The Book of the Dead.*

11. Ralph Waldo Emerson, "Ode" (1857).

9: PALM SUNDAY

1. Matt. 21:12ff., Luke 19:45ff.

2. John 12:20ff.

3. Zech. 9:9.

4. 1 Cor. 13:12.

5. T. J. Thorburn, *The Mythical Interpretation of the Gospels* (New York: Scribners, 1916), 167.

6. Ibid.

7. See Freke and Gandy, *The Jesus Mysteries,* 53–54.

10: THE PASSION

1. William Shakespeare, *Julius Caesar,* III.i.77.

2. *Toronto Star,* June 9, 2006.

3. Ps. 41:9.

4. Mark 14:20.

5. Mark 14:21.

6. Bloom, *Jesus and Yahweh,* 24.

7. John 12:4–6.

8. Simone Weil, *Waiting for God* (New York: G.P. Putnam, 1951), 89.

9. John P. Dourley, *The Illness That We Are: A Jungian Critique of Christianity* (Toronto: Inner City Books, 1984), 53.

10. Tom Harpur, *For Christ's Sake* (Toronto: McClelland and Stewart, 1993), 79.

11. Harpur, *Living Waters*, 62–64.

12. Celsus, *Celsus on the True Doctrine*, tr. R. Joseph Hoffman (New York: Oxford University Press, 1987), 143 n. 205.

13. Matt. 27:16.

14. For a detailed and fascinating set of alternatives here, see Price, *Deconstructing Jesus*.

15. Carl Jung, *Man and His Symbols* (London: Aldus Books, 1961), 61.

16. Mark 14:36.

17. Chopra, *How to Know God*, 170.

18. Maynard Solomon, *Mozart: A Life* (New York: HarperCollins, 2005).

19. Herbert Marcuse, *The Meaning of Death* (New York: H. Feifel, 1959).

20. Campbell, *Thou Art That*, 78.

21. Ibid.

11: ENTERING INTO GLORY

1. Bloom, *Jesus and Yahweh*, 5.

2. Ibid, 1. See also G.A. Wells, *Can We Trust the New Testament?* (Chicago: Open Court, 2004), 190, where he accuses Christian scholars of "perversity" in continuing to set aside "incident after incident" in the Gospels as "unhistorical," while the claims these make for Jesus are still accepted!

3. Ehrman, *Misquoting Jesus*.

4. Luke 24:13–53.

5. H.W. Bortsch, ed., *New Testament and Mythology, Kerygma and Dogma* (London: SPCK, 1960), 41.

6. Wells, *Can We Trust the New Testament?*, 192 n.

7. For a lengthy and detailed defence of the old conservative evangelical understanding of the Resurrection as a literal and physical event, see

Bishop N.T. Wright's *The Resurrection of the Son of God* (Minneapolis: Fortress Press, 2003). For a devastating deconstruction of Wright's position, see www.robertprice.mindvendor.com/rev_ntwrong.htm.

8. 1 Cor. 2:9.

9. It should be noted here in passing that Mark's account that says Jesus "was taken up into heaven and sat down at the right hand of God" is a later forgery. The ending of this, the earliest Gospel, has been lost, and all sound, new translations indicate that the real text ends abruptly at verse 8: ". . . and they said nothing to anybody for they were afraid." That means, among other things, that strange backwoods cults which feature handling poisonous snakes as a sign of their willingness to put "the Word of God" to the test and exhibit their depth of faith are really leaning upon a broken reed. The passage they quote was never a part of the original Gospel. In a word, it is fake. Bart Ehrman's *Misquoting Jesus* discusses this ending in detail for those who wish to explore the matter further.

10. Campbell, *Thou Art That*, 20.

11. Ibid., 48.

12: REACHING FOR TRANSCENDENCE

1. Robert Funk, *Honest to Jesus* (San Francisco: HarperSanFrancisco, 1996), 56.

2. For more on the lack of real history in the Bible, see *The Pagan Christ*, chapter 7, and on the web, especially the article by Ze'ev Herzog, "Deconstructing the Walls of Jericho," Oct. 29, 1999, at www.Haaretz.com.

3. Matt. 11:5.

4. Barnstone and Meyer, *The Gnostic Bible*, 45.

5. Arthur Schopenhauer, "On the Foundations of Morality," *Sämtliche Werke* (Verlag der Catta'schen Buchhandlung, 1895–98), 293, as quoted in foreword to Campbell, *Thou Art That*.

6. Dourley, *The Illness That We Are*, 69.

7. *The Confessions of St. Augustine*, Harvard Classics (New York: P.F. Collier & Son, 1937), 83.

8. Campbell, *Thou Art That*, 31.

9. Close examination shows that the passage differs from Bucke's solely in the fact that Ouspensky substituted "full awareness of an immanent [indwelling] God" for Bucke's phrase "cosmic consciousness" in one instance, and changed two or three other words to make the text more gender inclusive, for example "men" to "people."

APPENDIX A

1. See the ancient Egyptian parallels in *The Pagan Christ*.

APPENDIX B

1. *The Upanishads: Breath of the Eternal*, tr. Swami Prabhavananda and Frederick Manchester (Hollywood, CA: Vedanta Press, 1946), 17.
2. Ibid., 65.
3. Ibid., 126.
4. Ibid., 13.
5. Ibid., 20.
6. Gal. 6:8.
7. *The Upanishads*, 20.
8. Ibid., 21.
9. Ibid.
10. Ibid., 48.
11. Ibid., 59.
12. *Bhagavad-Gita: The Song of God*, tr. Swami Prabhavananda and Christopher Isherwood (Hollywood, CA: Vedanta Society, 1972), 141.
13. Many writers treat Krishna as a figure of mythology and question whether such a historical personage ever existed; or else they say he was a human hero who was later divinized. A similar controversy is taking place about the historical Jesus versus the mythic "Christ." So says Andrew Harvey in the Skylight Paths version of the Gita by Shri Purohit Swami (Woodstock, VT: 2001). Harvey goes on to say that in both cases it is impossible to establish the facts using any modern methodology. But, as Huxley in the Vedanta Society edition states, the historical issue is really beside the point.
14. *Bhagavad-Gita*, 29.
15. Ibid., 90.
16. Ibid., 88.
17. Ibid., 89.
18. Ibid.
19. Ibid.
20. Ibid.

21. Ibid., 90.

22. Col. 1:15–17.

23. Barnstone and Meyer, *The Gnostic Bible*, Gospel of Thomas Saying #77, 63.

24. See Patanjali, *How to Know God*, n. 51.

APPENDIX C

1. A. A. Barb, "Mystery, Myth, and Magic," in *The Legacy of Egypt*, ed. J.R. Harris, 2nd ed. (Oxford: Clarendon Press, 1971), 139.

2. Ibid., 140.

3. Ibid., 154.

4. Cf. A.A. Barb in *The Conflict between Paganism and Christianity in the Fourth Century* (Oxford, 1963).

5. Barb, "Mystery, Myth, and Magic," 157.

6. Ibid., 183.

7. Karl W. Luckert, *Egyptian Light and Hebrew Fire*, SUNY Series in Religious Studies (New York: State University of New York Press, 1991).

8. Ibid., 319.

9. Ibid., 319–20.

10. Ibid., esp. 320–21.

11. Ibid., 322.

12. Ibid., 323.

13. Ibid., 324.

14. Ibid., 324, 327.

15. Ibid., 293 n. 2, 293.

16. Ibid., 294, 295.

17. Ibid., 295.

18. Excerpts from Theodotus 78.2.

19. Luckert, *Egyptian Light*, 297.

20. Ibid., 57.

21. Ibid., 299.

22. Ibid., 302.

23. Erik Hornung, *The Secret Lore of Egypt and Its Impact on the West* (Ithaca,

NY: Cornell University Press, 2001), 43.

24. Ibid., 44.
25. Ibid., 45.
26. Ibid., 60.
27. Ibid., 73.
28. Ibid., 75.

Bibliography

Adams, James Rowe. *From Literal to Literary: The Essential Reference Book for Biblical Metaphors*. Bend, OR: Rising Star Press, 2005.

Allen, Charlotte. *The Human Christ*. Oxford: Lion Publishing, 1998.

Barnstone, Willis, and Marvin Meyer, eds. *The Gnostic Bible*. Boston: Shambhala, 2003.

Betz, Hans Dieter. *Essays on the Sermon on the Mount*. Philadelphia: Fortress Press, 1985.

Bhagavad-Gita: The Song of God. Translated by Swami Prabhavananda and Christopher Isherwood. Hollywood, CA: Vedanta Society, 1972.

Bloom, Harold. *Jesus and Yahweh—The Names Divine*. New York: Penguin Books, 2005.

Borg, Marcus. *Jesus and Buddha: The Parallel Sayings*. Berkeley, CA: Ulysses Press, 2005.

Brown, Raymond E. *An Introduction to the Gospel of John*. 2 vols. Anchor Bible Commentary Series. New York: Doubleday, 1966, 1970.

Brown, R.E., J.A. Fitzmyer, and R.E. Murphy, eds. *The Gospel of Luke*. New Jerome Biblical Commentary, 2000.

———, eds. *The Gospel of Mark*. New Jerome Biblical Commentary, 1989.

———, eds. *Matthew, A Commentary*. New Jerome Biblical Commentary, 1990.

Bultmann, Rudolph. *The Gospel of John: A Commentary*. Philadelphia: Westminster Press, 1971.

———. *Jesus Christ and Mythology*. New York: Charles Scribner's Sons, 1958.

Campbell, Joseph. *The Hero with a Thousand Faces*. Princeton, NJ: Princeton University Press, 1972.

———. *Thou Art That*. Novato, CA: New World Library, 2001.

Childs, Hal. *The Myth of the Historical Jesus and the Evolution of Consciousness*. Atlanta: Society of Biblical Literature, 2000.

Chopra, Deepak. *How to Know God*. New York: Three Rivers Press, 2000.

Cutner, Herbert. *Jesus—God, Man or Myth: An Examination of the Evidence*. Book Tree Online Catalogue, 2000.

Dodd, C.H. *The Interpretation of the Fourth Gospel*. Cambridge: Cambridge University Press, 1968.

Dourley, John P. *The Illness That We Are: A Jungian Critique of Christianity*. Toronto: Inner City Books, 1984.

Ehrman, Bart D. *Lost Christianities*. San Francisco: HarperCollins, 2005.

————. *Lost Scriptures—Books That Did Not Make It into the New Testament*. New York: Oxford University Press, 2003.

————. *Misquoting Jesus*. San Francisco: HarperCollins, 2005.

Harpur, Tom. *Living Waters: Selected Writings on Spirituality*. Toronto: Thomas Allen, 2006.

————. *The Pagan Christ: Recovering the Lost Light*. Toronto: Thomas Allen, 2004.

Hoffman, R.J., trans. *Celsus on the True Doctrine*. New York: Oxford University Press, 1987.

Johnson, Sarah Iles. *Religions of the Ancient World*. Cambridge, MA: Harvard University Press, 2004.

Jung, Carl G. *Man and His Symbols*. New York: Dell Publishing, 1968.

————. *Symbols of Transformation*. Translated by R.F. Hull. 2 vols. New York: Harper Torchbooks/Bollingen Library, 1956.

Keber, Werner H., ed. *The Passion in Mark*. Philadelphia: Fortress Press, 1976.

Kissinger, W.S. *The Sermon on the Mount: A History of Interpretation and Bibliography*. Metuchen, NJ: Scarecrow Press, 1975.

Koester, Craig R. *Symbolism in the Fourth Gospel: Meaning, Mystery, Community*. Minneapolis: Fortress Press, 1995.

Luckert, Karl W. *Egyptian Light and Hebrew Fire*. SUNY Series in Religious Studies. New York: State University of New York Press, 1991.

Ludemann, Gerd. *The Resurrection of Christ: A Historical Inquiry*. Buffalo: Prometheus Books, 2004.

Mack, Burton. *The Christian Myth: Origin, Logic, and Legacy*. London: Continuum, 2001.

————. *A Myth of Innocence: Mark and Christian Origins*. Philadelphia: Fortress Press, 1988.

————. *Who Wrote the New Testament?: The Making of the Christian Myth*. San Francisco: HarperSanFrancisco, 1995.

Meyer, Marvin W. *The Ancient Mysteries: A Sourcebook of Sacred Texts*. Philadelphia: University of Pennsylvania Press, 1987.

Patanjali. *How to Know God: The Yoga Aphorisms of Patanjali*. Translated by Swami Prabhavananda and Christopher Isherwood. Hollywood, CA: Vedanta Society, 1983.

Price, Robert M. *Deconstructing Jesus*. New York: Prometheus Books, 2000.

————. *The Incredible Shrinking Son of God: How Reliable is the Gospel Tradition*. New York: Prometheus Books, 2003.

Raglan, Lord. *The Hero: A Study in Tradition, Myth and Drama*. Mineola, NY: Dover, 2003. First published 1956 by Vintage Books.

Thompson, Thomas L. *The Messiah Myth: The Near Eastern Roots of Jesus and David*. New York: Basic Books, 2005.

The Upanishads: Breath of the Eternal. Translated by Swami Prabhavananda and Frederick Manchester. Hollywood, CA: Vedanta Press, 1946.

Wells, G.A. *Can We Trust the New Testament?* Chicago: Open Court, 2004.

————. *Did Jesus Exist?* London: Pemberton, 1986.

————. *The Historical Evidence for Jesus*. New York: Prometheus Books, 1988.

————. *The Jesus Legend*. Chicago: Open Court, 1996.

————. *The Jesus Myth*. Chicago: Open Court, 1999.

Wilson, Ian. *Jesus the Evidence*. San Francisco: Harper & Row, 1985.

www.earlychristianwritings.com/theories.html. For a list and summary of the positions of current New Testament scholars writing on historical Jesus theories.

Index